THE DELUSIONAL PERSON

THE DELUSIONAL PERSON
Bodily Feelings in Psychosis

Salomon Resnik

Translated by
David Alcorn

Foreword by
R. Horacio Etchegoyen

KARNAC
LONDON   NEW YORK

First published in 2001 by
H. Karnac (Books) Ltd.
6 Pembroke Buildings, London NW10 6RE
A subsidiary of Other Press LLC, New York

British Library Cataloguing in Publication Data

A C.I.P. for this book is available from the British Library

 ISBN 1 85575 262 X

10 9 8 7 6 5 4 3 2 1

Edited, designed, and produced by Communication Crafts

www.karnacbooks.com

Printed and bound by Biddles Short Run Books, King's Lynn

CONTENTS

FOREWORD

R. Horacio Etchegoyen

Salomon Resnik is undoubtedly one of the most original and productive psychoanalysts of our time. His philosophical, literary, and artistic background is impressive, and he has a deep understanding of psychoanalytic theories, not only because he is so well read, but also—and perhaps mainly—because of his skill, his considerable presence, and his originality.

Resnik was born in Buenos Aires and trained in Argentina. An associate member of the Argentine Psychoanalytical Association in 1955, he became a full member in 1957. He underwent training analyses with Luis Rascovsky and Marie Langer and was supervised by Heinrich Racker; he then had further analysis with Luisa G. de Alvarez de Toledo. He was one of Enrique J. Pichon-Rivière's first pupils, and he attended seminars by Marie Langer, Heinrich Racker, Celes Ernesto Carcamo, Arminda Aberastury, and other pioneering figures of the time.

Among his colleagues were Leon Grinberg, David Liberman, Raul Usandivaras, Willy and Madeleine Baranger, and Joel Zac, with whom he was able to establish a productive and on-going dialogue.

I met Resnik for the first time in Enrique Pichon-Rivière's famous psychoanalytically orientated psychiatric clinic, towards the end of the 1940s. Since then, we have been close friends.

In Argentina at that time, Resnik was doing pioneer work with psychotic children, and this enabled him to begin practising analysis with adult psychotic patients. This experience proved of particular value in his writings, especially for his paper on Cotard's syndrome (published here as chapter two).

In order to broaden his experience of life and complete his training, he travelled to Europe in 1957. He spent one year in Paris, attending lecture courses by Maurice Merleau-Ponty, Claude Lévy-Strauss, and Roger Bastide. At the same time, he was working with Dr Pierre Daumezon, one of the most brilliant French psychiatrists of the day, who gave him the opportunity to complete his training in classic psychiatry, especially in semiotics. Dr Daumezon put him in touch with the eminent English psychiatrist Morris Carstairs, who, on a visit to Paris, found Resnik's work with chronic schizophrenics particularly interesting. Through Dr Carstairs, in 1958 he was appointed consultant psychiatrist in the Netherne Hospital, Coulsdon, Surrey; this meant a move to England, where he was put in charge of a therapeutic community of young psychotic patients.

Resnik has always sought to develop his understanding of early object relationships as delineated in the work of Melanie Klein. Klein invited Resnik to attend her seminars and recommended him to Herbert Rosenfeld for further analysis, which in the event lasted for more than thirteen years. Resnik remained in weekly contact with Klein until her death in 1960. He became a guest member of the British Institute of Psycho-Analysis, where he attended seminars and had supervision with W. R. Bion, Hanna Segal, and Esther Bick. According to Salomon Resnik, Bion stimulated him into developing his own original style and way of thinking. Another important influence was D. W. Winnicott, whose seminars Resnik also attended before becoming a close friend.

After twelve years in London, he decided in 1971 to return to Paris, attracted as he was by the humanistic culture and way of life there and by the echoes these had with his Latin American roots.

Today Resnik is an international psychoanalyst, whose name is known throughout Europe, particularly for the way he has influenced a whole generation of psychiatrists in France and Italy. He has written books and papers in French, Italian, English, and Spanish. *The Delusional Person* is a book that brings together some of his major original writings. It was first published in French, then in Italian and in Spanish; now it can be read by English-speaking psychoanalysts. Two of his books, *The Theatre of the Dream* and *Mental Space*, have already appeared in English, the first published by Routledge and Tavistock (in their series *The New Library of Psychoanalysis*), the second by Karnac Books.

The title of this book, *The Delusional Person*, is a reference to the particular concerns of the author as to the ethical aspects of the transference situation: whatever the depth of regression in any given patient, we are always dealing with a *person*—from person to person. Winnicott's concept of personalization, an important part of his "primitive emotional development", was also a major influence on Resnik's approach and way of thinking. Other important influences on Resnik have come from Klein and some of her pupils, together with Paul Federn, E. Minkowski, and Paul Schilder.

According to Resnik, the idea of the person implies unity, integration, and identity. These are aspects that the psychotic loses in part (but never wholly). Resnik emphasizes the fact that the psychotic cannot accept the boundaries of his own body, since he cannot tolerate the limitations of daily existence and the concomitant idea of finite death.* The psychotic often has to leave his body behind, much as seafarers have to abandon a ship about to sink (the simile is borrowed from Jaspers). In his book *The Psychotic Experience*, published in Italian, French, and Spanish, Resnik states that the psychotic experiences a kind of metempsychosis: thoughts and feelings abandon his body to live a wandering, nomadic existence, forever searching for a place to "be". Resnik recently published in French a paper entitled "Wild Thoughts in Search of Shelter", inspired to some extent by Bion's ideas.

One of the most original chapters in this book concerns the experience of space in the analytic setting (chapter seven). For Resnik, space in the psychotic tends to multiply. In the same way, emigrating or wandering thoughts leave their private space within

---

*For clarity of exposition, masculine pronouns have been used throughout in general discussions.

the mind and spread far and wide into different spaces and times as well as into various unexplored and perhaps utopian places.

In the psychoanalytic treatment of psychosis, the split-off transference means that patient and analyst may share syntonic feelings and experience a "metempsychotic" itinerary until such time as the patient can return to his own body and accept his limits in a comprehensive way; he is thereupon better able to tolerate mental pain, even though this implies the risk of internal "commotion/emotion". The psychotic patient experiences a crisis during treatment when his delusional cosmic vision begins to fall to pieces, involving as it does a painful narcissistic loss. Therapeutic improvement implies abandoning his delusional *Weltanschauung* and accepting a self-image leading to disillusion and sometimes suicidal ideas.

During his delusional phase, the psychotic tries to impose on others his conception of the world. Sometimes he feels he possesses the magical power of transforming people into "things" that can then be manipulated and downgraded. When the patient reaches individuality in his own condition as a person, he can recognize and respect the autonomous existence of the Other. This is the level at which integration relates to what Klein called the depressive position, allowing the patient to establish normal links of reciprocity and interdependence; at this point, he can negotiate with other people instead of imposing his own point of view.

How can the psychoanalytic method contribute to the abandonment by the psychotic of his fascinating and illusory delusional world, exchanging it for ordinary principles and values—which may prove less attractive? This is not easy, but not impossible. The analyst must work through, with his patient, the process of grief and mourning with respect to fundamental changes in the personality and the way that life is experienced.

Resnik starts from three basic and inseparable premises. The first is the importance of language, thought, and identity—the fact of being a person in one's own right. The second claims that however deluded the patient may be, there is always a latent capacity for contact and help. His third point is that if we can discover an appropriate method of communication with the patient, we can establish contact with him so that he, in turn, can re-establish contact with the world. It is in the dialectic between the dependent infantile self and the omnipotent delusional self, between the psychotic and non-psychotic (neurotic) parts of the personality, that the psychoanalytic process can develop. Here, of course, Pichon-Rivière, Bion, and Herbert Rosenfeld have had a great deal of influence on Resnik's thinking.

The analytic situation involves a particular "encounter" that enables the transference process to make contact with the infantile self that at some time in the past was able to play with the mother (and father) but has been crushed by the narcissistic self. The narcissistic self blocks off communication with the infantile self as well as with the psychoanalyst in the paternal or maternal transference. At the same time, delusional narcissistic interference implies in itself a conception of life, a system of ideas or ideology that has to be decoded with respect. This is a major aspect of Resnik's technique: he believes that the analyst must show respect for the personality of his patient, including the psychotic parts. We cannot repair or rebuild a person if we do not respect him and preserve our own self-respect as a person/psychoanalyst. It is only through the understanding of distorted and distorting communication from the psychotic parts that we can create a space for exchange that can lead to re-establishing the unity of the patient's mind. On the other hand, the psychoanalytic setting has to be maintained: the analyst must not be confused with the patient or let himself be confused by him. Resnik differentiates between respecting the psychotic personality (and understanding it) and idealizing psychosis, quite another matter.

Resnik's technique is flexible but rigorous, and it preserves the *asymmetry* of the psychoanalytic dialogue. At the same time, Resnik can, with his patient, face up to the arduous task of reconstructing the destroyed links. The understanding of projective identification, normal and abnormal, is essential if the patient is to be helped to recover—through time—the split-off parts of his self. The intensity of paranoid and depressive anxieties is at that point critical, and narcissistic wounds appear as an inevitable drama, leading in the end to the recognition of otherness.

The idea of being a person, claims Resnik, has to do with a process in which the individual becomes aware of his own existence as different from others, yet in constant relationship with them. In other words, the presence of the mother as a separate entity enables the infant to discover his own self as well as that of his mother. Thanks to this, the child is able at the same time to conceive of the presence of the third party—that is, the father.

The process by which the child acquires his own individuality and identity in his relationship with others is what Resnik, following Winnicott, calls "personalization". It is a complex process that requires the presence of the father as an essential element in establishing links and patterns of social relationships.

If I were to summarize these comments, I would say that the psychoanalytic situation offers the possibility of studying the vicissitudes of the encounter between patient and analyst from a double perspective: diachronic or genetic, and synchronic or present. In the relationship between analyst and patient and through the dialectics of transference and countertransference, the destiny of the treatment will appear as an interplay between two people and two worlds; this involves a multiplicity of times and places that tend to reintegrate at a particular moment. As Resnik puts it, the process is not only "scientific" but also "ethical", helping the other person without invading his space or contaminating it with the analyst's own conflicts and system of values. This implies respect of otherness in a reciprocal manner.

Resnik's book should be read in a reflective way. I am personally grateful to him for asking me to write a foreword and for giving me the opportunity of reading this book once again with great emotion.

THE DELUSIONAL PERSON

Introductory self-reflections

This book is a revised version of an earlier work based on a collection of papers I wrote between 1953 and 1967, none of which has previously been published in English. In this new edition—more than 25 years after the original French edition —I thought it opportune to say a few words about my thoughts on the meaning that the book has for me today; I hope that these reflections will interest my readers. When I re-read what I then wrote, I do not feel I need to add too many comments, since I find my work as reported here still very much coherent with my present way of thinking. However, putting together papers belonging to different moments of my life was already a way of looking back on my itinerary. This new edition is still a re-thinking, and so a way of re-establishing dialogue with my self and with the sources of my learning and creative processes. Perhaps I should first of all say something about this itinerary.

I came to Paris in 1957 after completing my training in Argentina and becoming a full member of the International Psycho-Analytical Association.

Coming to Europe represented an old dream of mine. The son of Russian Jewish immigrants, I felt the need to come to the Old

Continent in order to make contact with my family roots as well as with my cultural aims. I had always been interested in French and Middle-European humanistic culture. To be in Paris for a year before going to London in 1958 to study with Melanie Klein and her group meant a very important pause in my fantasy of linking and integrating phenomenological psychiatry, psychoanalysis, and life itself.

In my early experience as a child analyst, I became interested in Klein's work and in problems of communication and early language. In fact, child patients suffering from autistic and psychotic syndromes made me aware of the importance of the early stages of development in the way that Klein theorized these. After my work with very regressed children, I became interested in working with schizophrenic patients. Dr Enrique Pichon-Rivière was my guide and supporter, because he felt I was very motivated for this kind of research and therapy. In the 1950s, as I was working with chronic psychotic patients in the mental hospital of Buenos Aires, Dr Emilio Rodrigué, an Argentinian, came back from London after his analytic training. I asked him to supervise some of my child cases in order to complete my training as a child analyst; this also gave me a vivid and creative image of his experience in London. He had been analysed by Paula Heimann and had had supervision with Melanie Klein. When I travelled to Europe for the first time in 1955 for the International Congress in Geneva, I met Ernest Jones, the Princess Marie Bonaparte, Mrs Klein, Bion, Herbert Rosenfeld, Hanna Segal—whom I had met in Buenos Aires—and that wonderful analyst and human being, Donald Winnicott.

At that time, encouraged by Pichon-Rivière and Rodrigué, I decided to complete my training in both Paris and London. During my year in Paris, I attended Lacan's seminars as well as seminars and lectures at the French Institute of Psychoanalysis, and I also followed the great French philosopher Maurice Merleau-Ponty's lectures in the Collège de France. I was very impressed by these lectures; I must say he was the greatest orator I have ever met. I was already impressed by his book on the phenomenology of perception (published in 1945). I had already read a seminar he gave in Paris, based on the child's relationship with the Other (Merleau-Ponty, 1955).

The present book, then, is a miscellany from different—indeed crucial—periods of my life. My first chapter—on personalization—is based on Winnicott's ideas. I translated it into English and sent it to him; he replied that he felt very "stimulated" by what he read. When I came to England, he was one of those who supported me morally and intellectually throughout most of my work in different institutions. I felt that he was an extremely authentic and spontaneous person in his life and in his work. I was already very impressed by the first Kleinian papers on psychosis, written by Herbert Rosenfeld, Segal, and Bion. I was able to have supervision with two of them during my ten years or so in London, and to have further analysis with Herbert Rosenfeld. In this latter, I was fascinated by the way in which he interpreted dreams in the transference. This encouraged me some years later to write my own book on dreams (Resnik, 1984).

My initial impulse, as I suggested, had its source in the analytic treatment of autistic children[1] and then developed further as I began to work with adult psychotics. After my years of work in London, I returned to Paris for a sabbatical year during which I put together several of my early papers on the subject of the psychoses (infantile and adult), which have become some of the chapters of this book. The second chapter, on Cotard's syndrome, was my thesis presented in order to become an associate member of the IPA. "Language and Communication" (chapter four) is based partly on Merleau-Ponty's phenomenological contribution and on my interest in the language of the body and non-verbal communication as expressed in the transference (with child and adult psychotic patients). I was already attentive to the "climate" of the session and the meaning of the nuances of silence as part of a private world that comes out into the open in a sensory and perceptual manner. Increasing intuition on the part of the patient or of the analyst is very important for me and for my ongoing research. This chapter, together with that on the analysis of an acute psychotic crisis (chapter five) were the papers I presented in order to be accepted as a full member of the IPA. As regards the other

---

[1]Melanie Klein (1930) discusses the problem of language and symbol formation in the case of a child suffering from what we would now call early infantile autism.

chapters, "An Attack of Catatonic Negativism" (chapter three) was a stimulating and difficult experience of silent, non-verbal communication; the chapters on countertransference (chapter six), the experience of space (chapter seven), and the schizophrenic world (chapter eight) are further developments on my entire experience as a person and as an analyst interested in problems of human existence and the importance of space and time, as two major coordinates of every relationship. Many of the ideas that I was able to publish and elaborate on in these past years have their roots in this book.

In my view, for these reasons, the publication in English of this work may—thoughtfully—bear witness to all the years that I was also an actor in that complex drama of the work that my patients enabled me to have as a life experience.

Transference begins with the beginnings of life, wrote Melanie Klein in her paper on transference (Klein, 1952). In 1979, I gave a lecture in the Sainte-Anne psychiatric hospital in Paris on "Transference and Life" based on Freud's first texts on the dynamics of transference. I described how to preserve the psychoanalytic setting and situation as a "field" that requires respect for and appropriate "distance" from the Other. I believe that dealing in such a delicate area of life, the most private and "sacred" aspects of each individual, can be felt at times to be an intrusion.

In these last years I have been impressed by Bion's final papers, as well as by Harold Searles' contribution to the study of transference and countertransference.

I have learned that in the psychoses—child and adult, including chronic cases—a part of the ego with syntonic ability is always preserved, even though the rest of the personality may be manifestly ill. The question is how to discover and reawaken this healthy part through that particular encounter we call the analytic situation. In the old way of looking at mental illness, the patient appeared to be "wholly" deranged. But it has progressively become necessary to think in a more dialectic way about the psychotic and non-psychotic aspects of the mentally ill patient. Behind his façade, behind the mask that the patient presents to us, there are always other clues that enable us to discover the person in his wholeness—the healthy part as well as the ill part of the self. It is always possible to discover some personal traits that have re-mained unchanged in spite of the illness; these go to make up his "personality" (from the Latin *persona*, mask). Sometimes we may even see the patient transcend his limits and become able to project sounds beyond this mask, vibrate his voice, show himself through gesture or grimace—in other words, reveal himself.

When Freud began his investigations into mental life, he did not believe that psychotics could develop a transference relation-ship (Freud 1914c). He located psychotic states at an auto-erotic and narcissistic (i.e. not object-related) level of regression. In devel-oping some of Abraham's ideas,[2] Melanie Klein formulated the hypothesis that, from the very onset of life, the infant is able to transmit his feelings to the mother (Klein, 1952).

The child's mental apparatus and ability to communicate are shaped through repeated contacts with the mother. This relation-ship helps the infant to perceive and to feel; conversely, the mother who is syntonically available for her child learns through these encounters what he is striving to transmit to her. The developing communication between mother and baby precedes the relation-ship with the father and forms the basis upon which the original models of object relations are built. The infantile ego of the adult patient, neurotic or psychotic, may dramatize in the transference these early relational patterns.

In discussing the relationship between mother and baby, I shall first of all look at its implications for the adult and his ability to identify himself as a person. The idea of *persona* is connected to the process by which an individual becomes aware of his own exist-ence as distinct from but in relation to other people. The presence of the mother as a distinct entity enables the infant to discover his own body as well as that of mother. Through his exchanges with her, the infant learns to identify with roles that he can spontane-ously dramatize. This playful experience promotes the develop-ment of his own image; he becomes able to identify the character

---

[2] In particular, Abraham's papers "The Psycho-Sexual Differences between Hysteria and Dementia Praecox" (1908) and "Notes on the Psycho-Analytical Investigation and Treatment of Manic-Depressive Insanity and Allied Condi-tions"(1911).

or characters he plays, while becoming more and more aware of his own individuality. His ego has at some point to be able to integrate these various *modi vivendi* in order to build up a complete picture of himself. The process by which he forges his own identity in counterpoint to that of other people is part of what Winnicott called personalization.

I call this book "The Delusional Person" because in these further reflections I made in Paris on my return from London, I recall what my last analyst in Buenos Aires, Luisa Alvarez de Toledo, said to me when I told her I was about to leave for Europe. "Don't forget that what happens between patient and analyst is not only a matter of object relations or ego mechanisms. It is above all a human relationship from person to person." Those two sentences left very significant traces inside me and suggested the title for this book. I thought also in those days that it was very important to be able to have the opportunity to have great teachers and to attend the major schools of thought, whatever the discipline. But what is more important—and this is a lesson I learned from Pichon-Rivière and from Bion—is to be oneself, to wear one's own "mask"—that is, to be spontaneous and authentic and to develop one's own style of being and working.

On precisely that point, I go on to explore in this book what happens when the process of personalization goes wrong, in particular depersonalization and its relationship to the changing experience of the body. In my discussion of Cotard's syndrome (chapter two), I study the mechanism by which the body is negated in whole or in part—in some cases certain organs are ignored, in others the whole organism is negated and the patient feels himself to be invisible. This is what I refer to as a *negative internal autoscopy*, in which there is a perception of something "missing", and in this sense we could say that what has been "erased" is still to some extent present. The organ or part of the body that is negated becomes both the sign and the seat of unpleasant or painful experiences that the ego has been unable to tolerate. This *locus* is like the trace of a depressive or paranoid drama which, though denied, reveals its presence through the very fact of negation. Hypochondriac anxiety, which is at the root of the denial, is first displaced then obliterated. The ego rejects what it cannot deal with, and the body becomes a reservoir for what I have come to call *internal projections*[3] and unconscious denial. Furthermore, the choice of organ upon which displacement of the anxiety-laden experience has occurred is not an arbitrary one. Choice of any given *locus* is a function of "body syntax"—the semantics of the body.

I have recently learned that my paper on Cotard's syndrome is still regarded as a classic work by French psychiatrists. The syndrome was described by Dr Jules Cotard in 1891, and my paper adds a psychoanalytic interpretation that is particularly appreciated; it has as a result been extensively quoted by colleagues writing other papers.

As regards conversion hysteria, as Freud discovered, it is characterized by displacement from the psychic sphere to somatic innervation—for example, paralysis, anaesthesia—that is to say, a functional change. Conversion raises theoretical questions about economic and symbolic interpretations—repressed representations are expressed through the body.[4]

In the case of hypochondriasis, we again find this "displacement from the psychic sphere to somatic innervation". This is what I call projection into the body, with the addition of an underlying delusional element.

Negation of the body and of its contents is also part of the autistic defence. What some authors interpret as "emptiness" would seem to me to be an example of negative internal autoscopy. In other words, it is less a case of evacuative projection (emptying oneself) than a negative hallucination of internal reality. If the autistic child succeeds in projecting the emptiness of his negated internal world outside his armour-plated shell, external reality then becomes empty too: the world, being devoid of all content, becomes meaningless,[5] leading to a nihilistic view of life. In his

---

[3] *Internal* projection means looking from a global somato-psychic point of view. But from the point of view of the mind alone, in hypochondriasis (and some somatic illnesses) and in depersonalization the body is experienced as being *external*, a kind of "alter body", in the sense that we speak of "alter ego".

[4] Some authors draw a distinction between conversion and somatization. In the latter, according to this view, symptom-formation processes other than conversion are at work; also, somatization is clinically easier to distinguish. To my mind, the issue is still an open one.

[5] Cotard and Séglas were the first to recognize this.

article on narcissism, Freud (1914c) stressed the importance of libidinal cathexis of the hypochondriac organ, and the same point was taken up by Paul Schilder, Melanie Klein, and Herbert Rosenfeld. The ego diverts its attention to an organ, which then becomes the body locus onto which conflicts have been displaced. In the same paper, Freud makes a connection between hypochondriasis and schizophrenia: in both cases, he points out, pathological narcissism plays a fundamental role.

With this kind of patient, the deciphering of body language is crucial to psychoanalytic investigation. The analyst-cum-semiologist attempts to decode the principles and the rules governing the patient's body language and its relationship to verbal expression. Freud's interest in archaeology is well known; he attempted to find in the object-as-sign traces of messages buried in the "past". The analyst-cum-archaeologist tries to observe, describe,[6] and interpret what is buried "in present time" in the unconscious: the data are revealed in the shape of symptoms or signs (this implies an "archaeology of the present"). Our biography does not lie "in the past", "behind" us—it is always present somewhere in our bodily mask. The interpretation of what is taking place on the verbal and body levels can never be more than a working hypothesis. A collection of data is personal and arbitrary, because every observer gathers what he feels to be significant; in this way he builds up his own semiological code, one he will feel comfortable with in his investigation. The "field" we explore here is the analytic one. The transference relationship between patient and analyst and its implications for the construction of the analytic field create a common language which develops into a fine-tuned instrument of communication.

In chapter three, I discuss catatonia, in which negation concerns motor behaviour.[7] The tense, armour-plated body wants nothing to do with reality: oppositionism. The patient loses touch

---

[6] Latin *describere*, meaning to write from (*de-*) an exemplar or model, to copy. From the Greek κρυπτος, is derived "decrypt": find the secret meaning, decode. The Latin *legere* means to gather, collect, then to read, with its compound *intellegere*, to choose from among [*inter-legere*], to read between the lines, and hence to understand, to perceive.

[7] We could speak also of "catatonic thinking", in which experience itself is petrified.

with his body and with his mental apparatus, he allows himself to be modelled by someone else just like a tailor's dummy (*flexibilitas cerea*). When psychic and body ego are fragmented, mind and body become two separate entities. There subsists nevertheless between them a hidden or lost link which has to be rediscovered. Once the analyst has revealed this hidden link, he can reconstruct the syntax of the fragmented language and attempt to read—to decipher—the dis-ordered and incomplete message. The preserved ego is hidden, but it can help the analytic investigation through body and mental expression—even though the message may be difficult to grasp.

To dis-cover the meaning of a given phenomenon and expose it to the light of day is to initiate a transference relationship.[8] The phenomenology of bodily "intentions" finds in catatonia a rich field to be mined. Non-verbal elements become particularly significant, given the apparent poverty of verbal expression. Thus, even when the patient does speak, it is his body that gives meaning to what he says. As to the analyst, the attitude that accompanies his words is also of fundamental importance. The patient is sensitive not only to what the analyst says, but also to what he *feels* and to the way in which he expresses it. If there is a discrepancy between the interpretation and the analyst's own frame of mind, this is what the patient will perceive; he will react to what the analyst does *not* say—that is, to something that, in spite of all his precautions, the analyst expressed in another manner.

I then go on in chapter four to examine different forms of communication in the psychoanalytic setting. Self-awareness and the experience of the Other are part of a mobile/"moving" context. We become aware of ourselves insofar as we are able to perceive other people as existing beyond the frontiers of our body. The ego invests the other with intentions, which in turn act upon it. This mutual *induction* implies the presence and impact of the body on another living organism. Between patient and analyst there is a phenomenon of reciprocal influences: the patient "does" something to the analyst, just as the analyst "does" something to his patient (this is what I call "impacting" into the other or "inducing"

---

[8] The Greek φαινομενον [phenomenon] is itself derived from the verb φαινεσθαι, which means to reveal oneself, to be shown, Hence, φαινομενον means that which is revealed, manifest. See also Heidegger (1927).

the other to behave in a particular way). Working through the transference and countertransference should allow us to translate this "concrete" phenomenon into a meaningful *verbal* dialogue. If all goes well, it will be possible to link the *mobility* or *circulation* of feelings and thoughts to a meaningful communication process; in this way, phenomena as yet "unnamed" can, thanks to creative symbol formation, acquire a "name" and hence meaning. Psychic mobility implies a living transference situation. I discuss also the meaning of the space "in-between" patient and analyst and the search for the appropriate "distance" between them in order to preserve boundaries, prevent confusion, and maintain an ethical recognition of the other's living locus in space. If, after a period of devitalization (in catatonic patients), life starts once again to circulate, the relationship acquires an organized rhythm of exchange though living time (Bergson's *temps vécu*).

Differentiation between subject and object is the starting-point for the concept of number. Acknowledgement of the mother–child duality gives rise to the idea of the self and self-identity (being oneself), and, by inference, of the idea of multiplicity. As Bergson (1920) put it, every unit encompasses a multiplicity of identical or differentiable parts. The unitary relationship within the mother–baby couple at the beginning of life implies the existence of potentially differentiable entities. Discovery of and working through this otherness (mouth and breast in part-object terms) engender the idea of number (first "2", then "1", then "3" as personified by the father).[9] For Melanie Klein, the nipple plays the role of the third element to the extent that the infant is able to distinguish this

---

[9] In my book *L'esperienza psicotica* (Resnik, 1986), I suggest that the original "gap" (almost in the sense of a geological fault-line) creates *discontinuity* from an initial stage of continuity and differentiation from an initial undifferentiation (syncresis). Therefore, space appears as something that separates (introducing three elements: *a*, the "gap", and *b*), though it also provides the opportunity for time-to-be. Separation in space corresponds to pause in time; a pause implies the existence of threefold rhythm (presence, absence, presence). From this void, a syntonic dialogue can be created in which, thanks to its three constitutive elements, two beings will confront each other (hence the number "2"). From this interrelational phenomenon, awareness of oneself (one's self, the existence of "1", the person) appears.

nourishing "phallus" from the breast. The primitive superego is already experienced by the infant as the nipple-tap, which regulates whether the contents of the breast are to continue to flow or to be turned off. The initial phase of communication or pre-communication is characterized by states of primitive confusion. Differentiation between subject and object becomes blurred. To clarify confusion involves accepting the passage from a world of continuity to one of discontinuity (splitting and weaning). This situation is constructed by means of what Winnicott called "moments of illusion", specific states of indeterminate exchange between the respective wishes and expectations of each partner in the original couple. Accepting the presence of the other implies accepting the other as a separate object or person. The infant refuses for some considerable time to accept the mother or part of the mother as being external to him. For Melanie Klein, the father appears as a "continuation" or extension of the mother's body (the phallic mother), until the picture of the combined (and then separate) parents appears. In my view, the birth of relational space gives rise to the presence of a third constitutive element: the space "in-between". I suggest that this space involves the unnamed presence of the father, the same father who, in the weaning process, comes between mother and child in order to separate and help them to wean from each other. In so doing, the father becomes a potential bridge, a link. In this sense, the link stands for the "structuring" father, who both separates and joins.

The pre-linguistic or "vocal gesture" phase can further our understanding of certain aspects of the behaviour of autistic children, schizophrenics, and schizoid personalities. When speech is absent, the meaning of a message may be revealed through vocalization or even through modes of silence. This is what I attempt to demonstrate in what I call the semantics of silence: silence is not a mere hiatus in speech, it is itself discourse. Silence is not necessarily negation of speech; sometimes it reveals the manner by which a withdrawn ego may become permeable, or how the gap may be bridged. The autistic person wraps himself in silence, and his message can only be made clear "silently".

In chapter five, I report the clinical material of a female schizophrenic to illustrate different types of expression and the part they play in constructing a polymorphous—or, better, polysemic—language, gradually fine-tuned by the analyst–patient couple. Both patient and analyst feel the need to communicate, and out of this need several linguistic techniques may emerge (to some extent, psychoanalysis itself is a quest for precisely this). I stress the importance of the initial encounter, in which our earliest relational patterns are reactivated and renewed. The modalities of the analytic situation mean that the analyst is both witness and participant in this encounter, and this gives him the opportunity to observe the patient and learn how he functions. The distance between patient and analyst—in space and time—is symptomatic precisely because it is so mobile. The patient may at times prove to be "far away" or even "entirely absent" from the analytic session: the fragmented mind of the schizophrenic is projected and often cut off from its "reservoir", the body. If projection and splitting are excessive, the patient feels impoverished and empty (the fragmented ego loses contact with the body and the self). In the analysis of psychotics, the infantile transference—in which the ego can express itself in a playful manner—is particularly significant. Puns and other plays on words (schizophrenic humour) and stammering or babbling (rudimentary forms of vocal expression) play a major role in the early levels of relationship between patient and analyst. The child-adult in a regressive state who has not forgotten how to play may induce in the mother- or father-analyst something of his own availability to participate in the play—but at the same time, in order to maintain the analytic setting, the analyst has to stand back and keep his distance. The more the patient is fragmented or disintegrated, the more variables have to be grasped and understood. That is why it is so important to preserve the analyst's role and the analytic setting (non-variable elements). But here the analyst is faced with a problem: how then is he to maintain adaptability and flexibility of expression? How is he to maintain the appropriate distance in order to follow the thread running through the material yet not lose himself? The distance between patient and analyst—necessary in order to preserve the setting—may be under threat when the patient projects himself pathologically into the analyst: one way to annihilate distance is to take possession of the other person. Another threat is when the analyst becomes too closely identified with his patient—the analyst could lose his "formal" role, his separateness as an individual. There is always an optimal distance from which the analyst can maintain his role as participating observer listening, watching, feeling, and attempting to understand—without becoming alienated or entrapped.[10]

The relationship between the transference situation, with its parameters of time and place, and the family environment can give rise to difficult practical and theoretical problems. Some analysts refuse all contact with the patient's family (they keep their "distance"). But children and psychotics are undoubtedly dependent on other people, and it is impossible to ignore this fact. When such a patient wishes to transmit some message or other to the analyst, he may do so either directly—through the words he says or enacts in his body (an action-message)—or indirectly (someone in his immediate environment acts as his spokesman or ambassador). It is therefore important to distinguish between indirect communication such as acting-out (doing something outside the analytic setting as a defence *against* communication) and the message transmitted via a third party (the transitional object *for* communication purposes). It is also important to think about how these means of expression—apparently external to the formal setting—can be put to use, while preventing the external world from intruding into and disturbing the internal workings of the analysis.

A further complication lies in the fact that, in the direct encounter between patient and analyst in any given session, there may be defensive "acts" (acting-in) by patient or analyst, as well as what I have called action-messages.

In a recent paper (Resnik, 1997b) in which I discuss psychotic hysteria in a borderline patient, I explain my views on neurotic and psychotic transference and countertransference problems in severely disturbed patients. I learned in supervision with Bion that it is very important to be aware of the kind of transference that

---

[10] "For every object, as for every painting in an art gallery, there is an optimal distance from which it must be looked at, an orientation in which it gives the best of itself; nearer or further away, and we have only a confused perception, too much or too little. This optimal distance gives us maximum visibility, and as with a microscope our focus is better; it is reached through a kind of equilibrium between our internal and external horizons" (Merleau-Ponty, 1945, discussing Schapp's *Beiträge zur Phänomenologie der Wahrnehmung*).

emerges at any one time. For instance, if a psychotic patient appears at a neurotic level, it is essential to deal with him *at that level*. This applies similarly for neurotic patients with strong psychotic tendencies—if they function psychotically, they must be treated at that level. With the patient described in my 1997 paper, the problem of negation emerges as destructive narcissism (H. Rosenfeld).

The next issue I discuss, in chapter six, is that of countertransference—and by implication that of transference—in the analytic field. This field is defined in terms of a particular place and time. The analyst is similar to the ethnologist on a field-work assignment: he is both witness to and participant in the civilization he studies; he is part of the field, his very presence unconsciously modifies it, yet he has somehow to maintain his position as observer. The attitude and position he adopts both determine how he collects and organizes the data and, in the process, influence the hypotheses he will put forward. He has to look at himself, dialogue with himself, and think about his countertransference, while keeping constantly in mind the fact that his way of thinking and his ethical position (value-system) have an impact on the patient–analyst relationship. Freud (1915a) wrote of the risk that the analyst runs when he finds himself in a situation in which he can be unconsciously influenced by the patient. In the same way that the patient transfers his infantile imagos onto the analyst, the latter projects aspects of himself onto the patient. Classically, we speak of a transference neurosis, but it would be equally correct to speak of transference *psychosis* when treating psychotic patients.[11] Indeed, a novice analyst may well fall into a "psychotic situation" (or find himself drawn into one). If, as Freud says, the analyst should not reject the feelings of love his patient has for him, he has to differentiate between these feelings and seductiveness—whether in the patient or within himself. Seductiveness serves narcissism, negates communication, degrades the relationship, and tends to develop into an erotic transference (false-positive transference).

I draw a distinction also between projection and *induction*. The former cannot be effective unless the latter—induction—stimulates

---

[11] For Kleinian analysts, analysis of neurotic patients should also seek to elucidate the psychotic mechanisms that form part of each individual.

in the other person an unconscious availability for introjecting what has been projected. Patients can use manipulative (conscious and unconscious) techniques—and in psychotics and psychopaths these can be quite powerful—in order to induce in the analyst a "disposition" to enact roles that the patient's ego attributes to him (alienation of the formal role of the analyst). I emphasize the vicissitudes or destinies of the object introjected by the analyst in the transference–countertransference situation. I base my discussion of the issue on certain concepts first formulated by Money-Kyrle (1956), concerning normal and abnormal countertransference. The analyst is in a situation corresponding to internalization: he listens, hears, and understands what the patient is saying. But the destiny of what he has internalized depends on his capacity to "metabolize" and think through what he has taken in. Some patients "over-feed" their analyst: they provide him with so many free associations that it becomes impossible to "digest" them. This is a defensive manoeuvre that the analyst has to address in the countertransference.

Another defence mechanism prevalent among psychotics is the attempt to prevent the analyst associating and thinking by providing him simultaneously with divergent and unconnected material. This "free dissociation" aims at alienating the analyst's free associations and preventing him organizing his thoughts.

In chapter seven, I continue my discussion of certain problems related to transference and countertransference, this time in connection with the experience of space within the analytic situation. Minkowski (1968), who was influenced by Bergson, studied the opposition between space and time in clinical experience. He pointed out (Minkowski, 1927) that schizophrenics in particular tend to spatialize time—transforming the experience of time into an experience of space. I would rather say that the schizophrenic cannot bear to construct his own personal time (the experience of time-as-duration) in terms of his internal vital rhythm, the prototype of which is biological rhythm. Excessive projection of this vital rhythm dehumanizes the individual and transforms him into a mechanical robot driven (or paralysed) by external forces—the omnipotence of the external or internal persecutor. Paralysis renders him inert and dispossesses him of his experience of life as ongoing; the projective process transforms individual time into what Minkowski (1927, p. 104) called morbid rationalism and geometrics.

The inner experience of time is ejected and manifests itself as dimensions of space. Freud (1911c [1910]) introduced the term *projection* in his discussion of paranoia,[12] claiming that self-reproach is repressed in a way that could be called projective. Self-accusation is transformed into accusations against others who engender mistrust and suspicion. In this way, the patient no longer accuses himself, but the accusations return to haunt him in the shape of delusions personified in the outside world.

What I attempt to describe are the vicissitudes, in unconscious fantasies, of the idea of space in its relationship to the experience of time. This is the case where a patient is physically present in the session but is mentally elsewhere: outside in the street, in another country, perhaps even on another planet. He has taken leave of his body and from that internal rhythm which he finds so distressing in his ongoing experience of life. The reservoir that is his body has rid itself of its contents and thrown them out into space. Sometimes the body itself is absent or negated, and this makes it difficult to "locate" the transference. In what *locus* in space is the patient? What part or parts of him are still in the session, and which are floating in the air? A patient recently told me of his "flying thoughts", wrapped in a cloud, that wanted sometimes to return home; the idea pleases him sometimes, but at others he is very much afraid of what such re-introjection might mean.

On other occasions, it is the analyst who is distracted, who is elsewhere, in some other space and time—"absent-minded". Where, then, is his observing ego? From what point in space can he look at himself and observe what is happening? It is not enough for the analyst to be "with" his patient through his comments and interpretations; it is just as important for him to know *where* the participants are. If, for example, a patient is speaking about his past, this may imply that he is going away (putting some distance) into some point in *space* he calls a particular moment in *time* ("the

---

[12] Strachey notes that the first appearance of the concept of projection—and indeed of the term itself—in Freud's writings appears in a letter to Fliess (Freud, 1950 [1892-1899], Draft H).

past") in order to escape the present and flee the *hic et nunc* of the encounter. The same may, of course, be true of the analyst. But sometimes one or other of the participants can establish a "long-distance connection" as they come back to earth.

The phenomena I have just described cannot properly be understood without taking into account those other elements we call thought, the conscious and unconscious world, imagination. The tendency to transform duration into potentially external actions is related to transformation of image-*thoughts* into image-*things*. Reifying thought in this manner belongs to the world of "concreteness". A patient in this kind of condition will describe inner or subjective space as though he were describing it objectively from some external location. The ordinary phenomenon in which a perceptual experience is transformed into images and thoughts is sidestepped, or at least, for whatever reason, seems not to have occurred. One of my patients called this "transportation"[13]—that is, the displacement of an event or an object from one locus to another (from external space to inner space). This is neither sublimation nor a true transformation of experience; it is a mere translation, a mechanical displacement in space.

It is impossible fully to understand a patient without some idea of his "personality" and his view of the world. In chapter eight, I discuss the question of *Weltanschauung* in relation to my clinical experience with schizophrenics. Karl Jaspers defines *Weltanschauung* as a way in which the individual as a totality expresses his manner of looking at the world and his conception of reality. An authentic encounter with the outside world implies a vision of one's own inner-ness. Philosophical thought has always been challenged—and nurtured—by the enigma of reality and its as yet unsolved mysteries. Deciphering these enigmas, attempting to solve the mysteries, implies giving meaning to what is unknown, identifying, naming; it entails penetrating the mystery that lies at the root of all mythology and religion, the source of every philosophical approach. This is mankind's *natural* metaphysics.

The schizophrenic's curiosity and fascination with the unknown are inseparable from his ontological anxiety. Since the psy-

---

[13] I shall explain this term fully in chapter eight.

chotic individual cannot tolerate the anxiety of not understanding, he tries either to deny his curiosity or to construct for himself his own "organized" world. He must rework and remodel this overtly painful confrontation with internal and external reality into a delusion (delusional system), thanks to which mystery is henceforth inhabited and the unknown known.[14] But if the psychotic patient cannot recognize his perceptions for what they are, his reality is peopled by unknown persons who surround him and become mixed up with his own projections (parts of the ego or internal objects).[15] External reality changes, it becomes foreign and bizarre; perceptual distortion of reality is substituted for transformed perception.

This change in reality is an important element for our understanding of the transformation of the world that the schizophrenic experiences during the acute stage of his illness. The entire outside world is altered and distorted by his projections (the self-centred view of reality). As the acute phase winds down, anxiety is diminished but self-centredness and magical thinking remain, thus colouring the external world in a very peculiar way: it is as though everything in the patient's environment is directly referred to him. Nothing exists *per se*, things exist only in relation to himself; this referential world observes him, listens to him, feels him, and thinks of him. His conception of the real world is, like language, structured; its particular grammatical rules are part of his personal self-centred culture and civilization. The analyst has the difficult task of understanding this language with its apparently bizarre syntax and temporo-spatial rules, incomprehensible to an outsider. But, in my view, every psychotic has within himself a part that has been preserved and that is potentially able to follow the rules of ordinary everyday life.

In the mobility of the transference, some phases are dominated by much more rapid rhythms than others; the meaning of this acceleration is often difficult to grasp. In any given psychotic patient, delusional aspects of the personality may alternate with

---

[14] In other words, the patient thinks he can recognize voices and images, which take on personal meaning for him.

[15] Hence the idea of "participation", as explored by Lévy-Bruhl (1928; 1949, pp. 151 ff.).

more neurotic ones. When the neurotic aspects are dominant, it is important to make comments or interpretations based on repression or other typical mechanisms of the neuroses. If an interpretation is made on a psychotic level, it will run counter to the rhythm of the transference; the same is true of the converse situation. When the self is being presented in a psychotic way, that is when the psychotic aspects of the personality should be addressed, together with the view of the world which it entails.

One of the characteristic phenomena of the transformation of the world in psychosis is illustrated by Schreber's experience of his body (Freud, 1911c [1910]; see also Schreber, 1955). In his account of his impressions of being transformed into a woman, he tells us of the pleasure he experienced in being penetrated. He goes through periods of negative internal autoscopy, in which he has no stomach, no intestines, no oesophagus. His delusion meant that he could always rebuild the world after his own fashion, since "powerful rays" would restore what had been destroyed and accomplish his transformation from man to immortal being (and vice-versa). It is, however, important to note that restoration was always incomplete, since some feminine aspects remained in his body, and these he would sometimes interpret as the stigmata of direct sexual intercourse with "God". Though "God" was at a great distance from him, Schreber invested him with "special" intentionality and powers.[16] Such projections into the distance, into some far-off locus in space, are typical of psychosis: the more the experience of an internal object or part of the ego is distressing or persecutory, the further away is the locus into which it is projected. When projections of this kind are massive, the self becomes emptier and emptier; the patient behaves as though he had no ego and no internal world. His body becomes an empty mental space, his thinking becomes impoverished and is gradually destroyed. Everything that once was inside is fragmented and scattered to the four winds.

Sometimes the patient will also evacuate the healthy non-psychotic part in order to safeguard it from destruction in his own

---

[16] In a recent paper (Resnik, 1998), I discuss in more detail the question of Schreber's delusional "transference" in relation to the pathogenic way in which he was raised as a child.

body. This can be expressed in the transference as projecting the good, healthy parts into the analyst; this is particularly true when the patient experiences deep trust in his analyst, who then becomes the depository of the patient's good health, the "bank" that keeps his "valuable objects" safe.

Re-introjecting the parts that have been projected is both desired and feared. Bringing together the psychotic and non-psychotic parts of the self, the good protective objects and the persecutory ones, may prove impossible to "digest" or difficult to "metabolize". The feeling of danger that there may be renewed contamination of the healthy part acts as a brake (resistance) on reunification. The task of the analyst-cum-semiologist is to explore the meaning behind this impossibility to unite different parts of the self.

The patient's world and his various concepts are expressed through verbal and non-verbal language. One of the principal functions of analytic work is to decode that language and use it in the analyst–patient "field"; this is what I mean by instrumentation, the "organizing" aim of the analysis.

My interest in the "field" and its spatial and temporal dimensions leads me to another important task, that of *synthesis*—that is, the reconstruction of the psychotic patient's fragmented and scattered world. This is what enables lost time and spatialized duration once more to be brought back into a living, temporal sphere. The experience of time returns to the analytic field, and in the transference restructuring processes begin to make their appearance. It has to be said that any kind of projection of parts of the ego, internal objects, and affects linked to them must, at least in the short term, impoverish the mind and deprive the mental apparatus of its perceptual and cognitive functions. Schizophrenics *do not like* their own mind, because it puts them in touch with the very painful and persecutory reality they refuse to experience. In turn, the refusal means that they become ever more detached from reality and from what they have projected into it. Attacking one's own mind engenders psychopathological disorders which, in the case of schizophrenics, can be extremely severe. Bion studied this topic in his paper on hallucination (Bion, 1958). This kind of attack provokes the expulsion of fragments of the sensory apparatus; the damaged parts then acquire independent existence—so that, if they enter into external objects and modify them, these become "bizarre objects" that are henceforth absorbed into the delusion. If the "eye"—visual ability—is expelled from the body, external reality is inhabited by a hallucinated object which spies on the patient.[17]

Dependence—a necessary part of the working relationship between analyst and patient—demands that the role of each be clearly differentiated. That said, the patient's regressed infantile ego refuses this distinction and tries to merge with the object or deny that there are boundaries between it and the object (the analyst in the transference situation). A semiological distinction between different aspects of the infantile transference and the delusional transference is worth studying in depth in the encounter with patients. In the infantile aspects, in addition to the regressed elements, there are progressive and syntonic elements capable of re-establishing a relationship. The delusional part attempts to impose its view of the world and refuses the relationship with others as subject/objects; it seeks to change others, to transform them into thing-objects, the better to manipulate them. Others do not exist as independent human beings, as persons; they are merely the *dramatis personae* of the world, "thing-objects". Given that the avidity with which the world is engulfed is typical of self-centred people, the therapeutic process cannot but call into question the patient's delusional and narcissistic view of the world.

Being called into question in this way is extremely distressing for the patient, who may feel that he will have to give up everything that, up till then, he valued within himself—his delusional ego; he may have to renounce his omnipotence and become "normal". Since his non-psychotic ego was decathected, to be cured means to lose his entire world and everything that he had idealized.

---

[17] For Bion (1958), in order to differentiate between normal and hallucinatory perception we must give semiological consideration to the following possibilities: "If the patient says he sees an object it may mean that an external object has been perceived by him or it may mean that he is ejecting an object through his eyes; if he says he hears something it may mean he is ejecting a sound—this is *not* the same as making a noise" (p. 67).

The countertransference danger, especially for novice analysts, is to idealize the world of the psychotic. If the analyst falls into this trap, instead of maintaining an attitude of exploration and helpfulness he sets up a collusive narcissistic relationship based on admiration for the delusional images, omnipotence, and magic typical of the patient's psychotic ego. All psychotics try to arouse in their therapist the latter's own narcissistic and omnipotent tendencies; to induce such a disposition, the patient—with guile and seductive cunning—will try to persuade the analyst that his delusion and eccentricities are reasonable and worthy of admiration.[18] The problem is compounded when there is coincidence between the patient's induction and the analyst's own narcissistic projections; his personal idealized view of mental illness prevents the analyst from taking full stock of it, with all its complexity and intrinsic value.

There is a tendency in all of us to admire magic and omnipotence, and in some cultural groups this tendency becomes an established part of life: one member of the group is hailed as the wise man or shaman. The schizophrenic's world is fascinating[19] and captivates the analyst's infantile narcissistic ego, which then loses itself in the Other, like Narcissus.[20] Kleinian and post-Kleinian analysts often speak of mental pain and the difficulty this causes for thinking. I would add that psychotic patients are unable to tolerate not only pain, but also pleasure—sometimes they cannot even stand their own existence. They are sometimes so fragile and sensitive that the very experience of feelings is unbearable. This is why they "decide" unconsciously to be petrified or frozen (Resnik, 1999). I have also learned that they are nevertheless able to think—in their own way—so that there always exists something that we could call "schizophrenic language", made up of bits and pieces of psychotic and non-psychotic experience.

I hope that this introduction will give a living picture of what I am trying to express of an experience that is otherwise very diffi-

---

[18] Throughout this book I emphasize how important the countertransference is in treating psychotics. It is also important to be able to tolerate negative transference and to understand the positive transference without falling under the patient's spell and letting oneself be manipulated by him.

[19] There is no doubt that the delusional world is rich and fascinating—a vivid and creative imagination is necessary in order to construct such a world.

[20] The narcissistic object relation negates the other's identity.

cult to transmit and to communicate. My first steps in the field of the psychoanalysis of psychosis are present here, as are the traces of my present—and future—developments, in the form of "after-thoughts". I hope that the English-speaking reader will be interested in this transcultural experience of life in a field that covers the greater part of my existence.

CHAPTER ONE

Personalization

> But the awakened one, the knowing one, saith: "Body am I
> entirely, and nothing more; and soul is only the name of
> something in the body."
> The body is a big sagacity, a plurality with one sense, a war
> and a peace, a flock and a shepherd.
>
> Nietzsche, *Thus Spake Zarathustra*

It is not without reason that psychotics seem to have a natural vocation for metaphysical and ontological problems. The psychotic is the "crowd governed by discord, a flock whose shepherd is often absent, a man who has escaped from his skin". He has no perception of the frontiers of his body; in his flight, he meanders between inside and outside. At times, he does not even know whether a given object belongs to him or not, or whether it is inside or outside himself. When the psychotic feels threatened, his whole existence loses its vital harmony, as though he were dispossessed of his own body; in the midst of ever-increasing perplexity, he searches for his own image.

In a psychotic crisis, the body image disintegrates and becomes fragmented; it runs the risk of being scattered throughout the world of objects. The individual loses his specific *individuum* and hence his very existence as a person. It is interesting to note that the Latin *persona*, derived from the Etruscan *phersu*, originally meant a mask used in the theatre and was then extended to the character as a whole; *phersu* corresponds to the Greek προσωπον (containing the notion of face), whence προσωπειον, a mask.

A mask is attached to character as a shadow is to a body. A shadow is a kind of body-mask—a costume that provides the actor with a double body, according to the French poet Antonin Artaud, a second set of limbs. Confined in his costume, the actor seems no more than an effigy, and each of us is like an actor when we project an image and become alive as a person through the crystallization of desire, inspiration, or vocation, expressed as our way of being.

Just as in Greek tragedy, a person can play several roles and wear various masks while still remaining a unique individual. The idea of the individual is always related to that of *individuus* (indivisible) and wholeness.

This being-as-a-whole protects itself behind—or expresses itself through—various masks. One of them holds the particular position of being closest to the individual's specific identity: his personality. The series of dualities face/mask, body/costume, fundamental/apparent, person/actor almost vanishes as we become aware of the territory that is our body and enter into possession of it. This, for each of us, is our particular "global" image.

Altering the face with make-up and the body with other adornments is not necessarily dissimulation or an attempt at protection; the very uniqueness of the resultant image is also part of the individual's means of self-expression. Tattoos, like masks, are a kind of hieroglyphics; the "physiognomist" can read the signs (the message) of the person wearing them.[1]

In a psychotic crisis, the various masks and roles available to the individual lose contact with one another and find themselves cut adrift, resulting in the loss of unity and the sense of being

---

[1] In Lévy-Strauss's view (1958), the duality face/figurative representation evokes "not only the graphic representation of the mask but the functional expression of a precise type of civilization (cultural mask), ancestral masks, totemic masks, masks of the gods . . .".

whole and unique. The psychotic loses himself in a world of plurality, he becomes a group-person—but a group in which individuals ignore one another and cannot even see one another properly, a group in which all communication has broken down. The disintegrating ego is fragmented. James (1950) describes the ego as an entity that is conscious of its own self (this is similar to what Jung calls the ego-conscious-of-its-*Selbst*); the individual-as-subject can look at himself as an individual-as-object. This duality implies the ability to look inwards, the existence of dialectic distance, a bridge—the symbol *par excellence* of connection as well as of distance. The ego is the place within each of us where we can dialogue with ourselves and with others.

Externalizing this inner dialogue means that we become visible as separate beings for ourselves as well as for others. "To have a body," says Merleau-Ponty (1945), "means to be looked at, to look at oneself (in-sight: inner perspective, looking inwards), to be visible" (p. 106). Freud (1923b) put the same point slightly differently: "The ego is first and foremost a bodily ego; it is not merely a surface entity, but is itself the projection of a surface."

The internal distance from the ego to the inner "me" enables my "self" to construct a three-dimensional image and to acquire identity. The distance from my ego and the world outside my "self" to other people enables me to acknowledge their identity. The discovery of otherness and of distance has a connection with categorizing space into "inside" and "outside", and hence with the ability to perceive the objective world. Distance and space lead to the construction of our own body image. To have a body and be able to imagine it—to see it with our own eyes—is concomitant with the ability to transpose this experience to our relationships with others.[2]

The body image does not concern the surface of the body alone; it is also a representation of the inside of the body (intra-body schemata); in hypochondriasis, certain organs are cathected in a special way[3] and are given a privileged position in the intra-body image.

---

[2] At one point in his development, the infant acquires the capacity to transpose to others the image he has constructed of his own physical existence.

[3] Schilder's term is *genitalization* of the part of the body concerned.

The body image is not a pure form in space, fixed for all eternity. Time and rhythm play their part in giving life and movement to this image. The idea of body image would be incomplete were we to ignore motor aspects; they are a representation-in-action of internal time.

Each individual has his own postural models and positions (schemata) which determine his relationships with others. As the schemata evolve and are transformed, the body image is constantly being remodelled and reconstructed. The concept of body image is a dynamic and personal one.

In a psychotic crisis, the individual feels himself to be in constant danger of losing his image and struggles to recover it. Yet he cannot do this on his own, because he keeps on losing himself. Merleau-Ponty (1955) again: "Man can only know himself if he leaves himself, that is by projecting outside himself in order to be dis-covered. In order to see himself, man needs mediators; these act as mirrors in which he attempts to find himself again" (p. 35).

We cannot see ourselves without the help of others. Even when I am alone, I am alone with respect to someone else. In psychoanalysis, the mediator and mirror are personified by the analyst. The patient sees himself in and through the analyst. Offering himself to the other's gaze, he learns how to look at himself (the observing ego), to make himself visible to himself, and to envisage himself as a totality within the frontiers of his body.

Freud's discussions of bodily ego and psychic ego do not always integrate both aspects. It would appear that for him the dominant notion was that of the self [Selbst], which some authors have tended to confuse with that of the ego.[4] Speaking of ego mechanisms, for example, Federn (1959) emphasizes what he calls the ego feeling and the ego boundary. He uses the term ego as an instance that confronts external reality. Federn does not mention personality directly, but he does hint at the notion when he discusses depersonalization.

------

[4] Melanie Klein, however, always differentiates between the two: the ego is the organized part of the self, influenced by the instinctual drives, over which it maintains control by means of repression. It establishes relationships with the outside world. The self encompasses the whole person, not only the ego but also the id and instinctual life as a whole.

Among psychoanalysts, Winnicott in particular explores the notions of body, self, and personality from a perspective that is both developmental and phenomenological. "For me, the self—which is not the ego—is the person who is me and only me. . . . It finds its natural place in the body, but may in certain circumstances become split off from the body or the body from it. . . ."[5]

If the shadow becomes detached from the body, the unavoidable implication is death—because a shadow is witness to the presence and opacity of the body. If the self leaves the body, this too is a kind of "death"; the individual is emptied of all content, all opacity—he is dispossessed of his quality as a person.

In the first months of life, says Winnicott, the process of "personalization" follows three tracks. Firstly, integration, the process by which the ego becomes unified (initially, the ego is not integrated[6]). Then follows personalization *stricto sensu*, with the feeling of "living inside" one's body,[7] where the self becomes organized. The final stage is that of realization: acknowledgement of reality in terms of space and time.

The process of personalization has much to do with the feeling of inhabiting one's body. Heidegger (1927) wrote of the relationship between "inhabiting" and "being", between residing and living—occupying space in such a way as to construct and enliven it. We build our space, we occupy it dynamically, we create our own habitat. In German, *bauen* means both to build and to inhabit.

The experience of our body gives structure to the personalization process. When a human being feels himself to be a person, he has already accomplished a great deal in his journey along the developmental road. Being a person always implies the existence of someone else; it is inconceivable for an infant to exist isolated

---

[5] Personal communication from D. W. Winnicott on the concept of self.

[6] On this point, Winnicott and Melanie Klein held divergent views. The former speaks of a non-integrated ego, whereas for Melanie Klein a primitive ego does exist even from the moment of birth. This rudimentary ego enables the infant to defend himself against anxiety arising between "inside" and "outside". For Klein—and here she follows Freud's original idea—birth implies the ability to survive the death instinct (the original internal persecutor).

[7] I would prefer to use the term *corporization* as a more specific way of describing the experience of one's body.

from the rest of the world. As Winnicott (1952) put it: "There is no such thing as a baby" (p. 99). There is always baby-plus-a-significant-other (the mother, and through her the father and the whole family structure). This is the basis for his description of early relational models.

Winnicott and Melanie Klein agree that it is once the infant can differentiate his relationship with his mother as a whole person distinct from all others that the father, the third party, makes his entry. Winnicott was interested in the "field" in which the mother–child relationship unfolds; he considered it to be structured by the interplay of forces represented by the emotional and physical exchanges between the participants.

The infant hallucinates a "personal" breast and projects this onto the real breast (illusion). However, the real breast and the hallucinated breast cannot coincide perfectly with each other for gratifying his oral expectations—thus the infant learns to make a painful distinction between them. This is what Winnicott calls the moment of dis-illusion.

As for the mother, her "primary maternal preoccupation" (Winnicott, 1956) determines how she handles her infant. This preoccupation or caring attentiveness is characterized by a special sensitivity which reaches its climax in the final months of pregnancy and remains at that level for several weeks after birth. Generally speaking, the mother does not remember this period; indeed, she tends to repress it. If the mother does not succeed in working through this experience, a post-partum psychosis may ensue; but ordinarily she will be able to surmount this "normal pathology".

The mother's attitude determines to a great extent that of her infant, but it must not be forgotten that she too needs a baby who will help her to fulfil her maternal role; mother and baby need each other to define their respective roles. Her ability to feed—in the widest sense—her baby, especially if it is her first child, depends on the way the baby approaches her and stimulates her. If the baby is a bad feeder and does not suck, she cannot have the feeling of being "awakened" to her role as mother and appreciated as a person. There is, too, the narcissistic mother, who uses her infant as an object of sexual pleasure, as a thing, or as her own property.

Kanner (1943) described a type of mother who is too cold and indifferent to "awaken" her baby; in his view, this is a major factor in early infantile autism.

The mother–child couple and the living history of their relationship is crucial for the future development of the infant. A baby experiences anxieties that he is incapable of taking on board alone; the mother has to take them in to a sufficient extent or in some other way help her infant to "digest" them. Working through anxieties over weaning enables the infant to acknowledge his mother as a person, and this in turn makes possible the development of a relationship with her on a symbolic level. The word "mummy" is adopted at a particular point in the biography of language as an acceptance of mother's physical absence. In learning the word "mummy", the infant accepts the substitution of a word for the absence. The symbolic representation replaces the real mother. There is a gap, a distance, between the real mother and her symbolic representation.

Winnicott explored in some depth the various mediators in the mother–child relationship, particularly in his discussion of transitional objects and transitional phenomena (Winnicott, 1953).

Different parts of the body (fingers and thumb in particular) or certain distinctive objects (a toy, a teddy bear, a corner of the blanket, etc.) are employed by the infant as transitional experiences of the originally desired object; these give rise to "not-me possession", something that is distinct from the self (hence the discovery of other-ness). The transitional field is the experiential zone between thumb and teddy bear, between oral eroticism and the object (auto-eroticism and allo-eroticism). The idea of illusion is essential to Winnicott's description of the encounter between mother and baby: the encounter between the breast hallucinated by the infant and the mother's real breast. The "good" mother has to help her baby to dis-illusion himself in a *creative* way, so that the infant can develop his own perception of reality and organize his own mental apparatus.

The dramatization of speech and act in the transference enables us to observe how the individual struggles to find himself as a person. It was when I made a "semiological" study of a session with a female psychotic patient with clear paranoid and hypochondriac tendencies that the issues behind becoming a person took on new meaning for me.

The patient, Miss L, was 27 years old when I began therapy with her. Her treatment lasted for four years, and the session I am about to report occurred some two years into the analysis.

The patient began by saying:[8] "I am not a person. When you're a person you *are* somewhere, people can see you and be seen by you, you have a body. To have a body means you can look at yourself and see yourself. It means standing upright and knowing that you're standing; it means talking and being wholly yourself. Only people who are not persons say something inside but remain outwardly silent, or else say something completely different."

From a phenomenological point of view, we could say that for this patient, being a person does not only mean *being* or being conscious of one's existence and of one's body; it means being *whole*, an integrated totality. To be aware that we exist implies some kind of relationship with our surroundings; it means seeing and being seen (Merleau-Ponty's "visible being"). If the frontiers of the body are to be clearly established in space, a clear distinction between inside and outside must be reached—the ability to envisage others as existing as well as oneself (the ability to conceive of oneself).

Later in the session, Miss L took off her coat and said: "Now I feel better . . . I don't feel so confined any more . . . With my coat off I feel less stiff . . . The more clothes I wear, the more I feel shut in and the less I am able to talk. If I could walk about naked, I could say everything I wanted to." She continued in this vein, sometimes talking to me, sometimes to herself: "What is a drop of water? Is it empty or full? What do drops look like when they fall? Are they empty, with something all around them, like soap-bubbles? How could we cut them in two?" Then she answered her own questions: "But they vanish. Should we measure them as a whole, and then naked, to see if they're still the same size? Yesterday I was on a bus, and I watched the raindrops falling on the window. But I couldn't see what they looked like, because they broke as they fell."

---

[8] Sometimes she would address me, but at other moments she seemed to be talking to herself, as if I were not there at all.

I interpreted that she wanted to know what she was made of. Was she just a series of little hollow pieces which needed clothes as a kind of shell to hold her together, or was she a collection of complete bits? I added that when she took her clothes off she felt much freer, but with no body—dispersed like raindrops, because she felt that her only body was the one that was shaped by her clothing. She would say from time to time that her clothes were as hard as steel, and so I added that she felt as stiff and unbending as steel because she needed a very solid container to save her from disintegrating and from becoming a disorganized heap of little fragments. Also, she felt imprisoned in her shell and had the impression that what was covering her did not belong to her. She felt that when she came to my consulting-room she was penetrating inside me, inside my recipient-clothes (projective identification[9]) and occupying my body space with all her fragments. In this way I became her shell (the containing mother), but as soon as she took possession of me she felt locked in and persecuted by me.

---

[9]Melanie Klein used this term for the first time in her article on schizoid mechanisms (Klein, 1946). The phantasy is expressed on various levels: oral (enter into other people or the mother in order to suck, empty, bite, take away, steal whatever is inside), anal, and urethral (attack).

The analyst becomes the container for fragmented parts of the self, cathected with various meanings, including sadistic possession via urethral and anal fantasies. This is one way of attacking or possessing or controlling the inside of the mother-analyst's womb. (The womb itself becomes the container for the bad parts of the ego—the bad self.) In attacking mother, I attack my own ego in the sense that it is part of the narcissistic object relation. Such hostile projections of parts of the self are cathected with omnipotence; the patient's curiosity does not correspond to a true desire for knowledge but to an attempt to control and dominate the analytic field (the analyst's body). In the case of Miss L, excessive projection of different parts of her mental apparatus results in disintegration and impoverishment of her self. However, this very impoverishment means that she is also projecting positive feelings and capacities—seeing, knowing, realizing, learning, thinking, feeling: in other words, the good self. When the latter aspect is dominant, the analyst becomes the container for the good parts of the self; the patient may well experience this as a loss or even as a massive outflow of her essential functions (projection of "good" feelings and certain valued aspects of the self makes for a good object relation and furthers the normal process of integration). Excessive projection of good aspects leads to idealization of the object and pathological dependence on it.

Her claustrophobic fears about clothes were experienced in the transference as being held prisoner inside her own body.[10]

After my interpretation, she said: "I am scattered and dissipated like smoke that comes out of a bottle and evaporates." I replied that it was therefore difficult for her to say anything, because for her speaking was equivalent to leaving her body and vanishing like smoke from a bottle. She went on to say that whenever she spoke she had the impression that a few moments later she would evaporate and become invisible.[11] Furthermore, she could see other people without their seeing her (invisibility is a mask). For Miss L, invisibility is the result of disintegration. As Bion (1957a) would have put it, minute splitting fragments her personality and encysts the objects in the outside world, transforming them into bizarre objects.

The feeling of being invisible and fragmented in space is combined with the desire to control the world in an omnipotent manner from any object-locus whatsoever. In her view, people did not know that she was inside objects, mingled with them and controlling them. This idealized megalomaniac feeling ran counter to integration, and hence she felt scattered. She was the bottle whose contents evaporated whenever she spoke; unable to communicate anything, all she could do was to empty herself like a bottle. In order not to disappear completely, she needed her clothes—her shell. They meant she could be seen, she would be visible, she

---

[10]Schilder (1950) mentions "altering the body-image with clothing". He shows how clothing, cathected as it is with narcissistic libido, gradually becomes part of the body image. Our clothes are part of our image, and they are experienced as integrated into our "anatomical" image. We identify with other people, adds Schilder, by means of our clothing. We change the postural image of our body by adopting the postural image of others. In this way, clothes can become a means of modifying completely the body image. Changing body image by means of clothing is manifestly related to getting inside mother's clothes, her skin, her body. This is the phenomenon Melanie Klein called projective identification.

[11]When we look at an autistic child, we notice how his feeling of emptiness is reflected in the way he seems to float lightly along. This emptiness, however, is not produced by "evacuating" parts of his internal world; it is the result of negative internal autoscopy, a hallucinatory denial of the self. I shall explore this phenomenon in chapter two.

would *be*. She would often tell me that she needed her sister to help her dress because she could not see herself. She could only fully realize who and where she was once she was in bed. I interpreted this to her thus: when she was in bed, she had a frame, a shell—the bedstead contained her and provided her with some kind of boundary. As a result, she could feel less scattered and more protected, like a foetus inside the mother's body (she was in the receptacle where all births take place); in the transference, the analyst's interior played a similar role. After each session, in order to remain "inside", she would go home, go to bed, and stay there more or less until it was time for her next session. In her fantasy world, there was no gap between sessions, simply a continuous state of non-differentiation with mother.

The protective shell—which as we know can become persecutory and claustrophobic—was sometimes projected onto the walls of the room: when she said she only felt safe once she was undressed, what she meant was that the walls were there to encompass and "clothe" her. In his discussion of the relationship between clothing and body image, Schilder showed how the image may vary continuously, swelling and diminishing in size. When my patient felt that her clothes were as hard as steel, she was expressing her fantasy of living inside the object, which, like a shell, became a kind of armour-plating imprisoning and shackling her.

All the same, this patient wanted to learn about herself and find out what she was made of—to discover what these drops of water really were, and why she had to have such thick armour. She wanted to know, to understand, and eventually to free herself from confusion. Whenever she felt persecuted by others, she would say: "They make fun of me. I feel disguised, but I don't know what disguise I am wearing. I despise them."

Here, the mask is present in the shape of a disguise from which she feels detached. She cannot know what mask she is wearing. She does not know who she is; she is wearing someone else's mask. Her voice, like her other messages, is also disguised—she does not speak in her own voice [*per sonare*]. Her mask is strange, or a stranger to her—she cannot find herself through it. When our mask resembles our inner self, the personality is identifiable as such and has a global sense of ontological security.

"I feel I have been placed inside a dead woman. Why can't I be set free? I look at myself in the mirror, but I cannot see myself. I can only see myself inside, like someone crying out so loudly . . . There are things outside me which move at very high speed; they attack me and sting me. If I were to represent them, I would draw lines and dots, but I don't know whether the dots are bright on a dark background, or dark on a bright background. Outwardly, you can see nothing. When people see me, they make fun of me. I remember I was "myself" when my father died. Before he died, I was anaemic, skinny, and I could not feel my body. But when he died, I suddenly became fat and bloated like a hippopotamus. I felt relieved . . . Then a naevus on my back became worse. I had it operated on, I was in despair and felt like crying all day long. I was left with a big scar, I felt badly damaged. Then the naevus started to grow again and it began to look like a bat. I swear it, I saw it myself."

I interpreted that this time she was making a link between her armour-plating and her father, on whose death she had felt free. She added: "It was a relief, like when I take my clothes off. I felt as though my fetters had been unlocked. I wasn't afraid any more. He loved me, but he made me ill and he wouldn't allow me to breathe. I couldn't be master of my own thoughts—he would always do the thinking for me. When he died, I put on weight, I became fatter and fatter and I felt much better. But it didn't last; I soon became a prisoner again."

I commented that she had felt relief at her father's death at first, but that afterwards she had become imprisoned inside herself (during this session with me she experienced me either as an enveloping mother or, at this point, as a father);[12] in her relationship

---

[12] As with her mother, her way of getting close to her father was to penetrate inside him by force (pathological projective identification) with the aim of controlling the internal object—but the result was a feeling of being imprisoned and persecuted. Melanie Klein (1946) derived claustrophobic anxiety from two major sources: projective identification with the mother, which leads to anxiety about being imprisoned inside her, and re-introjection of projected hostile objects which imprison and immobilize and turn into persecutors. We could say that in the present case, the patient had the same fantasy towards both parents and sometimes had difficulty in distinguishing between them— she felt that in every object relation the internal object would deprive her of her liberty and imprison her.

with her father, she had the impression that by forcing her way inside him (projective identification) she would mortally wound him. And so she had the impression she was inside a corpse, a fantasy which her father's death in reality had reinforced. On the other hand, his death enabled her to get rid of the father-armour, father-prison, false self—somebody else's mask.

This situation, however, did not last long. The persecutory fragments of her dead father returned in the shape of lines and dots that now persecuted her from inside. With no idea how to extricate herself from such a predicament, the patient tried to use a hypochondriac mechanism to focus persecutory death on a precise spot: the naevus on her back. She then felt that the only way to get rid of it was to have it removed surgically. She had been born with a malignant naevus, shaped like a bat, on her back. Her mother had told her that during the pregnancy she had been frightened by the sudden apparition of a bat. According to my patient, her mother had thereupon touched her back in precisely the same spot as Miss L was to have the naevus.[13] Thus the bat became a kind of copy of reality, a malignant shadow of the object. Her delusional hypochondriac fantasy or interpretation, derived from persecutory feelings projected onto a part of the body, coincided with a "real" change in her body which had become a materialization of her underlying delusional fantasy. Schilder quotes Freud, who called the phenomenon *somatisches Entgegenkommen*; a somatic predisposition or organic illness is thus ready to encounter the psychoneurotic tendency.

I interpreted this in terms of the naevus being the locus in which she was struggling to control the re-introjected persecutory father. On the one hand she had been freed, but on the other she had lost control of the object.

After the operation, the patient saw herself become fatter and fatter, like a hippopotamus, a fantasy that was related to feelings of grandeur and triumph over the father—a megalomaniac inflation. This is how the manic defence operates, with denial of the internal persecutors—the lines and dots that were attacking her. We could also look on the megalomaniac distortion of her body as the expression of her feeling that her body had no limits; this feeling

---

[13] This, of course, is the patient's fantasy of what had transpired.

compensated for her impression that she was feeble and composed only of water and emptiness.

I would now like to discuss more fully the desire to look inside oneself. Writing from a phenomenological standpoint, the French psychiatrist Sollier (1903) called this "internal autoscopic hallucination". Cotard (1891, p. 386) also described it as a symptom of delusional hypochondriasis. However, from a dynamic point of view, we could look upon it as an attempt to locate and to control the internal persecutors—in the case of Miss L, the lines and dots are "geometric" representations of her father and mother. As she penetrated further into her body space, however, the patient tried to deny her internal persecutors and the body that contained them. This is how she felt when she could no longer see herself in the mirror. This is a negative external autoscopy: a negative internal hallucination is projected onto the mirror, so becoming external. By becoming visible, she could not only control but also protect herself from internal and external reality.

Paul Federn (1959) describes the ego boundary as a kind of peripheral sense organ. The relationship between the ego as a dynamic entity and the ego boundary as a manifestation of ego integration is disturbed in depersonalization. In *The Ego and the Id*, Freud (1923b) writes: "A person's own body, and above all its surface, is a place from which both external and internal perceptions may spring"; and he added in a note in 1927: "[The ego] may thus be regarded as a mental projection of the surface of the body, besides [. . .] representing the superficies of the mental apparatus." Melanie Klein (1946) speaks of a primitive ego which is formed at the very beginning of life and also of a nucleus, the original internalized good object, around which the ego is organized. Good object relations make the ego feel secure and establish an even balance between projection and introjection. When persecutory anxiety is activated, the ego splits and schizoid mechanisms upset the workings of the normal ego. Nevertheless, splitting is a necessary step towards developing a capacity for dividing reality into categories. In the present case, the re-introjected persecutor located in the naevus was split off from the psychic ego. When this hypochondriac defence failed, the self felt invaded by "lines and dots"; the patient tried to first to control them and then deny their existence.

Ego integration and organization of the self depend on the good aspects of the introjected object and the ability to overcome persecutory anxiety. Excessive projection, albeit a means of getting rid of internal persecutors and controlling external reality, empties and weakens the self, and this in turn creates a high degree of dependence on what the self has projected into other objects. Similarly, excessive introjection gives rise to the feeling of being replete, overwhelmed, submerged.

Let me return to the process of ego integration and early object relations—that is, the link to the mother and its importance for personalization. The development of the self within the frontiers of the body and the expansion of perceptual experience enable the infant to discover the existence of non-self. Winnicott (1945) puts it thus: "I think of the process as if two lines came from opposite directions, liable to come near each other. If they overlap, there is a moment of *illusion'*—a bit of experience which the infant can take as *either* his hallucination *or* as a thing belonging to external reality" (p. 152). Winnicott insists on the importance of this experience for both mother and infant. He refers firstly to caring for the baby, keeping it warm, caressing, bathing, cradling and talking to it; and also to the baby's powerful "instinctive" tendency to gather itself together inside. What is important above all is the atmosphere in which the exchange takes place, and the way in which these "moments of illusion" are experienced. The encounter between the infant's "hallucinated breast" and the mother's real breast is always ambiguous, insofar as hallucinated experiences and normal (perceived) ones are mistakenly treated as identical.

Bion (1962) also explored the earliest moments of the mother–child relationship. He emphasizes how important it is for the mother to be able to "take in" and tolerate in her body the infant's persecutory anxiety. This enables her to send the anxiety back to her baby in a way that he can bear. If mother is unable to work through her infant's projections, all she can give him back is increased anxiety which he cannot assimilate.

The mother–child relationship is a fundamental experience that is decisive for the infant's future development. Some children have powerful *innate* tendencies such as greediness or aggressiveness that make the mother's task much more difficult. But if the mother has good emotional rapport with her baby, she will be able to address situations of conflict much more easily. If the mother is not in touch with her own feelings—in other words, if she is cut off from herself—the whole mother–child relationship will also be split and incomplete. Some mothers may be physically very close to their offspring, but not emotionally close. The infant takes in an image of a distant, impersonal, cold mother, and this increases his own splitting. The relationship becomes physical, mechanical, and mediocre from the emotional point of view.

Miss L will help me to illustrate this last point. In a preliminary meeting with her mother, I learned that breast-feeding had continued for an inordinately long period—almost three years—and that the mother had been in the habit of holding her daughter's hand until she fell asleep. Yet the patient described her childhood as being bereft of warmth and affection. The more the mother tried to "satisfy" her greedy daughter, the more the latter's demands increased—as did her frustration. Her avidity stimulated projective identification in order to take possession of the mother. In this way, the baby could feed herself from inside her mother; but, on the other hand, she felt confused with the object and unable to build the frontiers of her own ego.

This state of fusion with a mother in permanent—but distant—physical contact did not help the baby to override the confusion between her ego and that of others (here, the mother's). The patient once told me: "I was given everything—but without warmth. I was never *educated*, nobody ever told me what to do and what not to do." In the transference, she gave the impression that I was becoming the superego she had been unable to construct at that time.

The patient had been unable to develop a good relationship with her mother at an early stage, and as a result ego synthesis and integration had not been properly set in motion. She was also incapable of introjecting a good superego guide to lead her and tell her what to do and what not to do. On the contrary: she felt she had a very persecutory superego which attacked her from within and immobilized and imprisoned her from outside. In the transference, she used to ask me questions in order to make me play the part of the "good superego" that would give her guidance and keep her in touch with internal and external reality.

One day she told me that my words were changing into smoke and vanishing. In her view, I was not giving her what she wanted. When she felt I was again taking on the part of the superego-guide, her impression was that my words were "hard, hard as steel", penetrating inside her in order to stay there. The distinction between what is "good" and what is "idealized" is a very fine one in this patient; also, all the degrees from good to bad are lost in a manichean dichotomy between good/idealized and bad. Sometimes there is a confused overlap of two contradictory experiences reunited in a single message. When she said that my words were "hard", she meant that they gave her strength; when she added "hard as steel" as though she was idealizing the strength of my words, she was in fact negating and masking the severity and hardness of a persecuting superego.

She did not allow people to show kindness towards her. That hurt her. "I don't want to be treated as a person, I prefer not to be treated kindly; it would be like putting something bright on something dark, and by contrast, darkening it even further." As I have mentioned, from time to time she would see herself as made of drops of water (empty or full) or like fumes escaping from a bottle (her body-recipient) and vanishing into space, or again like something contained within steel armour-plating. It is not only the structural image she had of herself that is interesting to analyse, but also the textural image.[14] At times she would experience her body as made of sand or of wood. She wanted to penetrate inside her inner world and learn what those lines and dots were, the ones that attacked her from inside herself. She was not sure whether the dots were bright on a dark background, or dark on a light background; this gestalt-like figure showed her inability to discern what dominated her internal world—was it something bright and good, light and idealized, on a dark background, or bad dark spots on a bright and good background? She found it necessary to distinguish between the good and bad values of these internalized

---

[14] I have already discussed in previous papers (e.g. Resnik, 1997b) the "ontological" questionings of the psychotic patient: What is he? What is the nature of things [φυσις], the nature (texture and structure) of his own body? Of his own existence? Of the world?

objects[15] and to define more or less what kind of person she was in terms of these values. In her attempt to achieve integration,[16] she tried to differentiate between the objects contained in her internal world, just as she felt the need to distinguish between herself and others.

Acquisition of identity and achievement of authentic interpersonal relationships promote objectivity and judgemental capacity—ethical and rational. They signify perception of oneself as existing as an inhabitant of one's own body. When the body, which has also a social function, is able to acknowledge its frontiers, a lost world has been re-conquered, and communication—inextricably tied to recognition of separateness—is henceforth possible.

As Miss L put it, *to be* means "to look at yourself and see yourself; to stand on your feet and know you're standing; to speak and be aware that it's you who is talking; to be wholly yourself, to be a person."

---

[15] The idea of "good" and "bad" in terms of intrinsic value, in addition to their persecutory or non-persecutory vector, can be thought of as a stage on the path to ethical discrimination of reality. This phenomenon is part of the construction of a moral superego.

[16] Melanie Klein (1950) showed how the global view we have of ourselves and of others (whole-object relation) constitutes the "depressive position". Becoming aware of hitherto denied truth is painful; the entire developmental process goes through depressive periods corresponding to transitions from one state to another (normal mourning process).

CHAPTER TWO

Cotard's syndrome
and depersonalization

Some years ago, I analysed a female patient whose symptoms were depersonalization and negation of her body; these symptoms brought to my mind some of the clinical features described by Jules Cotard (1882–1884). I feel it may be of some interest to draw a parallel between the phenomenological aspects of the classic description and the analytic experience.

Cotard's syndrome

In 1861, Baillarger (1890) drew attention to a particular form of hypochondriac delusion which included feelings of destruction or non-existence of parts of the body; he had encountered these in cases of general paralysis, and in fact had thought them typical of and belonging almost exclusively to this ailment.

In 1880, Cotard read to the Paris Société Médico-Psychologique a paper in which he described a particular kind of hypochondriac delusion in cases of severe melancholia; he called it "delusion of negations". For Cotard, this delusion was a feature of certain severe forms of chronic melancholic anxiety. He describes six major symptoms: melancholic anxiety; the ideas of damnation and of diabolic possession (demonopathy); disposition towards suicide or self-injury; analgesia; hypochondriac ideas of non-existence or destruction of organs or of the entire body, of the soul, of God, etc.; and ideas of immortality and enormity (hugeness).

Classical French psychiatry calls this group of symptoms Cotard's syndrome (Czermak, 1986). The fundamental feature of the syndrome is the "delusion of negations" which is expressed in one of two ways: either by a negative attitude expressed as systematic opposition and contradiction (negativism), or in the unshakeable conviction that there has been alteration, destruction, absence, or non-existence of something. Cotard (1882–1884) classified these ideas into three groups. First, negation of physical aspects of the individual—the existence of certain organs is denied (hypochondriac delusion of negation). Then, negation of the psyche—there are neither thoughts nor ideas. Lastly, negation of the external world—neither people nor things exist. The conjunction of all three gives rise to what is known as "universal negation", in which neither the world nor the individual concerned exists.

This classification gives us an integral view of negation which is no longer limited to mere negation of the body. Séglas studied negation in terms of personality aspects, bodily and mental features, and the relationship between the individual and the world. He emphasized in particular the fact that such ideas are always secondary to some modification in the personality. The syndrome is above all, therefore, a symptomatic disorder that concerns personality development. It affects the internal world and the body that the patient inhabits; it is expressed by means of the body or in the external world, where it becomes manifest through projection.[1] For Séglas, ideas of negation are not specific to melancholia, they are encountered in various clinical contexts. Furthermore, the full-

---

[1] "Internal" (or "inner") world and "external" world are two concepts that I use a great deal in this chapter and throughout this book; it is therefore necessary to give some explanation of what I mean by them. The internal world is a set or conglomerate of experiences, created through our contacts with the environment and located in our body. For Melanie Klein, unconscious phantasies are experienced as part- or whole-objects which are in relation with

blown Cotard's syndrome is uncommon; we may come across similar cases that do not present all the symptoms listed. This does not invalidate the diagnosis. Séglas makes a distinction between typical and atypical forms: the melancholic delusion of negation on the one hand, and delusional forms of hypochondriac negation (in which paranoid mechanisms predominate) on the other.

Cotard described how the illness usually progresses from simple hypochondriasis, through the intermediate stage of delusional hypochondriasis, and finally negation. It is a matter of degree.

Other writers (e.g. Barbé, 1939, p. 183) use only two categories, according to whether melancholic aspects are a feature or not. They include in the latter category confusional states and the negativist catatonic form of schizophrenia.

Cotard and Séglas identified the ideas of negation prevalent in melancholic conditions, and their clinical examples show clearly the paranoid aspects. Cotard drew attention to the link between ideas of negation and hypochondriasis. In his view, if we make a thorough exploration of simple hypochondriasis, we are bound to come across delusional features, "either paranoid or depressive". Generally speaking, hypochondriasis and paranoid conditions have a very close relationship—hence the alternative name for hypochondriasis: somatic paranoia.[2] Analysis of hypochondriac patients is even more complex when the psychotic aspects are bound up with the symptom.

---

one another and with the ego. We can feel them alive and active within ourselves.

The "external" world includes fields of experience in which our contacts with real objects are given dramatic form; it is, however, to some extent also the product of our own projections.

Paula Heimann (1952) maintains that fantasies belonging to the internal world cannot be separated from those relative to the external world. Only limits to our descriptive capacity make them appear to be two different entities in reciprocal interaction.

[2] Hypochondriasis seems to be one of the very primitive defence mechanisms available to the ego. It is based on splitting body from mental apparatus. In order to spare the mind painful paranoid or depressive situations, the ego displaces them onto the body. If in spite of this the situation is still fraught with anxiety, an omnipotent ego is quite prepared to negate the existence of the organ or part of the body into which the painful situation had been projected.

The aim of this chapter is to combine the phenomenological aspect of the clinical situation—the ideas of negation—and its physical manifestations with the dynamic concepts of psychoanalysis. Analysis of psychotics gives us the opportunity to observe psychiatric descriptions "in movement".

The mechanism of negation

Freud (1925h) considered negation [*Verneinung*[3]] to be one of the earliest defence mechanisms because of its relationship to expulsion. He writes: "Expressed in the language of the oldest—the oral—instinctual impulses, the judgement is: 'I should like to eat this', or 'I should like to spit it out'; and, put more generally: 'I should like to take this into myself and to keep that out.' [. . .] the original pleasure-ego wants to introject into itself everything that is good and to eject from itself everything that is bad."

Anna Freud (1936) studied denial as a defence with respect to reality, and described how it becomes manifest in action and in words.

Bertrand Lewin (1951) examined the relationship between negation and exalted affirmation. What is important is the difference between "no" as an expression of opposition to some affirmation or other, and a magic or omnipotent unconscious denial (the manic defence). In Melanie Klein's writings, the mechanism of negation has particular importance, specifically in the paranoid–schizoid position. The bad or persecutory object is not only spilt off from the good object, its whole existence is denied, whereas the good aspects are exaggerated or idealized in order to be safe from persecu-

---

[3] Freud employs the term *Verleugnung* [disavowal or denial] as distinct from *Verneinung* [negation]. In *Verleugnung*, the defence consists in denying something that affects the individual —and to this extent is a way of affirming what he is apparently denying. Strachey adds a note on *Verleugnung* to Freud's paper "The Infantile Genital Organization" (1923e, p. 143), in order to call the reader's attention to the differences between *Verleugnung*, *Verneinung*, and *Verdrängung* [repression]. For Freud, *Verdrängung* is a neurotic defence mechanism, whereas *Verleugnung* is related to the psychoses (where repression is impossible and the patient turns to denial of internal and external reality).

tion. It is not so much the object that is negated as the object relation—that is, that part of the ego which is linked to the object and the part of reality onto which it is projected. In her view, denial of distressing and persecuting reality is accomplished by means of omnipotence. The unconscious translates omnipotent denial and negation to mean annihilation.

I would like to illustrate some of these issues by means of a clinical case in which the patient manifested symptoms similar to those described by Cotard in the syndrome of negation.

Negation and guilt

Miss L is the young patient I referred to in the previous chapter. From the outset of her analysis, it was obvious that strong denial along with manic and obsessive symptoms were being used in an attempt to avoid underlying melancholia.

I had been consulted by the patient's mother, who told me that her daughter had fallen ill after the death of the father: "On the day of the funeral, she was strange; she didn't seem to recognize anybody. Like the rest of them, however, she did show some outward signs of grief, but she seemed absent and distant, a stranger to what was going on. From time to time she laughed, saying everything was beautiful and in good taste. Then she would look at her dead father in surprise and say that she didn't know that thin person lying in the coffin, adding that if only she had a scalpel with her she would do a dissection" (at that time Miss L was training to become a dentist). This bizarre and depersonalized attitude was accompanied by a tendency to feel elated from time to time; this later gave way to obsessive rituals. For example, in order to reach the bathroom, she felt obliged to go through her dead father's bedroom in spite of the fact that a more direct route was readily available. Apparently she felt she had to ritualize the fact that she needed a father-figure between herself, her ego, and her pre-genital and genital life, in order to help clarify her confusion. On the other hand, there was some ambivalence in the fact that perverse fantasies of denial of her father as a superego figure were expressed symbolically—she imagined or hallucinated a flag which she wanted to burn—but at the same time she felt guilty at having killed and burnt her father, and so had to be punished. She later associated this need with the fact that she was at that point hospitalized and treated by electroconvulsive therapy and insulin. Her condition improved, and she was able to return to her studies.

A year later she had a relapse after undergoing surgery (removal of a malignant naevus from her shoulder). She was again hospitalized, then left the clinic after some improvement in her condition. This cycle was repeated several times during the following three years. Her mother said she was still bizarre and withdrawn.

Miss L is the second of three children. Her parents had not wanted another baby at that time. She was breast-fed for an unusually long time—her mother had a great deal of difficulty in weaning her (she was almost three years of age). During the consultation, the mother seemed to be somewhat distant, talking of her daughter in a very detached tone of voice. I could therefore imagine that the mother–daughter relationship was "mechanical" and empty of all emotion. The mother described the father as having been ambivalent towards his daughter. He died of uraemia. Immediately after the funeral, Miss L took to wearing a scarf that had belonged to him.[4]

My first encounter with Miss L took place in a private clinic where she had recently been readmitted after a relapse. She looked at me suspiciously, then began by telling me that she had "fixed ideas". These forced her to count things in threes and multiples of three. I had the impression that it was only from time to time that she was actually speaking to me; most of the time it looked as though she was talking to someone who existed only for her. She asked "essential" questions: "Where does water come from? Where does fire come from?" Then she went on: "Water is made from hydrogen and oxygen, but I don't know how they combine."[5]

---

[4] This scarf would seem to represent a transitional object which perpetuated the link with the father. It was also the "organ" onto which she displaced the feelings of loss that she denied in her depersonalized state.

[5] In this displaced and symbolic way, Miss L was expressing both her difficulty in communicating and her desire to communicate, as well as her interest in linking and in the way "essential" things combine.

I communicated to her my impression that she wanted to know where things came from, what their origin was, and how from two essential objects—father and mother (hydrogen and oxygen)—it was possible to conceive something new, a newborn baby.[6]

Miss L replied to this interpretation, saying that at home nobody ever explained anything to her, that her father and mother were too serious and distant for that. (This confirmed my impression of the mother's attitude during the preliminary consultation.) Her mother watched over her constantly.

I added that the aim of her questions was not simply to know the origin of things; by questioning me, she was attempting to "feel" what kind of person I was. She wanted to know where I came from, if I was going to be sincere and spontaneous, and if I was going to answer her. The attitude I adopted—listening to and trying to understand the symbolic meaning of her language, and not refusing her questions—enabled her to recreate a link with her father (the mediating scarf).

"Daddy was very affectionate towards me," she said. "I don't remember him dying . . . They told me I went up to him to give him a kiss. Once I saw a corpse dressed in white and that amused me. I don't like corpses, they make me laugh."[7]

The manic and obsessive defences are an attempt to deny her father's death and her own feelings of guilt. They are related to sadistic fantasies she often had about him (the desire to cut his body with a scalpel) and to the idea she had that the medication she had given her father during his final illness might have been for euthanasia.

The intensity of her destructive drives and of her anxiety and guilt did not allow her to work through grief and mourning and enter into the depressive position. Her inability to recreate and repair the object stimulated her regression to the paranoid-schiz-

---

[6] I have often observed that psychotics are preoccupied with ontological issues. Questions about the origins of water and fire are, for me, reminiscent of the pre-Socratic philosophers' questions about the origins of the universe.

[7] Her description of the events surrounding her father's death was identical to her mother's version. The patient spoke impersonally in order to deny the pain she felt and to keep all feelings about his death at arm's length. In addition, she used laughter as part of a manic denial mechanism.

oid–position (she split off the good and bad images of her father: her affectionate father, and the severe and distant one). Through her manic defences, she omnipotently denied the existence of a persecuting object. She controlled her father by means of her obsessive acts and rituals.[8]

As well as controlling the objects of her internal and external worlds, she had to isolate them because she perceived the danger that her instinctual drives would create. She said: "I'm angry with my mother, sometimes I'd like to kill her. That's why I stay in bed all day long. I only get up when I'm sure everybody else has left the house. In the evening, I'm very careful to put away the scissors or any other dangerous objects I come across."

At one point, she said: "There are things I can't say, I can't express. They are like drawings." She began to draw a gibbet, with a platform and thirteen steps—a number she associated to the date of her father's death. Then she wrote the names of three Nazis who had been sentenced to death; she added: "The first one is guilty, but he doesn't repent. The second one is better because he tries to make reparation. The third one is bad; he looks for excuses." Miss L told me that, in her view, I would dislike the last one most. Then she wrote "3 = 3" and said that three Capuchin friars were judging the three Nazis.

I interpreted this as two aspects of herself she was trying to balance out: the accusing part (the friars) and the accused part (the Nazis). In the transference, she felt accused and judged by me for all three aspects of her guilt with respect to her father. Of these three aspects, the one she considered the worst was the bad one which only looked for excuses and refused to admit guilt.

I added that her need to draw had a double aim. In the first place, it showed me how difficult it was for her to express herself directly; this explained why she needed some other means of expression such as drawing materials. Second, it demonstrated her need to make a confession.

---

[8] Her obsessive rituals are an attempt at recreating lost objects through repetition (counting them to make sure that none are missing, and that they all come in threes—the basic nuclear family: father, mother, baby and their various combinations). Her manic defences, however, are aimed at negating their existence.

Simple hypochondriasis and paranoid mechanisms

When manic and obsessive defences failed, Miss L felt both guilt and the need to be punished. Her guilt, however, alternated with hypochondriac and paranoid mechanisms. She said: "People annoy me. They talk to me. Everybody is mad. When you speak, I hear a buzzing noise. I have a headache . . . I'm angry with myself; I want to hit myself. I feel bitten and aching inside myself."

She tried to eject her internal persecutor along with the dangerous aspects of herself (the mad parts). Projecting these mad parts into other people convinced her that people outside were mad. In the transference, it was my voice that annoyed her.

The physical manifestations of the internal persecutor were the somatic and hypochondriac symptoms. She could not project everything into the outside world because it would then be entirely given over to dangers of various kinds, and she was afraid that these dangers would attack her (and therefore introjection was distressing). In order to safeguard the external world from her internal dangers, she needed to use her body; in this way, she could imprison everything harmful inside herself. She tried to defend herself against internal persecutors by appeasing them: "I want to sleep. I'd like you to give me a sleeping pill. Let me sleep."[9] "When my father died I envied him, because then he could relax without anybody bothering him. I want to die, because it's like going to sleep."

She was making sleeping the equivalent of dying; death appeased the internal persecutors and at the same time protected her from external ones.

In contrast to this restful picture of death, Miss L spoke also of a persecutory death: "People bother me, they upset me, they kill me. My father won't let me move or even breathe. He killed me."

The breakdown of her splitting mechanisms between good protecting object and bad persecutory object led immediately to confusion: "Everything is cloudy . . . Night and day are the same

---

[9] I think that it is always important in analysis to explore the meaning of medication with respect to an internal situation. Some patients need to put their internal persecutors to sleep (hypnotic or narcotic drugs), others to calm them down (sedatives), and still others to wake up some dormant aspect within themselves (stimulants).

. . . Nothing is good, nothing is bad, everything is the same" (unity in a mixture).

I interpreted her confusion in the transference as an inability to distinguish between what was good and what was bad in herself and also in me. She felt me to be good if she had a satisfying image of me; but I was bad whenever I became frustrating.

"I came here empty. You have to talk to me in order to fill me up . . . The worst days are the ones when I'm not with you, that's when I feel emptier than ever." Her oral demand was expressed in words that equated food with speech.

Paranoid anxiety alternated with periods of confusion: "They twist my bed and I can't untwist it. I'm twisted too . . . . I get mixed up between this place and my home . . . I mix up the days . . . I'd like to be alone, without anyone to annoy me . . . My father wouldn't leave me alone."

I interpreted her complaints, commenting that I, like her father, did not leave her alone: she felt I was pulling her out of her isolation and putting her in touch with reality that either persecuted her or increased her confusion.

She re-created the image of her father in her dreams. She saw him "ill, dying . . . He never stops dying". As soon as she had said that, she complained of an intense pain in her back, where her scar was. I commented that the father lying on his sickbed (in the dream) had turned into a vengeful and persecuting father. The scar was where she could feel him alive and punishing her, and she could not easily get rid of him. She was experiencing in her body her relationship with her father and what had occurred when he died.

When her father first fell ill, she had felt fine—as though she had forced into him the bad and terrifying image of persecuting death. It was only when her father was actually dead that the dead-father object returned to persecute and invade her (the naevus became a malignant tumour). The invasion of the naevus signified also the failure of the mechanism through which she located, contained, and controlled persecutory death in the father-persecutor.

Every time the father-persecutor appeared in the transference (or whenever he was personified as persecutory death), the pain in her back increased. From time to time—I was sitting behind her— I became the persecuting naevus attacking her in the back.

In order to defend herself against this paranoid situation in the transference, she would sometimes re-introject me as an idealized protector she could carry with her wherever she went. "When I'm at home, I feel I'm with you. I feel I take you with me when I leave the session. That way, I can talk to you and tell you everything I want for as long as I want."

Delusional hypochondriasis and body fantasy

"My head is empty, and inside I can see hinges and nuts and bolts. What side do you open the hinges on?"

Concepts like opening and shutting are reified in her thinking, and take the form of concrete everyday objects;[10] she wanted to know what to do in order to "open up", in what direction, and also when to "close" in order to be distinct from other people.

She described the nuts in an anthropomorphic way: "They have a head, a body, a washer, and a bolt. I pick them up in the street. I leave nails alone, because they hurt. The washer is important—thanks to it, the head of the nut and the bolt can hold on to each other without actually touching."

She was using concrete elements and structural terminology in order to find the solid, concrete, "nuts and bolts" of integration. Nuts and bolts represented a reparatory coitus (but not nails—they hurt).

From this union, this integration, emerges a possibility of differentiating and learning: what does "opening up" entail? and "closing down"? What is external reality? internal reality? When I fell silent, Miss L made as though she were in pain, and she touched her body in the region of her ovaries. I said that my words had been experienced as harmful nails rather than as nuts.

She wanted to hold on to me, but she knew also that some distance between us was necessary—a washer between nut and bolt. She said: "I see in my head bright lines which move at great speed and cross one another. I have to follow them constantly with

---

[10] Instead of images or thoughts, all that existed for Miss L were concrete objects that had not been subjected to mental and sensori-perceptual transformation.

my eyes. Now I feel jammed between two planks of wood. And now I see two stones, a big one and a smaller one. How can they be brought closer together without breaking?"

I commented that the lines she saw moving about in her thoughts were mummies and daddies having multiple intercourse, from which were born smaller lights (babies). Seeing this made her excited and aroused, but since she was afraid of different kinds of intercourse she was trying to control the situation; she wanted to separate the constituent elements of a couple, she would be the washer that keeps the daddy-bolt apart from the mummy-nut— but when she does get between them, she feels jammed in. In the transference she dramatized this situation, with the feeling that she was hemmed in by the two planks (erotic and persecutory transference). At the same time, she was responsible for the parents coming together or remaining apart in the transference; in her reified world, she expressed the desire that the big stone-daddy be reunited with the smaller stone-mummy without either of them breaking. She also expressed the idea of reuniting/separating by projecting her fantasies onto the analyst's body: "You, doctor, are in the lift when suddenly it stops; I see your head separating from your body." "Sometimes you are an accumulator battery which transmits electricity." As she made this last statement, she felt her chest and pubis becoming itchy and prickling.

She projected onto me the sexual feelings she was experiencing in her own body (erotic transference). The source of food and knowledge was erotically cathected and became a source of "electric sexuality".

She attributed to the analyst the role of sexual-energy accumulator in the transference relationship: "From time to time you are two stones, *Doc* and *Tor*. Whenever I'm afraid, I say the word "doctor" and the fear leaves me." (When a couple of magic stones are reunited, they have tremendous power.) "Sometimes you are God, and my life is hell because I feel tied to you everywhere you may be. If you see the door is shut, doctor, don't go in through the window. Because anyway the door can't be opened from the inside, the key isn't there. So don't go in, you can never be sure that the ground is solid."

I pointed out to her that when she projected so much into me, she became mixed up with me. She saw in me her own split-off hallucinated parts, and she tried to tie them together with magic. When she said the word "doctor", she could, like God, reunite the magical stones. On the other hand, she showed me how she cared for me when she warned me that I would have to watch my step if I entered her world. Her door was shut, there was no key, and the ground might not be solid. She needed to keep me "good", and so she warned me of the bad aspects lurking inside and outside herself. Pathological dependence on the idealized object, God, ended up by persecuting her, and her life became hell.

Negation of external reality

Up till this point, I have explored negation and denial with respect to internal reality. Now I would like to discuss the mechanism whereby bad objects are ejected and expelled. When external reality is constantly felt to be suspect, mysterious, and dangerous, negation of reality is the ultimate recourse.

Miss L told me that she had recently taken up her studies again, but reading was a problem for her: letters and words became persons who separated then came back together again (like *Doc-Tor*). The object split into two parts may be an attempt to differentiate between me as a doctor and me as a person in the transference. However, at the same time, Doc-Tor is a projection of her own splitting, or even of her splitting of the combined parents talking together in secret. "I hear voices, but not very clearly. It's like a murmur, two people whispering secretly . . . The world is full of shadows . . . The other day, I saw a shadow that looked like my daddy; it tried to attack me . . . I'd like to fall asleep. I walk as though I was asleep. I can't see anything. Everything is empty." Her desire was to come between the two parts of the parental couple, as between the point and the line, but the father returns as a persecutory oedipal superego.

Here she was externalizing her internal persecuting objects, first into her textbooks and then outside in the street. The internal situation with respect to her parents was: "they come together and then separate". She was dramatizing her voyeuristic arousal and her fears about the primal scene. The primal scene was felt to be persecutory, in particular with respect to the image of the superego father, the shadow who tried to attack her. The outside world was full of threats, inhabited by the shadows of her internal world, and as such was unacceptable. And so it was negated and denied—reality was "de-realized".

Freud (1936a) wrote of doubting external reality—the feeling of derealization—distinguishing it from depersonalization, which is unfamiliarity with some part of internal reality.

Negation of time

"Days just don't exist," she said. "Sometimes one day feels like a lot of days, sometimes almost nothing. When I come here it's day; when I leave it's night.[11] Day means remembering something. Night is the negation of day. On sunny days, I see daddy bright and good . . . Sometimes I can't link days together. There is a gap between them.[12] Time is something which gives me a great deal [nourishing time] and that has something to do with light and ideal; but at other moments it gives me little or nothing. Day does not exist [empty time].[13]

---

[11] Her experience of time was extremely variable. Sometimes, time would last for some fairly extensive duration, at others it would simply flash by. The passing of time could be either very slow, or very rapid. Again, time could appear infinite, or be reduced to nothing ("Days just don't exist"). This irregularity and estrangements show how difficult it was for Miss L to think out some notion of time which would be harmonious and evenly balanced.

[12] Her inability to link day with night and the fact that she considered night and day to be absolutely opposed to each other illustrate her manichean tendencies: the part of herself she identifies with night or blackness annuls the bright day part.

[13] The father is experienced as good and useful when he fulfils his role as *nexus*, the one who links days together. According to Melanie Klein and to Bion, the part-object penis is originally experienced as the prototype of the mediating object, the linker or *nexus*. The nipple—an oral penis—links the baby's mouth to the mother-breast. The father-penis is thus already differentiated from the mother, the nipple-and-breast. However, the very idea of a link suggests that there is some perception of a separating space experienced as a gap between objects. The penis-*nexus* vanquishes the anxiety aroused by the void: it is a bridge, an intermediary.

Day meant remembering—that is, recalling and recovering the bright father who made links (linking days).[14]

To remember is a way of finding again in memory the father who had been lost from her internal world. In the mind, the function of the nexus enables linking of thoughts and images in order to conceptualize.

Jules Cotard (1888) described a symptom he called "loss of mental vision" which he observed in melancholic patients with delusions of negation. Such patients can neither see nor recall absent objects in their mind.[15]

If recall is impossible, the lost object cannot be found again.[16]

For Miss L, time was undifferentiated and homogeneous: "There is no morning, no afternoon, no evening. Everything is the same." She did not distinguish between before, now, and after. Without integration (linking days together), she did not have the necessary boundaries for differentiating successive moments in time.

She added: "I'd like to leave this place, fall asleep and never wake up again." In her dreams she could possess whatever objects she wanted. In oneiric time, she could find her world, a world without end; being awake represented limited and demanding reality. Sleep is one way of rejecting the reality principle and negating reality insofar as it is finite and not inexhaustible. She

---

[14] Time here is characterized by oral intentionality. The father-penis in part-object relations provides what the breast contains (if he is a constant provider, he becomes the idealized nipple-penis). When he does not provide, time-and-breast are experienced as empty. The nipple-father embodies the "law" that allows the child to be fed or not.

[15] Mental images, *eidolon*, play an important role in thinking. We think in images or in imaginary representations of a perceived object. To accept an image as such involves accepting the distance that separates us from the original object. To accept the absence of the original object and put in its place a representation are the foundations of symbolic processes. Accepting the word "mummy" means for the infant that mummy-as-such is absent.

[16] For Melanie Klein, reparation is linked to the depressive position and is a structuring process with which the ego is required to come to terms. Guilt and depressive responsibility stimulate recovery of the damaged or lost object.

sought refuge in her eternally inexhaustible oneiric world, her dream world.

Negation of the body

When the hypochondriac defence fails in its aim of isolating and controlling the internal persecutor in one part of the body, omnipotent negation takes over. Its aim is to deny magically the existence of the persecutor and of the locus in which it has been placed. The extreme form of this negation involves making that part of the body—or the entire body—invisible.

At one point, Miss L said: "I see a man walking; he's carrying a very beautiful copper lamp. He stole it from a house." She associated to this as follows: "I saw a nun in the street; she had very beautiful eyes. She looked like the kind of idol that primitive tribes adore. I looked at her greedily as if to swallow her up."

This was Miss L's way of expressing her unconscious fantasy about stealing the all-powerful lamp-penis in order to possess her mother's body (the nun-mother). But in fact she took possession by means of her mouth-eye. Pregenital use of the phallus did not lead to a true relationship with her mother, but to a paranoid situation which was fraught with anxiety: "I don't have a body. My clothes are oppressing me; I'm inside something which envelopes me and won't let me be free . . . I'm very small. The walls are oppressing me . . . I feel something very hard inside my throat; it's pushing at me and preventing me from breathing. I'm frightened I won't be able to get out. Even criminals are authorized leave of absence."

She felt she was inside a maternal persecutory envelope, a feeling that she dramatized in the transference: "The walls are oppressing me." In this situation she felt weak and defenceless, attacked by the enveloping mother and by the father-phallus (who prevented her from breathing). This "intra-uterine" fantasy expressed the paranoid fear of having taken possession of the object which then controlled her and would not let her leave. Her paranoid guilt was related to the theft of the phallus and exclusive possession of her mother.

Negation of her body—"I don't have a body"—became transformed into negation of the world as a whole. The world turned into fog, confusion, dream. "I walk along the street, I'm upside-down among the people . . . Everything seems dream-like. People pass me by without moving . . . At times it looks like I'm being sucked into a void . . . They're sleepwalking. I'd like to beat them into waking up."

The image of herself asleep and confused is projected onto the people in the street. The part of herself that was fragmented and mixed up with ordinary reality was the stimulus for this picture of a dream-world. The outside world (container: the street; contained: the people) was negated in a veil of confusion. This veil was also the screen on which she projected her reality.

Miss L added: "I'd like to see daylight as soon as the sun starts to rise. I walk like a mechanical doll. I'm an imbecile." At that point, she sat on the floor and, holding on to a chair, went on: "I'd really like to know what to do in order not to be confused any more. I feel empty. I walk leaning forward; I'm holding this chair in order to avoid confusion."

Negation is here illustrated in several ways. Negation of the body and of the inside of the body ("I feel empty"), deflection of the body axis ("I walk leaning forward"), and negation of the outside world (image of confused reality). The chair was her point of reference, her anchor (inside herself or external, personified by me in the transference as an anchoring—but inanimate—object), which helped her hold on to reality.

"This body is not mine,[17] it's deformed. I'm in another body. I'd like to get out. I'll take you inside me and you'll come everywhere with me." Here, splitting[18] was a defence against confused reality: she located on the surface of her body (her envelope) everything she felt to be deformed and bad; inside, the idealized object (idealized ego) she would never be without, taking it everywhere with her. In her dual personality, she punished her envelope by beating it and making accusations against it: "It won't let me out. I'd like to

---

[17] There are two possible meanings here: either depersonalization (her body was foreign to her); or, through projective identification she felt contained in another recipient (claustrophobic and persecuting).

[18] Container and contained are here in the service of splitting: the recipient is in complete contradiction with the elements it envelopes.

get out and be elsewhere." (The persecutory enveloping mother was imprisoning her.) The body envelope signified the persecuting mother into whom she had projected herself, but also (occasionally) the envelope that preserved her from confused reality, when she did in spite of everything require to be hospitalized. The hospital-envelope with its "walls" protected her: "In hospital I feel less oppressed." The hospital was a super-envelope that allowed her to defend herself when she came out of the oppressing persecutory container (we have to be reborn in a safe context if we are to change and grow).

Once we had analysed and discussed this material, we decided that admission to hospital was indeed necessary. When she was in hospital she felt more relaxed and could take stock of the fact that she was not a living person—that is, conscious of herself as a person. In the clinic she acquired inner perspective, a way of looking at herself through the existence of other people. She commented: "They are different from me. They talk together. I feel ill when I look at them and realize that I'm not like them. I'm not a person, I'm nothing, and I'll never manage to be 'somebody'."

To become a person involves making reparation, to cause to "re-exist" something that did not exist previously. Her body image was fragmented and scattered, with no linking, locked inside a bizarre, distorted, and persecutory envelope. Her punitive paranoid guilt gave her the impression that to some extent she had no right to become someone ("I'll never manage to be somebody"). From time to time, she would again express an erotic transference through eroticized physical sensations (heat and itchiness in the genital area). She dramatized her desire to embrace the mummy-analyst by kissing the hospital bed on which she lay during her sessions. When she left the hospital, she said that she had no secure frontiers and no body. Once again, the envelope-surface became persecutory and oppressing: "The envelope squeezes me and leaves me body-less".

There is quite a clear relationship between not having a body of her own and not having boundaries—or rather, having the sensation of being unable to perceive her surface as her own.

Surface of the body, physical boundary, body, body image—all these took on various meanings for Miss L. Clothes on the surface of the body could be experienced in a strange and persecutory manner: "My clothes oppress me and prevent me breathing." For Miss L, clothing is not even a kind of skin, but someone else, a persecutory engulfing object (Bion)—or perhaps she is describing the claustrophobic experience of being stuck inside the object/ clothing.

Sometimes clothes did have contours, an armour-plating that provided her with frontiers, and at that point they were part of her real self: "When I'm all alone I can take my clothes off, but when I'm with other people I feel dispersed . . . I'm made of drops of water which get lost." At other times, she was "made of grains of sand" which were disseminated everywhere.

Clothes could also be a good object with which she tried to unite and integrate into reality (sometimes this union became eroticized and persecutory): "Daddy was good and kind, I wanted to be with him. When I was a little girl, a very nice priest [father] used to come to the house and he would tell me I looked very gentle. Clothes oppress me. I had a dream about the priest, I'm ashamed of it . . . I was pressed up close to him . . . I'd like to press up close to you."

Pressed and being pressed are two aspects of an enveloped/ enveloping object relation—sometimes idealized and eroticized (a paternal or maternal erotic transference with respect to me), at others persecuting and claustrophobic (her clothes oppressing her). Her father came back to life in the dream in the shape of an eroticized priest-father. When she said she was ashamed to tell me of the dream about the priest, she was projecting into me a paternal superego sitting in judgement on her.

Clifford Scott (1948), following in Freud's footsteps, emphasizes the importance of the surface of the body in constructing and establishing the body image. He adds that perception, imagination, conceptualization, and development of a sense of space and time are also involved in building up the body image.

Melanie Klein (1946) also stresses the relationship between integration and the idea of limits. She claims that we need good ego growth (an integrating nucleus or primary good object) in order to attain equilibrium between being on or inside the object (projection) and taking it in (introjection). Balance of this kind enables construction of limits between inside and outside, and it helps safeguard against confusion. Excessive or pathological projection weakens and empties the ego and gives rise to intense dependence towards depository objects or parts of the ego that have been projected into them. On the other hand, excessive introjection gives rise to feeling so heavily "full-up" inside that the ego cannot "digest" anything.

Delusions of enormity

Séglas (1895c), quoted by Cotard (1888), observed that ideas of grandeur appeared in the later phases of melancholic anxiety. Feelings of power and self-sufficiency take on a grandiose quality. Patients have ideas of immortality and immensity. Cotard grouped a certain number of delusional notions under the heading "delusions of enormity". Patients who declare themselves to be immortal are infinite not only in time but also in space, and find themselves in a gigantic world. This is a kind of megalomania of the body, with melancholia turning into physical (bodily) mania. Séglas considered this to be a pseudo-megalomania. The bigger one feels oneself to be, the greater the despair.

Delusions of enormity are related to loss of control over the body's boundaries. Miss L expressed this feeling as follows: "I feel bloated like a hippopotamus. I feel so enormous I can't get into the subway train." Becoming "bloated" like this meant that her ar-mour-plated shell had failed to contain her. One of the functions of her shell was to protect her from dispersion and consequent loss of identity; the feeling of infinity and the expansion of her body space also expressed her omnipotent power to take possession of space.[19]

Miss L continued: "I feel bloated and deformed. I'm so huge it seems I occupy the whole world. I don't know what's happening

---

[19] For me, expansion is a projective movement of body limits, but one that remains attached to the body. This is a more primitive mechanism than projective identification, which assumes that we project into space *beyond* the frontiers of the body, thereby detaching ourselves from it. I would add that some delusional features of obesity contain similar omnipotent fantasies of expansion.

to me: if I look at someone, a small child for example, he suddenly disappears from view as though he's been swallowed up."[20]

In my patient's case, delusions of enormity went together with a fantasy of monstrous pregnancy: "I haven't had my periods," she claimed. Her ideas of enormity linked to a delusion of pregnancy were sometimes expressed as fantasies of sexual intercourse with her father and with the analyst in the transference. She swallowed the penis-lamp and, at the same time, the baby contained in the paternal penis destined to be deposed inside the mother.[21]

Cotard and Séglas agree that the delusion of enormity is a pseudo-megalomania distinct from true megalomania.[22] In some cases, delusions of enormity may result in full-blown ideas of grandeur. In Cotard's view, delusions of enormity alternate with symptoms of negation, and this was indeed the case with Miss L.

Delusions of possession or internal demonomania

Miss L's brother paid me an unexpected visit, because he was worried about his sister's state of health.[23] Miss L was furious at this, and protested: "All the people in my family are false. I don't want them to come near you. I'm going to leave them. They don't love me, and they don't treat me like a person.[24] Being a person

---

[20] We have already noted the greedy oral quality that her eyes are capable of taking on. Eyes are swallowing implements that take possession of external reality and control it.

[21] I have come across this fantasy in a 2-year-old child (Resnik, 1963).

[22] Cotard observed that in the delusion of enormity, the delusional ideas retain their characteristic monstrosity and horror; this is not the case in true megalomania. Monstrosity is a manifestation of a terrifyingly sinister world which the manic mechanisms fail to hide. It is therefore pseudo-megalomania, since the manic idealization fails in its endeavours.

[23] In chapter five, I discuss some technical aspects of the relationship between analyst, patient, and the patient's family. I must make it clear that as a rule I do not encourage contacts between analyst and relatives, but I do sometimes accept unplanned encounters with them. The presence of family members may be of semiological value in approaching the group situation and may therefore lead to a better understanding of the semiology of the patient.

[24] She defined being a person in the following manner: "When you're a person you *are* somewhere, people can see you and be seen by you, you have

means being loved and having real parents. I feel I never had that. They treat me badly . . . I can hear voices talking to me. I think so hugely that it's biting me like a wild dog. It's a mad enraged animal running from one end of my head to the other and tearing me to bits." At that point, Miss L began to walk from one end of the consulting-room to the other. The dog was out of its wits as it scurried along in her head-room.

She did not feel appreciated by the united couple (the family and me as the personification of a united couple), but held in contempt. Unable to separate people or cut the links between them, she turned into a mad dog whose only aim was to tear everything to bits. But when she tore linking as an internal object in her head, she also tore herself to bits: "I want to hit myself on the head. The hatred I have for them is because of all that I've had to put up with. I will not calm down, even if I kill the whole world.[25] The dog won't stop at biting."

She was afraid the dog would bite because it was frightened: "I'd like to go away somewhere where the dog would be free without anybody hurting it."[26]

In this session I observed the duality between her verbal discourse and her body movements and attitudes. Verbally, she spoke of the dog in the third person, but when she paced up and down the room, she personified it and dramatized the scene in the first person. She was showing her deep and intense oral aggressiveness (biting) with respect to the primal scene. She was unable to channel her rage in a controlled manner. If she were to give it free rein,

---

a body. To have a body means you can look at yourself and see yourself. It means standing upright and knowing that you're standing; it means talking and being wholly yourself." See chapter one.

[25] It must be remembered that Miss L's relationship with her analyst had been "violated" from without—in this case by a member of her family, experienced as persecutory. In reality, her brother was also expressing the anxiety felt by the family as a group, the impossibility they were in of doing something about it, and their feeling of total helplessness.

[26] I mentioned earlier in this chapter in my discussion of hospitalization the relief and tranquillity provided by hospital walls experienced as protecting an out-of-control internal world which is also paranoid and laden with anxiety. Sometimes, too, overwhelming depression cannot be contained simply within the frontiers of the body.

she would annihilate the very objects she needed; then she would truly have been faced with a "lost world". That was why she wanted the dog to be free but not hurt or damaged; but the implosive concentration of this inexhaustible rage threatened to destroy her. Therein lay the reason for attacking and annihilating the dog inside her head by striking it, or for isolating it from the outside world in order to preserve her own world.

Self-injury and the idea of immortality

Miss L's attack on the primal scene aroused paranoid guilt expressed as a tendency to self-injury (self-punitive tendencies). During one session, she exposed one of her breasts. Pointing to the area around the nipple, she claimed to have noticed small dark blotches there: "They're ugly, and I'd like to get rid of them." She added that she carried a small pair of scissors in her bag, and she asked me to cut the blotches out. "If you won't do it, I'll do it myself," she said.

The atmosphere of the session was tense. After this moment of high drama, she relaxed slightly and said that the blotches annoyed her because they reminded her of the naevus and because "pregnant women have them". When she wanted me to remove her naevus/newborn-babies, she was asking me to punish her for being pregnant and having wicked ideas; it was also a way of destroying the persecutor located there (i.e. the parental couple united against her). Furthermore, we could look on it as an attempt at a radical though mutilating cure—by "removing" the illness. Depersonalization is a way of cutting oneself off from parts of the self and from reality. Here the physical reality of the cuts are expressed as a desire in her body—but in a concrete and material way (cutting, surgical removal).[27]

Miss L came to her next session wearing a bandage on her finger. She had hurt herself with the scissors when she opened her bag on the subway train. "But it doesn't matter," she said,

---

[27] This mechanism is typical of patients who have a tendency to undergo frequent operations. The problem should be seen as a psychosomatic one.

"because whatever I do I won't die of it. At home, I give myself injections without sterilizing anything, and nothing ever happens to me."

Cotard pointed out that, in cases of negativistic delusion, failed attempts at self-injury only serve to reinforce ideas of immortality: the patient takes survival to be proof of immortality. The idea of immortality is an expression of "temporal" grandeur, in the same way as the delusion of enormity is one of "spatial" grandeur. It is one way of denying finitude and anxiety over death. Freud (1915b) wrote of the tendency to avoid awareness of death. "It is indeed impossible to imagine our own death; and whenever we attempt to do so we can perceive that we are in fact still present as spectators. [. . .] No one believes in his own death, or, to put the same thing another way, [...] in the unconscious every one of us is convinced of his own immortality" (p. 289). For Freud, there is a kind of "natural depersonalization" with respect to the question of death.

Body, thought, and person

It is not only the body and the real external world as it is commonly perceived which can be denied. There is also negation of thinking. The patient has a tendency to deny part of his internal world, displacing anything painful or persecutory either into the body or onto the external world (which as a result becomes peopled by persecutors). This kind of displacement is a defensive manoeuvre to avoid madness "inside one's head". The terrified—and terrifying—world is either imprinted in the body as a fragment of language detached from the mind, or expelled into the outside world. The initial split between mind and body might be a dualistic defence against unbearable monism. In the first years of life, the body is used as a receptacle or depository for containing distressing experiences, and also as a means of expression: the body is a primitive but essential language. Freud himself drew our attention to this tendency in referring to the narcissistic and auto-erotic phases of development. The infant tends to express his desires physically—early fantasies and mental experiences are mainly sensations. The imaginary world is still part of a sensory and concrete world.

Occasionally, however, as in the case of Miss L, it is not enough to displace thoughts; she had to negate thinking altogether. "I feel my body, but I am empty of ideas. I have no thoughts . . . but it's not that they've been taken away from me." Sometimes she would say the opposite: "I am invisible, as though I was just a thought floating without a body . . . I am nothing but thought."

We can follow in this patient the vicissitudes of negation: body, then thinking, then the external world.

The split between mind and body, according to Scott (1948), is a duality whose roots are to be found in a primal splitting of the ego. The aim is to locate the dangerous and persecutory elements in one part of the whole in order to preserve the rest. This is a very primitive defence against the paranoid image of the death instinct.

Melanie Klein (1946) describes primary active splitting of the ego. In her view, following Freud, it is the *active* projection of the death instinct which favours survival. Mind and body are part of the same unit: the individual. The body is the locus, the space inhabited by the internal world through which it maintains contact with the external world. We are anchored in our body, as Merleau-Ponty would have put it; but being anchored can mean either integrated within the body or being held prisoner there (bodily claustrophobia). Again, we may escape the experience of our own body and anchor ourselves somewhere else, in another body (pathological projective identification).

The "classification"[28]—internal world, body, external world—may serve defensive processes above all else. The ego tries to rid itself of a painful experience (persecutory or depressive) by placing it in one element of the triad in order to preserve the other two. If the painful situation remains threatening even after this, the ego feels endangered and employs omnipotent mechanisms to negate and obliterate it.

Excessive classification is one way in which patients "cut up" wholeness in order to manipulate anxiety in space and avoid contamination.

---

[28] Classifying reality and establishing categories are part of the normal process of differentiation. When, however, this becomes too obsessive, we lose touch with the necessary ambiguity for relating flexibly to the world.

Séglas described negation of the psyche, of the physical personality, and of the outside world. The combination of all three is what he termed universal negation.[29] In Miss L's case, negation oscillated between these various aspects.

She missed two sessions, and on her return she said to me: "I missed two sessions because I needed time for doing what I wanted—walking. I stopped and asked a priest where I could go ... It's my own business ... You don't have to know why I didn't come."

This was her way of expressing her desire to become a *person*. I interpreted this as her need to possess her own time, intimacy with herself, and also as her need to orientate herself in space and have a place of her own.

Talking of her body and its shape, she said: "I don't like this bed, it has a curse. I don't feel this body is mine; I'd like to go somewhere else." The bed gave her body limits that she did not herself possess—or, if she did, they were felt to be foreign to her. Also, it protected her from confusion, provided her with shelter and gave her warmth. "People look at my body ... I know it's deformed ... My body is a square thing that walks, a walking cube." She was expressing here her desire for a body, her own body (and not one that "borrowed" its frontiers from the bed in which it lay). She became aware of her body space, moving from two-dimensional (a square) to three-dimensional (a cube). She was expressing her need for an *identity* (awareness of her self, self-consciousness). "I saw a man who looked like a foreigner. He was in an office, asking for an identity card ... He had no nationality ... People were laughing. He wanted papers in order to belong somewhere." She wanted to acquire an identity, not be a "for-

---

[29] Another patient in analysis with me went through an acute phase of catatonic stupor with intense negativism. He said: "I feel empty .... I'm in a bed without a mattress. There's nothing inside me ... I'm in the wind you listen to .... I'm in the branches of the trees ... I'm in the table ... I'm in the water that's being wiped up now [a nurse was mopping up water in the courtyard] ... I had a shadow underneath my skin; it was my soul. I don't have it any more ... I'm no longer alive, I'm dead, I'm nothing, there's nothing left of me."

Here, extreme negation is connected to a projective mechanism that scatters parts of the ego all over the world of nature (see chapter three).

eigner" any more, and this was personified by the man who decided to take risks and confront reality. Overcoming splitting was a way to reintegrate the world through discovering a "place" for herself in space and in time—becoming a person.

* * *

The similarities I discovered between Miss L and some of the symptomatic aspects of Cotard's syndrome led to this attempt to relate classic psychiatry to the dynamic psychoanalytic way of thinking.

Cotard's and Séglas's descriptions are always refreshing to read, and their phenomenological intuitions are first class; above all, they took a global view of their patients, a perspective that is often lost in the minutiae of present-day scientific specialization. Even certain psychoanalytic techniques can be one-sided—for example, if we concentrate solely on defence mechanisms, or object relations, or personality, we lose sight of the fact that something much more global is at stake.

Psychotics find it very difficult to handle depression. If they are unable to depersonalize (depression without emotion), they try to depress the analyst through what I call "induction" in order to get rid of their depression. It is in the countertransference that the analyst must work through this manipulation and attempt to detect the role the patient is trying to make him play.[30]

The analyst needs empathy in order to identify with his patient's projections without allowing himself to be alienated or to lose sight of his role as analyst. Through his countertransference, the analyst orientates himself in the transference experience and takes up position as an observer. Phenomenological description of the field is part of the structuring instrumental grammatology that analyst and patient construct together. In order to decipher something that is constantly changing, it is necessary to describe and to classify the material in the analytic field. Semiology—the science

---

[30] Miss C, a psychotic patient, was speaking of her depression in a monotonous tone of voice. After a while, she asked: "Are you depressed? You are! I feel much better!" (See chapter six, where I discuss countertransference in more detail.)

of signs—plays a major role in this part of the task. Semiology to some extent is a state of mind. Exploration is done slowly and carefully, without precipitation. Psychiatrists of the old school, in addition to their intuitiveness, had this ability to explore patiently and persistently. The psychoanalyst, with his dynamic perspective on therapy, brings a particular kind of mobility to his consideration of the various clinical cases described in psychiatric terminology (the unconscious is dynamic).

Perspectives in the therapeutic process are many and varied. In the case of Miss L, what I found revealing for my work—her experience of her body and its relationship with the outside world—led me to concentrate on the physical and paranoid aspects. In some sessions, however, depressive elements were also present. Psychotic depression is almost always tinged with persecution. It is therefore important to make a semiological distinction between paranoid depression and "depressive" depression, the latter being the expression of a more integrative ego process.

Depersonalization can take various forms. Schilder (1951) claimed that perceptual disorders and alterations in body image result in alienation from reality as a whole. Hypochondriasis, he wrote, has much in common with depersonalization and forms part of a splitting mechanism that troubles the whole structure of the body image. Scott (1948) claims the mind–body duality is the result of a primary splitting mechanism. The child who lives in each of us as adults often has difficulty in seeing things as a whole. Freud (1936a) wrote that depersonalization and the impression of strangeness (minor depersonalization) are part of the wider phenomenon of derealization (the feeling that we do not recognize reality as such), which is the projection of the feeling of strangeness into the external world. We could speak of a sense of reality and a sense of the unreal[31]—the ability to perceive and tolerate another kind of reality foreign to everyday occurrences. Every scrap of our reality is draped in our intentions or modelled to some degree by

---

[31] For André Breton and other poets, the sense of the unreal has a poetic and creative dimension. Keats called "negative capability" the ability man has to know in the midst of uncertainty, mystery, and doubt that he exists. Shakespeare also had this ability—and, I would add, Freud too.

them. In the delusional conception of the real world, an almost complete transformation occurs. What for us would be unreal is, for such a patient, incontrovertible reality. The world exists only with reference to himself; if this referential tendency is very strong, the world becomes the product of his omnipotent creation. The feeling that we possess magical powers is related to infantile omnipotence and engenders a referential and self-centred view of the world.

Delusions of enormity and feelings of immortality are part of this omnipotent conception of reality. Control of space and time is one way of denying finitude and rejecting the idea of limits, while organization of the internal world involves the idea of finitude as well as that of otherness. The internal world flourishes in a body that can house it. A body unfit for habitation is one that, in the self's paranoid situation, is the depository of internal catastrophe; the debris of the implosion is either ejected from the territory of the body and dispersed throughout space, or accumulated in a locus-organ (or in the locus of an absent organ). In Cotard's syndrome, chaos and catastrophe are denied or disguised. Every psychotic crisis has to do with the idea of chaos. The analyst has to be able to tolerate disorder and to sift through the debris in his search for lost meaning; in this way, he can help his patient re-create his own order, his world, his own experience, his feeling of being and being alive.

CHAPTER THREE

An attack
of catatonic negativism

I n a congress presentation in 1868, then later in a paper published in 1874, Kahlbaum described catatonia as a particular
form of psychic and muscular disorder.[1] He identified the four
fundamental symptoms: catalepsy, negativism, hyperkinesia, and
organic-vegetative disorders.

The cataleptic patient is, from a motor point of view, immobilized and paralysed as though he were in the grip of a "seizure"
(the Greek κατα–λαμβανειν means to seize upon from below).
From a psychic point of view, he has no intellectual initiative and
may even suffer from a kind of petrification of thinking. The patient seems to have lost all experience of his body, over which he
no longer has any control; it becomes a thing-object which can be
manipulated by other people, much like a puppet or a doll. In this
condition, classically known as *flexibilitas cerea*, the robotic body is

---

[1] Séglas (1895a) and Chaslin (1912) introduced Kahlbaum's ideas into
French psychiatric thinking, but they disagreed with Kahlbaum's claim that
this was a specific illness *per se*; to their way of thinking, it was to be regarded
as a syndrome.

very clearly in a state of mechanical dependence. When the feeling of being a "thing"—for example, an articulated body made of wood—is projected onto the outside world, the world as a whole becomes bizarre; external space seems to the patient to be inhabited by wandering robots made of wood.[2]

Passivity, however, is not absolute, for sometimes a particularly inflexible state of hypertonicity can occur: *Spannungsirresein*, or "tense madness"—the classic name for catatonic catalepsy.[3] Just as tiredness can be thought of as a somatization of depression, so muscular tension can signify a struggle between non-integrated parts of the personality, or discord between two worlds—internal and external.

Negativism is a disorder of activity in which there is passive or active resistance to any prompting from the internal or external world. Either the patient *cannot* react or he *refuses* to react—or, again, he may do the exact opposite of what is requested of him. Examples of negativism include refusal to take food or to answer questions, urinary and faecal retention, motor inertia, and contradictory movements.

Bleuler (1950) added the idea of internal negativism:[4] the ego's opposition to feelings and instinctual drives is based on a contradiction between an impulse and what Kraepelin (1907) called a counter-impulse. One expression of this would be, for instance, when the patient acts in such a way as to contradict his expressed desires. This contradictory behaviour is reminiscent of the mind–body duality and more specifically the idea of dissociation, which can operate not only as a split between mind and body but also as a dislocation and partition of mental activity itself [*Spaltung*].

Discussing the split between mind and body in the time-honoured manner may seem contradictory when the argument of this book is that bodily expression is meaningful as a kind of proto-language in which the body is the vector of thought.

---

[2] See Leonora Carrington (1944), quoted in chapter eight.

[3] This may exist in isolation or be associated with other clinical conditions such as hysteria or *corpus striatum* catalepsy.

[4] Kraepelin had included catatonia in *dementia praecox*; Bleuler substituted the term schizophrenia for this, and catatonia became one of the clinical forms of the latter illness.

Changes in tonicity, alterations in facial expression, absence or profusion of similar or different movements—all these are part of the semantics of the body. Akinesia (suspended motility[5]) implies intra-psychic blocking, and hyperkinesia is a discharge of "mechanical" functioning when mental processes accelerate. Wernicke (1900) described hyperkinesia as "an excitability of psycho-motor functions", whereas Bleuler considered it to consist of "arbitrary" movements which are "pseudo-spontaneous" and stereotyped. Such stereotypes can be motor (movements, posture) or verbal and can also apply to thinking.

Alongside the semantics of the body, there are semantics of physiopathology: organic-vegetative disorders (vascular, metabolic, etc.) including dehydration (resulting from the refusal to take food) are phenomena whose meaning can be difficult to grasp.

Many psychoanalysts have explored catatonia.[6] Herman Nunberg (1961) emphasizes particularly regression to the phase where action is substituted for verbal discourse. He refers to the communication difficulties that we encounter with such patients and describes how their apparently playful behaviour can seem nonsensical to the casual observer. He adds that patients can develop negative transference when the persecutory coloration is strong enough to prevent development of a positive transference. The most striking characteristic is the exceptional powers of memory that these patients show (Bleuler had already remarked on this) very early life events are recalled with quite outstanding clarity. I would add that the past is present as though "imprinted" in the body.

Nunberg highlights two features common to both catatonia and hysteria: dramatization and anxiety. The difference between the two is an economic one. In acute catatonia, it is mainly the body that is cathected with libido, whereas in hysteria, though the body is cathected, there remains sufficient energy for objects to be cathected also. On the phenomenological and dynamic levels, catatonic dramatization does not have the same theatricality, seduc-

---

[5] Stupor and the *flexibilitas cerea* of catalepsy are two examples of this.

[6] These include John N. Rosen, F. Fromm-Reichmann, Federn, Wexler, Eissler, and Knight in the United States, and the Kleinians Herbert Rosenfeld, W. R. Bion, and Hanna Segal.

tiveness, or elaborate manipulation of the environment as we find in hysteria. The patient is too preoccupied with his own tragedy and its catastrophic impact to want to have much to do with the outside world. Anxiety about death is denied or paralysed and, as a result, eludes all forms of mental representation—it can be expressed only through the body. In catatonic dramatization, a sinister atmosphere reigns, which again is not the case in hysteria. In the experience of petrification, it is as though death itself were present. The paralysed self is reified, time is suspended; only death anxiety remains.

In this state of stupor and petrification, the eyes are all that remain alive: behind the catatonic mask, the eyes look out at external reality in terror. Most of the time the body is stationary, but some isolated movements or almost imperceptible attitudes are there to signify the attempt at communicating an incomplete message.

An essential part of the analyst's task is to identify these signs in the transference and explore their meaning. A clinical illustration will help us to clarify this point. After an appendectomy, an 18-year-old man suffered from delusions and an acute attack of catatonia; the operation had apparently caused his delusional hypochondriac anxieties to come to the fore. Later, negation took over—he claimed to have lost not only his appendix but indeed all his organs. As a result, he had feelings of emptiness and an intense fear of death.

These symptoms were described to me by the patient's mother. During the acute phase, she had remained beside her son to protect him, trying to calm his excitement and his anxiety. After a few days the crisis was over, but the parents decided to consult a psychiatrist just the same. In our first meeting, the mother told me that, as a child, her son had always been somewhat strange, shy, and withdrawn, remaining aloof from other people—including other members of the family. When he began school, these tendencies worsened. He had difficulty in expressing himself, and academic achievement remained limited. He and his twin sister were the youngest of the family; they had four older sisters.

In our initial contact, I found him withdrawn and uncommunicative. Most of the time he glanced at me suspiciously; his aloofness and almost inexpressive attitude was interrupted from time to time by sudden unmotivated smiling (hebephrenic mask) and mannerisms, in particular a repeated staring at his hands. In order to have some idea of his intellectual capacity and ability to express himself, I suggested he draw something on a sheet of paper; he was at first hesitant, then drew a bizarre human shape, so huge that one sheet of paper was not enough to contain it (the legs were missing, the contours imprecise, and the overall grotesque and static appearance seemed to confirm what an earlier psychological test had said about the patient's low intelligence).

At another moment in this first interview, the young man placed his hand on a sheet of paper and drew around the outline. I interpreted this as an attempt to get in touch with me. He was drawing his own contour in a space that was opening up for him. Shortly after this, he gave me a photograph of himself and showed me a love letter he had written to a young lady. I took this to be proof that he was beginning to trust me and also that he needed to find in me a depository for his intimate and personal objects.[7] As I read the letter, I was struck by the quality of expression and the affectionate tone of the writing. The discovery of such remarkably contradictory elements in the patient's personality led me to question the diagnosis of oligophrenia recorded in his medical file.

For more background information, I asked the mother to tell me about her son's early years. She said that at birth, delivery had been quite normal for the twin sister but much more difficult for him. Also, the sister had been breast-fed for much longer; the patient had only briefly been breast-fed by his mother, then a wet-nurse took over until he was 4 years old. In early childhood he seemed to have developed quite normally: first words at 1 year of age, walking at 14 months, and toilet-trained at age 2 years. "He was a lovely boy," said his mother, "but he did seem quite strange at times."

---

[7] One of the typical features of the development of a positive transference with psychotic patients is the need they have to test and to explore the analyst in order to be sure that they can deposit in him their good and precious objects so as to protect them from any internal danger or attack. Negative transference has more to do with projection or evacuation of bad and persecutory parts; the patient will try to get rid of these by projecting them onto the analyst.

The information she gave me reminded me of Kanner's clinical description of early infantile autism (Kanner, 1935, p. 111). He pointed out that such children do badly on psychometric tests, which is why they are often considered retarded; but, he adds, "it is usually emotional interference which prevents them from communicating and makes them appear mentally deficient".

If we consider the appendectomy to be the precipitating factor, we could say that surgery seems to have prompted the emergence of the psychotic personality from behind the mask of mental deficiency. This diagnosis appeared much more satisfactory to me and led me to propose psychoanalysis to the young man. I warned the parents that crises similar to the one he had gone through might occur again during the treatment, and that it would be necessary to find some way of continuing the analysis even if their son were hospitalized.[8]

In his first session, the patient proved apathetic and hypobulic. Some time later, he became anxious and began to express hypochondriac fears. His anxiety took the form of psychomotor agitation,[9] and he paced aimlessly up and down; for the first time he left

---

[8] When confusion with reality is at its height (loss of ego boundaries through excessive projective identification), hospitalization enables the patient to feel protected (it provides him with boundaries that he himself has lost). At the same time, the analyst has the advantage of continuing to analyse the negative transference without interrupting the treatment.

[9] The patient's behaviour could be interpreted as a kind of liberation through action from "tense madness" [*Spannungsirresein*]. I quote from a private correspondence from Professor Maldiney of Lyon (one of the most important philosophers in France exploring the phenomenology of madness and art): "*Irresein* is the classic word for madness in the sense of losing one's reason. However, if we dig deeper into the etymology of the word, we see that *Spannungsirresein* contains a strange contradiction. *Irren* means to wander aimlessly. *Irresein* properly understood means 'to be wandering'. So the patient is in a tense kind of wandering. Wandering is the immediate consequence of the tension—hence the coexistence of two contradictory ideas or feelings: tension/retention as opposed to free, unbounded living. The 'aimlessness' is the counterpart of the unknown goal of the tension."

This *strange* and unresolved contradiction often leads the psychotic to adopt further splitting, thus entering on a behavioural cycle equivalent to what Freud called the compulsion to repeat. Such behaviour does not resolve the issue, precisely because its aim is "wandering" and changeable. Unable to accept contradiction, the psychotic transforms it into dissociation. There is no longer a coming together (centripetal motion) but separation (centrifugal).

home and wandered about for a whole day without any precise aim. After this hypomanic phase, he suffered from sialorrheia and had a compulsive tendency to spit; he claimed that he was being poisoned and was obliged to spit in order to get rid of the poison. He reported the following story: "One day I was at the swimming-pool with the girl to whom I wrote the letter I showed you. As I was looking at her, I felt the wind and the sun's rays attacking me; they were infecting the freckles on my skin. Then I felt that little by little the freckles were changing into an invasive cancer."

In this unconscious fantasy, the forces of nature (sun and wind) appear as external persecutors; they become embodied in the freckles on his skin, and later "materialized" in food, which he was already beginning to refuse. His sialorrheia and compulsive spitting were attempts to expel the persecutors. With his world becoming more and more dangerous because of his projections,[10] he expelled the "poison"—but at the same time emptied himself. The development of a hypochondriac delusion, the intensity of his anxiety, and his family's difficulty in tolerating and containing all this led me to suggest that he be hospitalized.

In hospital, he would spit compulsively. In addition, he used to vomit after each meal; subsequently, he refused all solid food, then liquids too. He had ingested "a whole lemon", he said. Later, he stopped spitting—but stopped talking too: the mechanisms whereby he ejected and took in had both become paralysed. The aim of the paralysis was to prevent re-introjecting objects from the external world which, since they had been expelled in such a ruthless way, had become even more terrifying.

The young man's whole physical demeanour expressed deep anxiety: his hollow cheeks and the sad and anxious expression on his face bore witness to his inner drama. Lying prostrate on his bed, incapable of any kind of motor activity, he remained totally indifferent to any prompting from outside. In addition to his stupor, he was completely mute and all his muscles were tense (catalepsy)—the very image of catatonic negativism. When I tried to make contact with him, he replied in mime: raising his right arm,

---

[10] The idea of "peopling" reality with one's projections confirms Ernest Jones's (1925) work on the social aspect of speech in the symbolization process. We discover reality by projecting ourselves into objects and naming them.

he placed it on his stomach as though for protection. I reminded him of what he had said about the lemon, saying that he had kept it inside himself like something good which had come from the doctor. It was the "good lemon" he was trying to protect against threats from outside. I added that in order not to lose it, he had stopped talking, spitting, defecating, and so on. His arm was there to protect it and to set up a barrier between the dangerous outside world and something good that he needed to keep inside himself (he was responsible for peopling reality in this way).

This interpretation helped him to see things more clearly. He paused, then brought his hand up to his forehead, as though to show me that the badness was located there. I remembered a nurse had told me earlier that the patient kept on saying, "The madmen are attacking me"; he was expressing by word and action his fear that he was being driven mad. Madness was "outside" and in its persecutory manner might force its way into his head.[11]

This was the unconscious fantasy behind the meaning he ascribed to his mental illness.

When I clarified this fantasy relationship to his mental illness, experienced as external to himself in the way that I myself was, he protected his face with one hand and clenched the other fist threateningly. This was an expression of his ambivalence. Then he raised his arm as though, having decided not to fight any more, he were

---

[11] According to Pichon-Rivière (personal communication), being frightened out of one's wits is the result of sudden and unavoidable re-introjection of madness experienced as persecutory.

A technical remark here: in treating schizophrenics it is important that, if the patient is hospitalized, the psychoanalyst should introduce—in a manner appropriate to each situation—some elements of the patient's life as they have been reported by the nurses or other staff in contact with him. Insofar as the patient has lost the notion of contour, in the sense of a clear distinction between inside and outside, the setting of the session is dislocated and it becomes necessary to widen the analytic field. A hospitalized patient talks in "sign-language", using the staff as intermediaries in order to avoid direct, unmediated confrontation with the doctor, who is sometimes felt to be dangerous. Data transmitted indirectly can be looked upon as "associations" that are just as important as those of the session itself, on condition that the "locus" where data collected in this way converges is the formal setting of the session—the "laboratory" where all this can be worked through.

surrendering. After I interpreted his attitude towards me as oscil-
lating between hatred and fear, he looked at me attentively as if
trying to figure out my intentions—how kind or how malevolent I
might be. His fear appeared to diminish, and for the first time since
the beginning of his illness he came towards me and clasped one of
my hands in his. His eyes, and the look on his face, were much
more relaxed. A few moments later, he began making rhythmic
movements,[12] with one of his hands touching mine, as if to suck
my fingers—expressing his desire to be nourished by a good
breast. When I interpreted this to him, he spat and said in a jerky,
stereotyped manner: "Die in reverse, die in reverse." I added that
as his fears about me calmed down, he could see me as good; and
this enabled him to come into physical contact with me like a good
mother whose hand-breast was giving nourishment to his hand-
mouth.[13]

---

[12] There can be no rhythm without separation, without discontinuity.
Rhythm gives life and movement to any sequence of feelings, thoughts, sensations, instinctual drives, and biological forces in the organism. Rhythm confers
meaning in a harmonious way to the *dia-logos* between human beings and
within the self—for Freud, the ego was first and foremost a bodily ego.

[13] I use symbolic expressions such as hand-breast and hand-mouth, because
I consider that in profoundly regressed states (i.e. to very early infantile
phases) communication is much more effective when sufficiently "pliable"
terms are employed to express the more primitive unconscious fantasies. It
was therefore important to apprehend the meaning ascribed to his hand in
terms of his coming closer to me. I mentioned that in our first session together
that, when he placed his hand on the sheet of paper, this was his way of
making contact with me. I was the sheet of paper—unfamiliar and therefore
feared, but also the "screen" on which he needed to project. According to
Schilder's studies of body image, hands are one of the first elements to be
integrated into the initial schema; it represents for the infant in his "praxis" the
instrument for communication *par excellence*. Hands are used for doing, taking,
and manipulating objects in the surrounding environment (Heidegger's *Zu-
handenheit* expresses the idea of togetherness through instrumentality). A
means of relating to objects, hands are also an expression of the whole being
[*pars pro toto*]. When the patient placed his hand on the sheet of paper, he was
himself "figuratively" (in a gestalt sense) there on the white background. The
hand drawn on the paper later became a messenger when he wrote signs
inside the shape he had drawn: he wrote his name, followed by other names
along the fingers, his way of in-scribing and de-scribing the *dramatis personae*
of his internal world.

From then on he was once again able to take in something good from me. He no longer had to fear an inner void. And once he had introjected something "good", he could again project: he spat, then brought one of his hands up to the sleeve of my jacket and slipped it inside, saying: "Die in reverse, die in reverse". I commented that by slipping his hand into my sleeve, he was expressing his desire to put himself inside me as if I were a womb; in saying "die in reverse", he was telling me of his desire to go back inside the analyst-mother and be reborn differently and "well-made". The unconscious fantasy of death and rebirth appears frequently in analysis—improving and changing are experienced as a transformation into some other unfamiliar person. To be cared for and cured means change, and that involves abandoning part of one's self and one's old ways.

Later, the patient pronounced a new phrase: "Died a girl, died a girl." This, I think, was an announcement of the difficulty he had always encountered with respect to his twin sister. Noticing his refusal to share me with others (jealousy with respect to members of his family who from time to time asked to meet me) and the guilt he then felt, I said to him that he wanted to come into my mind and leave it safe and well (in order to be reborn differently) but that this was experienced as being dangerous for his twin sister. They could not both coexist inside the same womb, as though for one to live the other had to be sacrificed—as if the placenta (the internal or uterine breast) could not be shared.

After this, he stroked my hands and my face (and especially my chin). This was a gesture particular to this young man—he would frequently stroke my chin. In stroking me he was also stroking himself, since at that point he was as yet unable to differentiate between my body and his own.[14]

He fell silent, then his expression changed, as though he had had a flash of enlightenment. He said: "Died a boy, died a boy." I deduced that he was taking on the part that had been left behind, the empty and near-dead part (illness meant being empty and dead), in order to save the other, his sister. He felt very guilty

---

[14] At other times there was some degree of differentiation: I was his mirror, the mother-mirror of whom Winnicott wrote, in which he could see himself and encounter his "self".

about being re-born and sacrificing his sister; he needed to make reparation by sacrificing himself.

At the end of the session, the patient began to stare fixedly at a glass of water standing near him. I held out the glass to him to see what would happen. He clung tightly to my hand and brought the glass up to his lips to moist them slightly (he did not drink, as though afraid to sip the water in case he might use it all up). I interpreted that he needed me very much and that was why he was holding on to me; he wanted me to stay with him all the time and always have something to give him. He wanted me to be constantly able to provide him with something, like a source that would never run dry. The session ended, and he looked upset as I left; just as I was taking leave of him, he motioned to me to come back.

His refusal to take food persisted for several more days. Immobile, his eyes deep-set, his cheeks pale, his whole body clamoured that he was suffering from some terrible distress. In addition, he had all the symptoms of dehydration: discoloured lips, dry tongue, weak and rapid pulse, low blood pressure, hypothermia, reduced micturition, and so forth. He had to be rehydrated; he was put on a drip (glucose and chloride serum with protein hydrolysate). He accepted it passively, making no resistance.[15]

---

[15] Where the refusal to eat occurs in a persecutory context, food is, generally speaking, experienced as a dangerous persecutor (projection of destructive tendencies) against which the patient has to protect himself by preventing "intrusion". The same is true of anorexia, though to a lesser degree. In the case of this young man, however, it was not food that was felt to be dangerous, but his own mouth—his mouth-cavity—because of the possibility that it might contaminate everything coming into contact with it (food being just one example).

As in many other cases of this type, the patient had managed to keep the "good object" inside himself—or, rather, the "idealized" object, the whole lemon—in order to safeguard it against all external objects that might threaten to contaminate it. His mouth—the part of his body experienced as really dangerous—was, through splitting, kept at a safe distance from his stomach where the good object-lemon was, and also at a safe distance from anything good that might remain in external objects.

From anorexia to catatonic negativism there is a whole series of significant degrees of oral involvement. Greenacre (1953) emphasizes that anorexia is a defence against a depressive condition, an expression of helplessness when

When I arrived for the following session, he greeted me with fists clenched, an angry look on his face. I said he was furious with me for abandoning him in spite of his attempt to hold me back last time (this was the feeling I had had in my countertransference). He looked slightly afraid when I said that, so I added that he had felt not only anger but also fear of his own aggressiveness, which he had put into my words and the food offered him. Demanding satisfaction and inability to tolerate frustration are typical of regressive conditions: resentment and aggressiveness appear at the slightest frustration and contribute to the re-emergence of paranoid feelings.

He stared at the drip, then at the glass of orange juice standing on his bedside table. He seemed to be trying to tell me something, but I did not understand what. He continued to stare at the orange juice, and I decided to bring it closer to him. He hesitated; bringing the glass up to his lips, he pushed it away again, but without putting it down. I interpreted this as his ambivalence towards me (expressed as a desire to take in through the mouth, orally, together with the refusal to do so). He remained like that for a few moments, then he raised the glass high in the air, his arm stretched out stiffly in a quasi-vertical position (cataleptic attitude). Maintaining this posture, he put one finger inside the glass—the impression was that of a second "drip", which he wanted to "drink" in a greedy but non-oral way in order to preserve the "sanity" of the food. With a satisfied look on his face, he picked up another glass in his other hand and raised that high in the air too. With both arms stretched upwards like that, he had a strangely pathetic look.

The "pre-natal" tone of this picture (it was as though he were surrounded by food that, in his unconscious fantasy, he was receiving through a multitude of umbilical cords) led me to comment that he was satisfying his desire to "die in reverse"—that is, to enter inside me and be gratified by a multitude of inexhaustible

---

faced with the demands of reality. The inability to work through depression and tolerate loss is the hallmark of a weak ego unable to overcome the psychotic anxieties of the paranoid-schizoid position. Palazzoli-Selvini (1963) reports cases of anorexia which are so severe that the symptom is almost unique—a kind of mono-symptomatic psychosis; the body is negated in a total refusal of orality.

breasts. After this interpretation he remained impassive for a moment or two, then, still maintaining his bizarre posture, he exclaimed: "Enter in reverse, enter in reverse." I thought it helpful to complete my earlier interpretation by adding that he did not want to be fed through a dangerous mouth; he was afraid that his teeth and saliva might destroy the food or contaminate it and transform it into something dangerous. That was why he could only accept food if it "entered in reverse",[16] by some other means, in order to avoid passing through the dangerous mouth.[17]

In the same session, he again tried to bring one of the glasses up to his lips, but once more refused to drink. In spite of my explanations, he remained distrustful. I made as though to bring the glass up to my own lips, but he stopped me in a state of great anxiety. I interpreted this as a desire to protect me: he needed me, and could not tolerate the idea that he might lose me.[18] After these explanations I decided to drink a little water in spite of his anxiety. A few moments later, once he had seen that nothing had actually happened to me in spite of his fears, he appeared less worried.

In cases like this one, where there is profound regression, we sometimes feel in the countertransference that we have to play the role of the guardian of reality; "reality-testing" in this sense of the word may indeed prove quite effective. The profoundly regressed patient, like the very young child, has almost limitless demands, and his insatiability knows no bounds; in order for him to adapt to reality, he must be shown that there are limits to his desires.[19]

---

[16] "Reverse" meaning "from another direction".

[17] Abraham (1924) explored the meaning of the mouth from the point of view of ego development. He analysed in particular the cannibalistic phase corresponding to dentition, relating it to the infant's unconscious oral-destructive fantasy. Here, the degree of malignancy attached to the patient's mouth (teeth and saliva) corresponded to the intensity of his oral-destructive tendencies.

[18] Herbert Rosenfeld (1952) explores confusion in psychotic patients and relates it to the loss of boundaries between the individual and his objects, resulting from excessive projective identification (in this, Rosenfeld follows Melanie Klein). Here, the patient was confusing his mouth with mine.

[19] Winnicott (1945) emphasizes the importance for the infant of certain concrete experiences: as his sensations become more refined, he develops the idea of contour. Through his contacts with his first object, the mother, the infant gradually constructs limits to his desires.

In this case, giving the patient an opportunity to distinguish between fantasy and reality enabled him to have a better idea of where he stood in his actual relationships with others.[20]

Shortly after this, I could see the results of my dramatized interpretation in the patient's attempts to work through the interplay of the transference. Though he still maintained his negative attitude towards food, he indicated that he desired to be fed through his mouth as long as it could be done indirectly—through a gastric tube. Though I had been worried by his overall state of poor health, I had not felt it advisable up to that point for this particular means of nourishment to be employed, because of its traumatic effect. Previous experience with other cases had taught me that feeding through a gastric tube is often experienced as "oral rape" and only increases the patient's paranoid anxieties. Struck by his apparent acceptance of the tube, I tried to think about his motives; perhaps my testing of reality (the water I had drunk) had allowed him to verify the inconsistency of his fantasies (since a part of him projected into me—the water in the glass—had survived) and thereby to distinguish fantasy from reality. The tube was more acceptable, not only because it was another umbilical cord, but also because it let food pass through his mouth, the danger zone, without coming to harm.

This observation led me to the conclusion that it is necessary to act in as flexible a way as possible and remain attentive to what each specific case demands. I feel that any therapeutic act, including the most ordinary of psychiatric procedures apparently devoid of any psychotherapeutic function, can be and indeed *must* be included in the treatment protocol, if we feel it a necessary and effective means to continue the therapy. It must of course be brought into the transference and explained to the patient (it is, after all, part of the "drama"); the fantasies he creates about such acts have to be analysed, and the corresponding equipment (drips, tubes, etc.) must not be dissociated from the dynamics of the trans-

---

[20] Nowadays, I would not *act* in the way I did—I would simply interpret. I ought to have worked out in my countertransference the fact that the patient was attributing to me by induction the role of the "non-dangerous mouth". I would therefore nowadays simply have underlined the splitting without acting it out myself (split between the good mouth he had projected into me and his own bad dangerous mouth).

ference. The doctor–patient relationship should be thought of as a global structure "in movement", constantly demanding identification of the roles and functions of each element or person in the situation and recognition of their impact on the transference and countertransference. In so doing we are not straying from a psychodynamic attitude; on the contrary, the much more flexible approach I adopt enables a wider understanding of the therapeutic situation and thereby opens up multiple possibilities.

To conclude this report, I should add that shortly after the second test of reality—the gastric tube—the patient's fears about food disappeared completely. For the first time since the acute phase of his illness began, he accepted the food his mother brought him and ate it directly through his mouth without any "intermediary". I saw this young man eating with unbridled avidity and pleasure: he was like a rosy-cheeked baby stuffing himself, pushing the food in with one hand while grabbing a second helping with the other. From that day on, his feeding habits stabilized, muscular tension decreased, other functions (language, micturition, etc.) became normal, and the catatonic syndrome disappeared.

Conclusion

Without treating all issues exhaustively, I have discussed certain significant elements in this chapter:

- The psychodynamic features of an attack of catatonic negativism, focused particularly on a problem with feeding.

- Different aspects of the treatment of a psychotic patient of this type. It was possible to make contact with the patient only at a very primitive level of his relationship with others—before verbal language exists. Pre-verbal and body communication had to be analysed in order gradually to discover meaning.

- The necessity of a flexible attitude to help us employ in each specific context all effective means at our disposal. Psychiatric procedures are not to be set against psychoanalytic ones; on the contrary, praxis demands that they be combined in an appropriate way.

CHAPTER FOUR

Language and communication

My analytic experience with psychotic patients has taught me that problems of language are a regular occurrence, particularly when it comes to the complete message cycle, from emission to reception.[1] Sometimes it is the patient's own language that is highlighted—body language, words, dreams, the semantics of silence, all of them "traces" and signs that the analyst has to decipher—at other times it is my own, in the way I formulate my interpretations, for example. My verbal expression, my comments, my interpretations are the result of a complex process. I am like a witness, I describe, I read what is written in the

---

[1] This chapter was inspired to a great extent by Merleau-Ponty's lectures in the Sorbonne and in the Collège de France, the first of which were published as *The Child's Relationships with Other People* (Merleau-Ponty, 1955). As a child and adult analyst working with psychotics, I have always been interested in descriptive phenomenology, particularly in relation to formal exegesis of experience and the impact of interpretation on it. When I came to Paris in 1957, I was fortunate to be a pupil at the Collège de France, where Merleau-Ponty gave his Wednesday lectures. In my year, the theme of these was "On the Nature of Things".

object-phenomenon, I take notes, I organize the gleanings gathered from the analytic field in a way that is inevitably arbitrary, and I translate all this into words.

If I have sufficient empathy with the patient and his means of expression, my remarks will be in tune with what he is communicating. Patients are constantly communicating—through body posture, words, silence—even though the message may not always be clear and explicit; in the interplay of the transference, previous models of object relations are recreated, and I am introduced to the *dramatis personae*, recalling past scenes and playing them out in the *hic et nunc* of the transference. A patient's past is not behind him; it is alive within him even though he himself often ignores the fact. What is repressed or projected out of present time is sometimes revealed explicitly, and sometimes in a confused and disordered manner. In other words, the patient's infantile ego—probably mirroring the first years of life—goes from a state of non-differentiation to one of differentiation. As he navigates between the two, the infant does not know his own body as such; he can neither discover nor use his "body tools" for communication.[2]

Communication presupposes that two distinct entities exist: someone to broadcast the message and someone else to whom it is destined. Even before language appears, a rudimentary form of communication exists. Scheler (1913) refers to an initial stage of pre-communication characterized in particular by the role that the body plays: the most primitive of intentions are revealed by the body.

In comparison to the abundance of coenesthetic experiences, the infant, says Merleau-Ponty, has only minimal experience of his "visual body". He cannot see—indeed, he will never see directly—certain areas of his body, visible only in a mirror (reflected image). The image of someone else's body[3] ("body image") is built up from

---

[2] More precisely, communication in these very early stages of life is incomplete and confused. From time to time a message is formulated, enabling the infant to enter into a relationship with his original object, the mother. A stimulus emitted by the infant awakens in her, by "induction", the possibility of picking up and decoding the baby's desires.

[3] Merleau-Ponty describes this experience as follows. "There is the me I call my 'mind'; there is the image I construct of my own body through the medium of touch or coenesthesia—the interoceptive image of my own body; there is a

intero- and exteroceptive stimuli acting on the perceiving ego. The infant obtains an image of himself and of his contours which enables him to identify himself relative to his surroundings. This primordial classification of space—body and not-body—is constantly acting on the "position" of the body (Head's "postural schema", 1920). Variability in position provides an image of the body in movement, rhythmed by the personal experience of time, itself an ongoing development.

Lacan (1966) stresses the importance of the mirror stage for development of the "I", and he describes how we accept our image through a jubilant awareness of our body. Thus, a gestalt of the "whole body" is reached, an essential marker, adds Lacan, in the history of each individual. The mirror stage is a drama that organizes and structures ego identification: the non-integrated and fragmented part-images of the body finally become integrated. This dynamic construction has both symbolic and operational features. Awareness of body experiences enables the infant to get to know his own body and that of others. Bion (1957a) describes two different possibilities for the structural process of the self. First, the various fragmented aspects, projected outside the body, may be re-introjected according to a normal anatomical and physiological order. This results in a coherent, articulated gestalt. There is, however, another possibility, which occurs when the fragmented aspects are massively scattered far and wide, thereby losing all contact with the ego. Introjective reconstruction in this case is incomplete or incoherent. Contact between different parts of the self pays no heed to anatomical or physiological order, resulting in a distorted and bizarre body image. This false reparation is an agglomeration of bizarre objects (breakdown in the ego's synthetic function) and is typical of schizophrenia.

In normal interpersonal relationships, a proper balance between projective and introjective phenomena is required for the other to be perceived correctly and for the "I" to develop. Interper-

---

third element, the body of another person as I see it—the visual body; and finally, a fourth element, hypothetical, which I have to reconstruct or guess at, the "mind" of the other person, the feeling that that person has of his own existence, insofar as I can guess at it and imagine it through what he shows me by his visual body."

sonal relationships are manifested phenomenologically as "movements" in which bodily intentions are dramatized through actual
behaviour.

The infant becomes aware of himself and others insofar as he
"experiences" his own intentions in the other person's expressions,
and the intentions of the other person in his own gestures. In this
dyadic context, each partner takes into his experience the projections of intentionality of the other (reciprocal induction).[4] As I have
said, the infant gradually becomes aware of his body, its frontiers,
and of other people. Personality is shaped by the continuous evo-
lution from a state of non-differentiation to one of differentiation,
and from there to the point where a stable personal identity is
acquired.[5]

The pattern of confused object relations observed at the beginning of life reappears in the transference when patients in analysis
dramatize the original situation. In analysis, psychotics possess the
ambiguity of both models (confusion and differentiation), super-
posing them—one *on* the other—before it becomes possible to integrate them—one *with* the other.

The mental pain of being separate from mother hinders differentiation in the dyadic relationship, encouraging in the infant a
fusional relationship that is both confused and proto-symbolic.
Inhabiting one's body in full awareness of one's existence as a
person is complex. It can only be envisaged as the outcome of a
fundamental experience: the relationship with one's first object,
mother. Winnicott called "moments of illusion" the ambiguities by
means of which the mother–child encounter becomes organized:
fragments of experience that the infant can apprehend either as a

---

[4] I draw a distinction between projection and induction. In the analytic
context, where the patient is physically present, induction is an operation that
arouses in the analyst the disposition to introject what the patient has projected
(induction operates also in the direction analyst–patient). Projection, like introjection, belongs to the sphere of the imaginary; induction, because it requires
actual physical presence to operate, belongs to action.

[5] Esther Bick (1968) describes in infants a state in which the various parts of
the personality are not differentiated from parts of the body. Her hypothesis is
that at the beginning of life there is no primitive binding force to link them
together. The baby needs to be held passively together by the surface of his
body, the skin. Melanie Klein states that the containing function of the skin
depends on the introjection of a good containing object—the container-mother.

hallucination or as something belonging to external reality. The vicissitudes of this communication experience contribute to the creation of our first models of sociability. In this primitive relationship, the nature of physical contact[6] provides the original model for future encounters.

Loss of limits and transitivismus

In the pre-communication phase, the infant tends to feel himself merged with his surroundings; recognizing the other person as such signifies realizing that he is "outside", in the external world. The idea of a frontier delineating "me" from "not-me" requires the acceptance of the other as "outside". The inability to tolerate "being outside", in open space, stimulates the need for projection into the other—not, in the first instance, in order to communicate but to be "inside" again, to avoid being outside the other and at the mercy of the unknown laws of the external world. This kind of projection into the other person is part of what Melanie Klein called projective identification. It is a mechanism that weakens the ego and empties it of the experience of its own existence. In psychiatry, this phenomenon—sinking into the other, merging with him, and losing oneself as a result—was called by Wernicke transitivismus, and is highly typical of schizophrenic patients.

Herbert Rosenfeld (1952) put it thus: "As soon as the schizophrenic approaches any object in love or hate he seems to become confused with this object, and this is due not only to identification by introjection, but to impulses and fantasies of entering inside the object with the whole or parts of himself in order to control it" (p. 106). In the transference, pathological projective identification is experienced as a state in which the patient loses himself inside the analyst.

This kind of projection intensifies when paranoid anxieties increase. The schizophrenic needs to be *inside* the other (possessing him from within) and to control reality rather than be in contact

---

[6] As I suggested above in the discussion on personalization (chapter one), a relationship dominated by intense eroticized physical contact hinders rather than encourages the growth of the infant self.

with it. This defensive need can also be expressed in the intro-jective sense as a requirement to swallow the "outside" and con-trol it from within. Avidity can be of service here. At this level, the mouth can break up into several parts, projecting itself into differ-ent loci in space and from there swallowing up as much as it can. This "occupation" of space need not be limited to orality; anal and urethral elements come into play as the patient projects all manner of desires and body contents in order to refashion reality in his own way.

Verbal language is a "normal" projective phenomenon, always linked to the body. Communication brings into play various modes and levels of expression. This implies that we have to take into account not only language as a set of verbal symbols and signs, but all other types of expression alongside speech itself. In addition, there are primitive fantasies that remain impossible to express; they remain internal, isolated, and as though foreign to us.

The infant becomes part of the community insofar as he can articulate his desires by means of messages. Body language—the original vehicle for communication—is expressed through move-ment, gestures, facial expression, and all manner of conversion symptoms. In psychosomatic medicine, "conversion" is part of the semantics of the body.

Preverbal communication dwindles when the infant succeeds in "accepting" speech. In order to do this, the ego has to mature and accept "rules": as it opens up its horizons, it has also to accept that a gap separates it from the object.

Etymologically, communication implies putting in common, linking, establishing relationships *with*—hence the idea of trans-mission and dramatization of the message. Such a context de-mands two clearly identifiable poles: subject and object.

The function of language

Verbal language might be expected to be the linking device par excellence, yet speech is not synonymous with communication. The pre-linguistic phase includes some features of communication. Sounds are to some extent "vocal gestures", addenda similar to pseudopodia. At this stage there is no link to the other, no true *dia-logos*, simply a voiced extension of the body. Sounds become more and more efficient as the infant learns how to project himself beyond his limits. At the babbling stage, he learns how to play with sounds and to share them with his mother. The latter may or may not take part in this play, depending on her own capacities for contact with her child. The father is also included in the exchange, as an object distinct from the mother.

Interaction between internal and external worlds develops from this original encounter. Jakobson (1969) says that the "baby" language that adults adopt when talking to an infant is deliberately adapted to the young infant's phonemic equipment. The adult who is able to play with the sounds and movements of his children is revisiting his own infantile ego. The infant's capacity to learn speech depends to a great extent on the parents' capacity for playful empathy. The child begins to create his first words by "modelling" his phonemes on the relationships he establishes with his parents. Progressing from phonemes to word-phrases is a major step; the infant learns to create vocal symbols. When he is in full possession of language, the child can formulate sentences in which "I", "you", and "we" are differentiated. Organizing words into sentences requires use of different types of grammatical link; the acquisition of grammatical structure is proof that the nascent organized ego is able to communicate with itself (intra-communication) and with others (intercommunication).

Melanie Klein argued that it is only towards the end of the first six months that the infant becomes integrated. She used the term "depressive position" to describe the infant's capacity to overcome splitting, a typical feature of the paranoid–schizoid position. The process is a painful one, involving differentiation between the child and others, and between his various drives and feelings. In the depressive position, the infant is able to accept the breast not as an extension of his own mouth but as part of a whole—the mother. The mother becomes a specific entity, and the infant discovers his own wholeness. Separateness stimulates feelings of frustration in the infant (mother is no longer in continuity with him); at the same time, feelings of guilt are awakened because of his attacks against the object of his desires.

The voice is a means of expression that at first is closely bound to the body; it is experienced as part of the body, another gesture, another action. The transformation of voice and vocalizations into representations belongs to the "biography of symbols". The ability to form symbols has its origins in the differentiation inherent to the depressive position. Learning to speak symbolically is a painful as well as creative process: for example, the infant has to accept that the word "mummy" implies the absence of mother as a real object. The *word* "mummy" is not mother, but a substitute or replacement expression for her. The schizophrenic's inability to tolerate absence compels him to experience absence in a hallucinatory manner, as concrete presence. For the infant, play is the medium by means of which he dramatizes and attempts to work through the issue of presence/absence.

In the analytic experience, we can observe how words are sometimes undifferentiated from parts of the body. For the schizo-phrenic in particular (concrete language), emitting sounds may be experienced as sending fragments of the voice into vocal space; this is one way of projecting himself into the analyst (projective identification) in order to control him. "Occupation" of others is motivated also by the patient's desire to attack the source-object (source of learning and knowledge, in the case of the analyst). In other contexts, the schizophrenic's often monotonous speech and delivery aim at pacifying the analyst and perhaps putting him to sleep whenever his presence becomes too persecutory.

One of my patients was in the habit of boring me with his droning voice. In my countertransference, I felt this to be a con-certed and persistent attempt to force his way inside me by "bor-ing" into my mind. His way of putting it was that by boring me with his monotonous voice, he was dispersing himself. The persist-ent dispersion and boring implied a concrete attack on my ability to think and to communicate verbally with him. A "boring" noise is a means of action that has no symbolic value; it operates in a reified world. The schizophrenic's "magical" thinking is invested with concrete powers with which he can penetrate other people and control them and, more generally, attack and control reality. Discussing the laws of omnipotent magic in primitive peoples, Frazer (1959) refers to an implicit logic in which thinking is as concrete an act as digesting.

Gestures and communication

In each individual's make-up, there are specific primary forms of communication that are often more direct than speech. Anxiety in some patients is so intense that it cannot be put into words. Since, however, they do need to express themselves, they use other means in order to communicate. They sometimes employ expressions that, though they might be less elaborate, are more dramatic, more figurative, and more sense-oriented than ordinary speech. I would like to illustrate some of these points with the help of material drawn from the analysis of a schizophrenic patient.

The patient, Albert, was a young man of 18, in the throes of an acute psychotic crisis. I met Albert for the first time in his own home. He was refusing to come out of his room, thereby cutting himself off from the rest of his family. He was told who I was through the locked door. He reacted by suddenly opening the door, rushing out of the room, and standing squarely in front of me. He was very tense and looked at me arrogantly; impassive and apathetic, he asked me what I wanted. I replied that I had been called in by his family because he was withdrawn, had no contact with anybody at all, and, from what I could see of him, was very tense. He smiled, as though mocking my words, and declared that since he had not asked to see me he had nothing to say.

I stayed where I was, observing him from a distance, and I interpreted the fact that he had come out of his room as perhaps after all an attempt to "open up" and be helped. His narcissistic attitude of superiority would not allow him to accept the fact that he was ill. I respected his territory, making no move to get any closer than he would allow. He realized that I was respecting his personal space; after a long silence, he again smiled—but this time in a more expressive and spontaneous way.

After another silence—less tense this time—I noticed that his eyelids were constantly fluttering. I could not understand the meaning of this, until I began to feel in my countertransference something resembling loneliness; the patient was alternating between opening up to my presence and closing himself down again. I felt helpless with respect to this indifference. After some moments, I decided to say aloud what I was feeling: I wanted to get to know him inside, but he was shutting me out all the time with his eyelids, as though he didn't want me to penetrate into him through his eyes.[7] Also, by opening and closing his eyelids repeatedly, he was trying to control external reality. I was outside him, in an open space far beyond what his eyes could encompass. Given that I was an unknown quantity, he needed to control me and to keep me at a safe distance because of his paranoid anxieties.[8]

After this statement, he stopped fluttering his eyelids, adding that if I wanted to see him as he really was, then I should take advantage of the time-lapse between two flutters. I interpreted what he said as a sign of positive transference, a manifestation of his desire, in spite of his fears, to be "seen", understood, and helped. Being seen is also seeing through the eyes of someone else.

On another occasion, this time in my consulting-room, he sat down in front of me and began to stroke his face with his hands, touching his chin, his nose, then his eyes. Then, with his fingers, he began to open and close his eyes in a mechanical way (the earlier fluttering was now being performed by means of an external movement). He continued to do this in a ritualistic way for several minutes. I looked upon this "play" as a thread running from the previous meeting, a link between similar events. The repeated rhythm of this gesture implied the desire to keep to the rhythm of our initial encounter (organization and conservation of time). The gestured message was also an erotic visual expression of his anxieties, a "masturbating" rhythm that enveloped him and occasionally isolated him from me by describing in space a kind of repetitive circle within the perimeter of which he cut himself off.

As an item of body language, the fluttering had various meanings, depending on the context. Sometimes it was more of an eroticized attitude (which prevented communication and knowledge) rather than an exploratory one.[9] At other times, it was a true opening-up, an attempt to make contact with external reality.

---

[7] He felt that his ocular cavities, the holes in his mask, were coming under threat. In respecting his territory, I was also respecting the mask of the ill person.

[8] I have often noticed that young infants use their eyes in a magical way to "fix" and control objects belonging to external reality.

[9] Desmond Morris (1966) made an ethnological study of the psychology of animals living in cages. He draws a distinction between what he calls exploratory tendencies and others which he calls anti-exploratory. He observed that in

I said these thoughts aloud; the patient stood up, went quickly to the window, looked out, then sat down again. I said that this dramatization was the expression of an internal commotion, as if he had suddenly felt the need to get out of himself and go to the window—the "eye" of the room—to explore with impatient curiosity what was going on outside. The walls of the consulting-room had become the frontiers of his "extended body". His personal space oscillated between his original frontiers (anatomical body) and those of the room able to control him (fantasy body). Expansion and contraction of his body defined a spatial rhythm[10] that varied with the scansion of his stereotyped movements. The patient wrapped himself up in this rhythm-mask as if to protect himself from his surroundings. Once he was safely behind his mask, he could begin to explore external reality (through his eye-window). I too was trying to explore his world and make contact with him by deciphering and putting into words the semantics of his body. A true process of communication uses the most highly developed means—speech—but in order to use sounds as words, it is necessary to "go out through the window" and open up one's horizons. To go beyond vocal gesture and body symbols means going beyond the limits of the body—towards the birth of speech.

The analytic situation is nothing if not dynamic. Its structural and structuring—and sometimes de-structuring—dimension is the expression of a gestalt in motion. The experience of what transpires in the analytic field adds further movement to its inherent dynamics and creates changes in structure. Patient and analyst increase their learning through these movements and exchange of messages, with transference and countertransference being inter-

---

situations of intense stress caused by physical isolation, animals become less sociable and more withdrawn and begin to perform stereotyped movements of an erotic nature. This attitude implies rejection of reality. The animal's own sexual body becomes the object of desire and is used to discharge extreme claustrophobic tendencies; some animals even inflict injury on themselves. This eroticized hatred directed against oneself reminds me of the attacks psychotics make against their own mind (as well as on their body). What in psychiatry is called mental deterioration could be looked upon as the result of gradual self-inflicted injury to the mind.

[10] Rhythm is a rudimentary form of conferring a temporal dimension on body space.

dependent aspects of the dynamic exchange. A given expression or sign from the patient may be a signal, a device, that indicates to the analyst what to do or say.

For another example of body language, I shall refer to a young psychotic patient called George who tended to make bizarre movements as though he were constantly being taken by surprise. When I asked him what was going on, he replied: "I'm opening then closing. If I open, my instincts will gush forth in bits and pieces, so I close in order to stop them getting out." Then he began to speak in a jerky, "bitty" way. I interpreted that what he called his instincts were aspects of his internal world which he experienced as highly dangerous for him; that was why he had to control them or make them less dangerous by fragmenting them. And since at one point he had said: "I can't go on talking because everything gets cut up when I speak", I added that he expressed his fragmentation not only in the "cutting" movements of his body (the startled jerks) but also through his cut-up bitty words.

Dramatization of his body enabled the patient to express both a primary existential issue (open up to the world or cut oneself off from it) and a means of defence against the uncontrolled rush of his instincts; the defence consisted in cutting and fragmenting his link to the world (hence the "bitty" words). Words were not differentiated from physical reality, they were neither abstractions nor true concepts; the signifier merged with the signified. Symbol and symbolized were experienced as parts of the same thing.[11]

---

[11] Alvarez de Toledo (1954) describes the process of symbolization of speech as a projection of "organs" and "functions" onto objects in the external world:

Projection is performed via the voice, speech and various means of projective identification.

This is followed by identification by displacement or substitution (a mechanism described by Jones and by Ferenczi).

The object invested with projections and displacements is introjected (introjective identification), with its representation becoming a symbol.

The concrete physical (bodily) elements of the perceptual experience and corresponding fantasies are repressed. Partly deprived of emotion and desexualized, they are transformed into mental representations. The objects as such are outwith the sphere of thought, whilst their images do belong to this sphere.

At one point, George said: "I can't express myself, I can't transform my thoughts correctly into words. My movements are the result of my instincts, which I confuse with thoughts." His difficulty in displacing and transforming echoes his difficulty in sublimating (transforming actual reality into something else, a representation) because of his paranoid anxieties (his "instincts" were experienced as terrifying objects); this made it impossible for him to project by means of speech in order to communicate. The fact that he could transform thoughts only into movements and not into speech was indicative of his fear of expelling terrifying objects through vocal projection beyond the frontiers of his body—and in so doing, lose control of them. Gestures, on the other hand, are always physically connected to the body, and therefore they protect external reality from being invaded by the "instincts".

George was preoccupied by the destiny of his instincts, and he had to verify the effect they had on me: he would ask me how I reacted to his messages, and he would observe the impact of his projections while listening attentively to my replies. My comments and interpretations were occasionally felt by him to be dangerous (the consequence of projecting his terrifying objects). Depending on the intentions he projected into my words, they would be either good or evil. He expressed his paranoid fears in the transference (return of his projections) by becoming withdrawn from time to time or by attacking my ability to think (the starting point of my "reactions" to him). These attacks were destined to strike at my ability to think in order to disintegrate me and put confusion into my mind. Integrating comprehension thanks to my interpretations had become something "real" and therefore dangerous for him. He was careful not to fall sleep during the session—indeed, he had to struggle against his desire to do so; had he fallen asleep, he would have been at my mercy. He would rub his eyes and say: "I have to struggle against sleep. Sleep is trying to force itself on me, to prevent me thinking and to neutralize me. I have to fight against it. It's like fighting something unknown. I'm afraid in case I've opened up too much."

I commented that he was afraid in case I would take advantage of his "openings" to get inside him disguised as sleep or some unknown person, and then try to force myself on him and neutralize him as an individual. George associated me with the authoritarian figure of his father, of whom he was indeed afraid—especially when his father became angry, lost control of himself, and became "as furious as a tiger".

The patient's attempts to communicate with me were contaminated by projection of his "instincts". These projections turned me into a cannibalistic persecutory oral superego (the tiger) who would invade him and tear him to pieces. Entering into communication with himself also became dangerous, because he would then be in contact with an internal superego object that frightened him. With no control over re-introjection of his own projections, he felt defenceless and exposed to attacks from inside as well as outside. In such a situation, it is not only the meaning of speech (the signified) that counts, but also the intentionality of the signifier (the carrier). Various aspects of the voice (gentle, harsh, warm, cold, etc.) as signifier take on meaning in themselves.

The young infant reacts to his mother's verbal and gestured messages and discovers signs in the sounds long before he discovers symbols. De Saussure (1967), writing about the production of sounds, observes that phonologists tend to ignore acoustics. The impression produced on the ear is probably simultaneous with the motor image of the organs that shape it.

Sound production is the result of interplay between exhalation, articulation, vibration in the larynx, and nasal reverberation. Exhalation in itself has no differential value, but the presence or absence of nasal reverberation does give a characteristic note to phonemes.

In the regressive context of the transference, the phenomenology of sound is particularly significant. Opening and closing are extremely important, whether on the part of the emitter or on that of the ear which controls the intake of words (aural opening and closing).

Oneiric language

The theory of dreams played a crucial role in Freud's thinking—the "royal road" to knowledge of the unconscious. The language of dreams enables us to decipher the messages our unconscious sends us. In ancient times, dream-interpreters considered dreams to be signs or prophetic announcements. The dream message, which required interpretation for its obscure message to be revealed, was related to the need to communicate with others by means of dreams. Signs and symbols were originally transmitted through verbal language. Artemidorus of Daldis, who lived in the second century of the current era and was an inspired interpreter of Greek and Roman culture, classified dreams into speculative and allegorical (i.e. with symbolic and metaphorical content). Speculative dreams correspond to visual images as direct expressions of the signifier (like the dreams of young children, according to Freud). Allegorical (meaningful) dreams represent something beyond that which they purport to show. Artemidorus stressed the importance of the immediate linguistic expression and the word-plays that dreams often contain. For him, the best example of dream explanation—Freud quotes this example—was the capture of Tyre by Alexander the Great. The siege of the city was making Alexander impatient and uneasy, and one night he dreamt of a satyr dancing on his shield. Aristander, the dream-interpreter in the king's retinue, divided the word for satyr into σα and Τυρος [= "Tyre is thine"]. Taking the interpretation as an announcement of what he had to do, Alexander the Great marched into and conquered the city.

In the first part of his book on dreams, Freud (1900a) observes that even in the pre-scientific period of dream interpretation, ordinary people had the obscure feeling that some hidden truth could be unveiled through the language of dreams. Though the idea that dreams are a message from the unconscious is crucial to Freud's theory, his emphasis on the causal nature of repressed desires tends to push to one side the strictly linguistic aspects of oneiric expression which played such an important part for ancient dream-interpreters: the dream considered as a message.

For Burdach (1838, quoted in Freud, 1900a), dreams are a symbolic way of representing reality. Dreaming is proof of the capacity to symbolize or to communicate by means of symbol-instruments. The schizophrenic finds it difficult to dream—or, rather, to grasp the fact that he is constantly in a dream or in a delusion without being able to differentiate between them. To dream means to be able to wake up and know that we have been dreaming; the fact that we can distinguish between dreaming and being awake is an indication that we are able to distinguish dreams from reality. The gap between manifest and latent content in the schizophrenic's dream is so narrow that his almost naked dream thoughts are confused with real objects—in other words, with the landscape of daily reality (Resnik, 1987).

Let me come back to the story of the patient I have just been describing. George had a dream in which he was in *a circular building several storeys high. He and I were looking out of the fourth-floor window, and I was transparent.*[12] *A tiger was looking at us from a third-floor window. Since George was afraid, he and I both jumped out of the window in order to escape from the tiger.*

George associated the circular building to the ceiling rose he could see in my consulting-room. "In the dream," he said, "*the building was beautiful, but a lot of it was in ruin. There was a lawn the colour of this couch.*" He related the window out of which we had jumped in the dream to the window in the consulting-room. "I think my body is divided into different parts, maybe different floors. The tiger is on the third floor with its dangerous 'instincts'. I'm on the top floor and you are behind me, just like here." He touched the wall beside the couch, brought his hand up to his mouth, bit it, then rubbed his chest.

I interpreted the dream to him as follows. He was the tiger, scratching at the wall with his claws as though to break out, then biting himself because he could neither leave nor allow anybody else to leave. He then squeezed his hands with his fingers (a mouth-squeeze which bites). "I bite like someone trying to stimulate you, squeeze you, so that you'll be linked to me," he said; "I need to wake you up and make you react, so that you'll be with me all the time." I replied: "Yes, but the stimulus has been deflected— you in fact bit your own finger, perhaps to protect me from that biting impulse."[13]

George wanted to be linked to me, to the various parts of himself, and to the storeys or levels of his body image, but his cannibalistic tendencies had so invested the means at his disposal that

---

[12] He probably wanted me to be transparent for him.

[13] Another way of looking at it would be that he was trying to wake me up as an internalized object projected into his finger.

this attempt at communication was fraught with fear and aggressiveness.

Through the dramatization of the dream, his gesture-language, and his associations, the patient was expressing a desire to communicate, a desire that ran counter to his manifest behaviour. The aim of his desire as manifested in the dream is to look out of the window (his eyes) at what is going on outside, and in this way to link up with other people. The problem is that he has to be split in order to protect what he loves from his own dangerous impulses. Development of insight means the capacity to see oneself—to come outside in order to look at oneself—and relate to different aspects of one's "building" (the body). This process is fraught with anxiety, because the patient has to relate to ruins—i.e., something inside him which has been destroyed. The beauty of part of the building is an idealized compensation for what is felt to be damaged or ruined inside himself.

I observed that communication implies creating links, uniting, combining—and these are all present in the dream in various forms. Stimulate, scratch (George was at one point scratching the couch), squeeze—all are references to an attempt at "trying his hand" at relationships with other people and at controlling his cannibalistic tendencies in order to prevent the desire actually being accomplished.

I cannot overemphasize the importance of this dream and its interpretation, and also of the relationship between oneiric language and its "dramatic" clarification through the transference. The dream that the patient reports in the session delimits the structural configuration of the message. Past experiences coincide with present sensations. The dream and its oneiric language, thus extended in bodily space, provide the body with a means of expression. The idea of levels of relationship with others (the storeys in the dream building) is expressed in the transference through different modes of relationship with the analyst (gesture, oral, verbal); this is what forms the interchange of messages. Oneiric language is translated into gestures, facial expressions, words, and so forth. Freud himself argued that linguistic expression played a mediating role. The dream, a world of "hallucinated" and principally visual images, is linked in its narrative drama to body language as well as to speech.

Object relations and early verbal expression

Semantics of the body and speech are brought together when the first phonemes appear, when acoustics and articulation integrate (vocal gesture becomes articulated sound). The ability to project ourselves vocally beyond the frontiers of our body is a necessary condition for discovering others (moving from the body to open space in order to discover what lies outside).

Early linguistic expression is based on gesticulations (body and sounds) by means of which the infant tries to make contact with the surrounding world. These are indicative of both his desire for and the possibility of going beyond his limits. There is a dialectic relationship between going beyond the limits and constructing a "true" frontier, an interface that can be used for communication. In his first object relations, the infant makes contact with the world through the mother. His mother-world thus becomes an essential link with the wider environment.

Language is an instrument by means of which an individual reveals his intimate being and his desire to bond with others. The study of body language is closely related to that of verbal expression. Merleau-Ponty (1955) said that "the idea we have of someone would be superficial were we not to go back to the origins of expression, to find the silence underneath the noise of words and to describe the gestures which for the first time broke that silence" (p. 39).

We could say that the first gesture is a prelude to the first cry, which in turn foreshadows the first word—that is, the way in which we externalize ourselves through the act of opening up to the world.

A rough outline of the communication process could be broken down into the following stages (based on Marcel, 1927):

- communication as thought,[14] which we formulate "inside" in a kind of communication with ourselves (intra-communication);
- the sensorial and motor means of transmission (the body in the case of pre-verbal language, the voice for speech), as well as extrasensory or parapsychological means;

---

[14] Or, rather, what we *call* thought, with its unconscious implications.

- conversion of thought into externalized language through these means of transmission;
- confirmation of reception of the message by the other partner (intercommunication).

In order for thought to be externalized, it must first of all be formulated within the self (consciously and unconsciously). Intra-communication normally takes place in the mind and is subjected to the ego's synthesizing and integrating function. When intra-communication is distorted, the different elements are not assimilated by the ego; they remain foreign to and isolated from the rest. Appropriate contact between thoughts or fantasies[15] and the ego furthers better integration of the internal world.

Melanie Klein claimed that intra-psychic integration depends on the capacity to surmount paranoid anxiety and its corresponding splitting mechanisms. This is the node of what she calls the depressive position. The "former" defence mechanisms typical of the paranoid–schizoid position are employed in the depressive position as "devices" for differentiation in the context of whole-object relations. Distinguishing between good and bad values within that context is proof of the ability to classify reality taken as a whole and plays a major role in symbol formation.

Following Freud's views on symbolism, Jones (1919) demonstrates the successive homologies the infant makes as he gradually constructs appropriate symbolic tools. The infant's paramount experiences are displaced onto representative objects through a series of substitutions. Separation anxiety at each new stage is the primary model of this ability to "move on". To separate implies being able to move from one stage to another through a diachronic series of identifications. According to Freud, the reason for these displacements in symbol formation lies in superego frustration and prohibitions. The aggressive reaction against these and fear of the superego stimulate the search for other more acceptable objects.

---

[15] Though they are conceptually different, I use "thoughts" and "fantasies" to denote a certain type of representation in the psychic domain. The habitual use of conscious and unconscious fantasies has the drawback (which is at times also an advantage . . .) of oversimplifying the multiple degrees of representation that can be differentiated semiologically.

Jones insists on the importance of reality components as stimuli for communication; external reality invites us to make contact with it.

The infant tends to attribute intentionality to objects in his environment. His world is therefore inhabited by meanings for which he himself is to a certain degree responsible (through his projections). But in order to invest objects in external reality with significant content, the infant has first to run the risk of going beyond the frontiers of his body. Usually in their initial analytic session, children observe the playthings and other objects at their disposal before deciding to "come outside" and inject life into that reality. It is up to the analyst to "name" that reality in order to discover the child's projections. This done, a play-language can begin to develop within the analytic field.

For Melanie Klein (1930), the forerunner of symbolization is the fear that the infant feels with respect to his own aggressive impulses directed against his original objects. Projected aggressiveness spreads terror throughout reality, and this stimulates the search for substitutes. Paranoid anxiety with respect to persecutory situations is a determining factor in encouraging the formation of symbols.

Freud and Abraham had already explored projection and introjection. Melanie Klein argued that they are in operation from the moment of birth.[16] Projecting certain elements and introjecting others experienced as external indicate that there is already some notion of limits and frontiers in operation. The ability to differentiate between internal and external reality and between different impulses is part of Klein's depressive position. In perceiving mother as a whole- and not as a part-object, the infant becomes aware of his own existence. Interpersonal relationships result from the recognition that in reality there are two objects which can be differentiated from each other: mouth and breast on the part-object level, and mother and child on the whole-object level. In discovering duality, the infant becomes aware of singularity and of multiplicity; he as an individual is *with* some other person, and there

---

[16] I imagine that there exists an initial state of confusion which later appears in the transference, as Herbert Rosenfeld suggests. I have discussed this topic, *passim*, in several papers.

exists a third person, father, who represents the beginnings of multiplicity.

The original models of object relations determine various specific types of infantile dependence. The young infant's avidity and envy are concentrated on his original object, mother. If these tendencies are very intense, the normal relationship between them may be disturbed. Jealousy appears in relation to the third object, father—the person who interferes with the dual relationship (see Klein's 1928 study of the early stages of the Oedipus complex).

In the depressive position, partial experiences become whole; the persecutory object and the idealized object are brought together, and ambivalence is born from the proximity of these antithetical feelings. The infant loves and does-not-love, contradictory sentiments clash, and feelings of responsibility and guilt come to the fore. Satisfaction and frustration come together and engender ambivalence.

A higher degree of integration of contradictory aspects occurs in ambiguity, a more elaborate product of contradiction. In ambiguity, there is a "non-antithetical" confrontation between different realities, with a tendency to perceive them as a comprehensible *unit*. With the dialectic implications of ambiguous behaviour, the individual develops his ability to synthesize experience. In so doing, he becomes a *person* (the personalization process).

Communication and the oral zone

William Stern (1962) put forward the hypothesis that at the beginning of life the space that the infant's mouth can apprehend and explore represents its territorial limits. As part of our body, the mouth can contain and introject whatever exists in "apprehensible" space. Spatialization operates through opening outwards, but in order to establish a frontier with the world a closing movement is required. Through such openings and closings, the primary existential position is dramatized and given physical (bodily) expression.

Melanie Klein (1936) argued that the mouth is not to be thought of merely as the original erogenous zone; it is also the primary instrument of praxis, because it makes connections with primary objects. Wallon (1975) claimed that it is not only the mouth but the entire respiratory apparatus that enables the infant to acquire the notion of space. The body, he said, is above all a "body which breathes". The newborn's first "introjection" is the gulp of air he takes in at birth; air is the original "milk" he sucks in from the world. Psychosomatic respiratory disorders like asthma are perhaps related to disturbances of this primary experience.

Angel Garma (1956) proposed the idea of an oral–digestive organization that follows on from the initial sucking-in of air. Both, he argued, contribute to the development of an "apparatus" capable of projecting and introjecting, a typical feature of the infant's first months. Both mother's milk and "milk" from mother-world are indispensable. Recalling Winnicott's idea of the hallucinated breast as an anticipation of the infant's encounter with his first object, we could postulate that he anticipates the world, still intangible and undifferentiated but desired and just as indispensable as the mother-air.

The behaviour of one of my young patients was illustrative of this. As I entered my consulting-room, he was already there, lying on the couch with one finger in his mouth. As I sat down in my chair, he sucked on his finger and said: "I'm filling up." He added that he had found the consulting-room empty before my arrival, to which I commented: "You're filling up in your mouth [mouth-space] the emptiness you'd felt when you came in here; you missed me" (and because of that he had needed to feed himself with his finger, with the "hallucinated breast" he had created "on" his finger).

He then took his finger out of his mouth and began telling me of a concert where the orchestra would be playing Stravinsky's *Rite of Spring*; he was to be one of the musicians. I interpreted that he felt much more calm now that he had filled up the emptiness in him; he had received something from me, and now he wanted me to be an audience and suck the good music that it was only "*right*" he should give me.

This patient was communicating with me by means of his mouth-space and the sounds it produced,[17] and at the same time

---

[17] The means of communication I am referring to here are based on a kind of sensory transmission (composed of signs, signals, and symbols more or less

he filled himself with my nourishing words (he could "digest" them because they were comprehensible). In return, he wanted to give me something good coming from him—he felt it was only "*right*" that he should dedicate it to me. Through his mouth he expressed his oral impulses (oral, respiratory, and digestive) and fantasies—by his movements, his sounds, his words. He expressed the most primitive of intentions by means of his "mouth body space" in a figurative way.

Speaking and listening

Speaking is an apparently significant utterance through which we attempt to encounter others in the most sophisticated way we possess: speech. We cannot study speech, however, without first investigating listening and understanding. In ordinary language we say that we fail to hear someone properly, when in fact what we mean is that we have not understood. Listening and understanding are associated in a complex system of relationships and meanings. Acoustic phenomena are probably as ancient as visual phenomena, and they are obviously closely related. The ear "observes" carefully what is transmitted to it through speech.

In situations of paranoid transference, the ear can become an instrument for dosing and controlling introjection of sounds and words it is wary of for some reason. Occasionally, a patient will press his ear against the cushion, or block it with a finger. Hypoacousia in the transference may express the patient's desire to withdraw into himself and keep the analyst's words at a safe distance.

Hyperacousia in the transference, on the other hand, is often experienced as a sudden and unexpected opening up, or as the analyst's voice flooding in. Tonal characteristics, such as a rasping or abrupt voice, may be felt to be very dangerous. This is typical of certain disorders of symbolization in which speech is more of a

---

elaborate and precise). What in parapsychology is called extrasensory perception could be conceived of as a primitive system that ordinary sense perception is unable to explain. Such means of transmission lie "beyond" those we are accustomed to.

deed or an action than something that is "spoken". Even when speech is taken as something spoken (i.e. meaning overrides action), the defence may be that the patient is not listening or that he does not understand what is said. Negating meaning is a way of not grasping significant content; the person who is not listening cannot understand the message. Furthermore, we can hear without understanding—for example, when we listen to something said in a foreign language.

In the countertransference with schizophrenic patients, the analyst's difficulty in understanding is not a rare occurrence. This is not merely the consequence of a structural or syntactic difficulty; it is more the result of the morbidity of the message—which diffuses its madness into the analyst's space in order to drive *him* out of his mind. Such attacks against thinking are a feature of the psychotic part of the patient whose general attitude is one of hatred for reality and for processes of thinking related to reality. Apprehend, listen, comprehend—they mean for the analyst in his countertransference taking in and thinking through the respective roles of signifier and signified as they are expressed in the transference message. That is why it is important in my view to draw a distinction between hearing and listening. We hear whether we want to or not, but we listen because we have the intention of so doing. Listening is not such a passive attitude as is hearing; it is more an active manifestation of expectancy.

In the "concrete" thinking of the schizophrenic mentality or the psychotic part of the ego, words take on material values or characteristics in the same way that food, for example, does. In such cases, listening has the sense of "oral-aural sucking".[18]

In situations of major regression, all body apertures (nose, eyes, etc.) have an oral-receptive component through which the patient tries to take in food (word-food).[19] In one patient, for instance, the desire for "aural sucking" was evidenced by a clearly visible rash

---

[18] Alvarez de Toledo (1954) argues that words can take on the concrete qualities of milk, blood, urine, or faeces. In such a situation, the relationship with the analyst is more like "communicating vessels" than real communication.

[19] See my remarks on this point in the chapter on catatonic negativism (chapter three).

on the ear corresponding to the side on which I was talking to him.[20] Somatic affections of this nature show how receptive organs can become eroticized.

Hearing and understanding constitute two different phases of incorporation. In the transference, both patient and analyst may have difficulty in distinguishing between "hearing", "listening", and "understanding": they may be stuck at one or the other of these stages, or they may confuse the different levels of the sensory–perceptual–cognitive chain.

I have, up to this point, always referred to speech as communication, but it may also *interfere* with communication. This is particularly true of patients who suffer from very strong paranoid anxieties. In some cases, speech can be used to bore the analyst, hypnotize him, send him to sleep, or anaesthetize him in order to take up residence inside him rather than communicate with him. Occasionally a patient will weave an impenetrable web with his word-sounds, preventing anything from passing through, closing down all communication, and cutting himself off from the other partner. It is as though he has taken a scalpel and sliced through the *dia-logos*. This is one way of using words paradoxically—in order to say nothing. Such obstacles to communication may be necessary in situations where, for example, only indirect communication is possible.

Silence and communication

Silence, like speech, can be a means of or an obstacle to communication. We "temporalize" our experiences—that is, we situate them in sequence and in so doing attempt to make sense of our own history. The analytic experience teaches us that historicity as subjective reality is organized in contrasting rhythms. Speech stands out against a background of silence; conversely, silence occasionally holds the foreground.

Interpersonal relationships are structural and formal (they are a *gestalt*), and time is the backcloth against which they take place;

---

[20] See also Abraham (1913).

time can be mobile or, in the case of catatonia, frozen. The laws governing mobility form an articulated system whose structure is defined by the degree of internal equilibrium and by the capacity to be oneself, a person in one's own right. Gestalt psychology is no longer limited by a static concept of form; it admits of a continuous series of restructurings and as such is inherently dynamic.[21] Structural mobility is expressed as a rhythm that, with its varying tonalities and nuances, makes the experience unique. In this movement, sounds, speech, attitudes, gestures, and silence alternate. I have already discussed most of these aspects, and I will now concentrate on the last of these—silence.

In ordinary life, we tend to see speech and actions on the one hand and silence on the other as being in a contrasting figure-to-background relationship. However, the relationship may equally well function in the opposite direction, with silence appearing as the "figure". This possibility is quite clearly evidenced in the analytic experience, in which moments of "silence" are not interruptions in the flow of speech but a true discourse in itself with its own semantic structure. Some silences are tense and withdrawn, others relaxed and open. Some are permeable to communication, others are impenetrable and block all attempts at dialogue. The autistic patient even builds a fortress of silence and hides behind its walls. He does this not only to put a safe distance between himself and reality, but also to preserve his own frontiers from being overrun. An ego that is not wholly integrated or that lacks internal cohesion experiences every approach as a threat to its already weak integrity. The autistic person is bound and gagged by silence, a silence that nevertheless maintains him safe and sound behind its ramparts. Time, like everything else in him, is silent. Sometimes this wall of silence moves out into space and goes beyond the limits of the body; such "expansionism" aims at creating an atmosphere of silence that will surround and immobilize other people too. In the countertransference, the analyst may experience this as an inability to mobilize his thinking or to express himself.

---

[21] Von Ehrenfels (quoted in Meyerson, 1948) was the first to study form in relation to temporality (the principle of "transportability" of melody).

There is a geometry of silence. Sometimes, like a straight line, it penetrates; at other moments, like a convex surface, everything it encounters just bounces back off. Yet again, it may be an avid concavity that sucks in silence (oral silence). In autistic patients, the silence may appear to be emptiness, but it is an emptiness that is filled to the brim—his inner world is so distressing, persecutory, and chaotic that he has to reduce it to silence and hide it away by denying that an inhabited internal world could ever exist. This is what earlier I called negative hallucination or negative internal autoscopy (see Introduction). The patient sees himself as empty of all organs and of everything a body should contain; his omnipotence is working on behalf of negation of internal reality. However, if he negates external reality, it is the whole world that becomes empty and meaningless (solipsistic conception).

The greedy child who lives on in the adult sucks and swallows, hiding himself behind silence. Sometimes a word will suffice to interrupt this. Silence may take possession of surrounding space with no loss of boundaries.[22]

Insidious silence is difficult to detect; we discover it only once it has already penetrated. I once had a female patient who used to remain silent for minutes on end. Later, she was able to associate this to the actions of a mole; it was her way of burrowing silently into other people. In my countertransference, I could feel this silence-mole burrowing into me. She was attempting to take possession of me.

Between silences that block all communication and those that are projected and penetrate insidiously, there is a whole series of significant degrees. They vary from the most rudimentary of all—the gesture of silence—to those that anticipate speech. Like speech, silence has its own language, its own hidden devices that can support communication or block it completely, depending on the phenomenology of the encounter. In order to appreciate visibility, we must have some clue as to what invisible might be. Silence is related to darkness, to the unfamiliar with its cortège of mystery;

---

[22] I believe that the primitive self, before it can project feelings and thoughts, tends to "expand" the ego, in the same way that an amoeba will try to reach an object without leaving its own limits, i.e. without "coming out" into the open. See the discussion on Cotard's syndrome in chapter two.

but we must not forget that the role of mystery is to encourage us to undertake the adventure of exploration and discovery.

Summary and conclusion

Communication is a way of expressing and transmitting the way we live, feel, and think; it is the dynamic substratum of every encounter.

Communication is also movement from one situation to another, from one "locus" to another. The ability to move about in space by means of verbal language is related to our earliest experiences. The infant has to break free of his natural boundaries and project himself beyond his "contours" in order to make contact with the object, mother. Melanie Klein (1940) argued that initial object relations are models for adult relationships. The infant's first gestures, physical and vocal, indicate his need for intimacy, his desire to express himself and to make himself understood. The original pattern for this experience is constructed within the mother–baby relationship; they form a couple, and this led Winnicott to claim that a baby does not exist (i.e. in isolation). When we think of an infant, there is always someone else involved, taking care of him, watching over him, listening to him. What exists is the caring couple.

Jakobson (1969) said the same about language in the young child. No language belongs exclusively to the infant world; it is always the product of an exchange between two worlds, parents' and child's. The result is a phonemic, gestured, and social transaction. The features of the infant's early relationships determine the way in which he approaches the world, as expressed in his "character" and personal behaviour.

I refer in this chapter to the "mouth-space" as a particular zone in the body where what is inside intersects with the outside world. By means of this "hole-zone", the infant tests reality before adapting and entering into a series of exchanges with others (introjective and projective mechanisms).

Primary or pre-linguistic communication is part of the "gesturing body". True communication occurs when we discover our own individuality through our encounters with others; we discover too our own reactions to otherness. The origin of the word-as-symbol is the movement of body language beyond its own frontiers, into the discovery of space and "not-me". To communicate is to transmit something, but the latent message can become manifest only if the frontier between subject and object can be crossed—otherwise, communication would not indicate linking and transmitting, but entry into a confused syncretic relationship. A clear idea of the boundary between ego and outside world involves the feeling of being "oneself" and possessing one's own body. The individual acquires an identity, and thus becomes an integral and integrated person with the ontological structure of being-in-the-world.

The capacity for differentiation, argued Melanie Klein, is rooted in the development of the idea of wholeness, organized through the depressive position where words take on the structure of language. The infant stands apart from mother, his impulses become more differentiated as do the values (good or bad) of the object towards whom they are directed. The ability to discriminate determines the capacity to displace and transform (sublimation).

The idea of transference is comprehensible only within a psychoanalytic phenomenology of the encounter. Freud said that we transfer the *imagos* we each carry within ourselves. In the transference, two phenomena are in constant interaction: the interpersonal relationship and exchange with the other participant, and the clarification of an inner encounter with its corresponding intra-communication. True communication with others is possible only when intra-communication and ego integration has been accomplished.

My interest in phenomenology—obvious in my writings—stems from my experience as a clinician. The phenomenological aspect of my discussions owes everything to my attitude towards clinical matters, where I am a witness who simultaneously describes what he sees and reveals himself for what he is. In the fragments of my analytic fieldwork reported in this chapter, I have tried to study conscious and unconscious communication, verbal and non-verbal. I emphasize the role of non-verbal communication as the Ariadne's clew of psychosis. The highly specific position in which the analyst is placed makes possible his role as participant observer.

The analyst-witness needs to communicate to his patient his perceptions of and thoughts about a situation in which he is directly involved. The guidelines, the reference points for such disclosure, is his countertransference. To put it another way, the analyst as a person must translate into words what he has felt. Interpretation is *logos*, which is never more than a hypothesis that requires confirmation through the interplay of the analytic encounter.

Different perspectives within the analytic field can make a very useful contribution to the construction of the "analytic laboratory". The essential art of every analysis consists in creating the necessary links and operational instruments for this laboratory to "work".

CHAPTER FIVE

Body language and verbalization: the analysis of an acute psychotic crisis

I n this chapter I discuss the analysis of a female psychotic patient whom I treated over several years. I deal particularly with the period corresponding to the acute psychotic crisis; it was then that primary models of object relation appeared with maximum clarity in the transference.

In the previous chapter, I referred to the idea of communication and in particular to that rudimentary form of communication consisting primarily of body language which is so typical of both the young infant and the psychotic adult. I return to that theme here and deal particularly with its influence on the transference situation. The first encounter with the patient is, to my mind, fundamental because that is where in the dual relationship between patient and analyst the initial patterns of contact emerge. Analysis reactivates models belonging to the patient's past in a new context in such a way that the analyst can observe them; the analytic field of operations gives us the opportunity of observing how the analytic phenomenon is "born". The past integrated with the present takes the form of primary relational models dramatized in the *hic et nunc* of the session. The ways in which this occurs are unpredictable; they are the consequence of the need to communicate. The analytic session is the experiential field in which the analyst is both observer and witness.[1] Arranging what he has discovered in some kind of order and using it in the transference relationship help to structure the field.

With psychotic patients, who have difficulty in distinguishing fantasy from reality, it is necessary to include the reality principle as a basic operational instrument. The different forms of negation of reality can only be studied within a "realistic" framework. As the analytic process develops, different types of communication come into play, and a semiological study of them becomes necessary. In the present chapter, I give examples mainly of dramatization and playful language.

It will be helpful if I start by giving some details of the patient's past history.

Anamnesis

Anne-Marie is 31 years of age, an attractive, elegant, and likeable young woman.

From the outset, my attention was drawn to her sudden changes of mood. Sometimes she would be a very sophisticated adult, expressing herself coherently; at others, she would behave

---

[1] I recently attempted to explore the idea of *witness* —someone who is present, who observes and evaluates what is given to him to see (his other senses play their part too). His very presence implies some degree of participation in whatever occurs in the ob-served situation. *Servare* means to keep safe or preserve, and the prefix *ob* over or against. Observing has both an ethical connotation (observing a rule) and a spatial one of distance and position: to watch over (physically and morally). The role of witness is a determinant factor for the constitution of the analytic field; the analyst observes, listens, "feels", and bears witness in the presence of his patient to what he has been able to perceive and comprehend in the countertransference—this what we mean by "interpretation". The analyst's responsibility is to preserve and re-spect a situation in which he is simultaneously actor and spectator. This raises the issue of supervision of trainee analysts. We may ask ourselves how it is possible for a supervisor to judge a situation where the "witness" is someone else. What we call supervision can prove useful on condition that the super-

like a graceful little girl; and occasionally she would be cold, aloof, almost unable to talk or—when she did speak—rambling and incoherent.

According to her mother, Anne-Marie had been a sociable child, imaginative and intellectually advanced for her age. People liked her. She was apparently her father's little pet, and this increased her narcissism. She was the eldest of four children. After her came a sister who, as a young adult, had undergone lobotomy because of a schizophrenic degenerative process.[2]

When she was 6 years old, Anne-Marie became very obviously withdrawn; this coincided with the parents' decision to separate. (The relationship between mother and father seems to have been plagued by conflict almost from the start.) In addition, she suffered from *pavor nocturnus* and had a tendency to kleptomania.

One of the typical features of this family was its instability: they frequently moved house, and the father's profession (he was a journalist) took them abroad a great deal.

During puberty and adolescence, Anne-Marie apparently made friends without any particular difficulty until, when she was almost 18, she met a much older married man and had an affair with him. Shortly after he abandoned her, certain schizoid traits of character became more pronounced. She withdrew more and more into herself and was unable to make contact with other people; she suffered from insomnia, felt abulic and depressed, and feared she was going mad. She said she could feel something "strange" inside her head, but she was unable to be more precise.

At one point, she flew into a rage with her father's second wife, who was pregnant at the time. Anne-Marie attacked her compulsively and caused a miscarriage. Anne-Marie then fell into a deeply depressive state which, given her previous symptoms, led to her being hospitalized.

---

vision session is a kind of reactivation of what the *in situ* witness perceived and attempted to think through. The supervisor becomes an indirect witness; his task is to stimulate in the trainee analyst the capacity to apprehend significant material *in situ*—and this through an experience that occurs elsewhere, in the supervision session. If the latter is useful and creative, the trainee analyst's ability as witness will be improved.

[2] I had in fact been consulted by this sister a year before I met Anne-Marie.

In the clinic, she tried to commit suicide. She was given ECT and insulin; after three months she had improved sufficiently to leave the clinic. The diagnosis was schizophrenia.

Shortly after leaving the clinic, she married—apparently persuaded to do so by her father, who was about to leave the country for a considerable length of time and wanted her to be in safe hands. During the honeymoon, she met the man who would later become her second husband (he too was much older than she was). She married him a few months after divorcing her first husband.

She appeared to adjust quite well to married life, but about eighteen months after her second marriage she had another breakdown. As in the previous instance, she became withdrawn and insomniac, and her behaviour became strange; for instance, she would laugh out loud for no apparent reason, hide away in her own house, and become agitated to the point of attacking her husband. Again hospitalized, she was free to leave after one month. A year later, she was hospitalized once more, after another breakdown with similar symptoms.

Her behaviour during this new hospitalization resembled that on previous occasions. She was puzzled, immobile, and wept silently in a supplicating manner. She gave the impression of being nymphomaniac, but when questioned about her sexual life she claimed to be frigid and sterile. She wanted to be a mother, and she complained she was not being given enough to eat. The diagnosis again was schizophrenia, and she was treated by insulin and ECT.

Again after three months she was able to leave the clinic. She went back to her husband, even though after each breakdown she felt more and more estranged—in fact, two years later they separated for good.

Her lifestyle became more and more unorthodox. Her second husband died, and she had an affair with a man we shall call Mr G; they decided to live together.

For the next two years, she appeared to be fairly well adjusted, though she did consult a psychoanalyst, mainly for her alleged frigidity and sterility. She was also upset by the fact that she was losing interest in things and was beginning to have doubts about her relationship with Mr G. She also expressed the desire to be a mother and to be "whole" again.

Shortly after this she began analysis, but as her anxiety increased she interrupted this treatment, afraid that the analysis might set off another breakdown. That same year she fell ill with hepatitis; as a result, her father, who lived in another town, came to visit her. He was critical of her unconventional relationship with Mr G.

Some time later, conflict broke out between Anne-Marie and her lover. She became suspicious of other people, and in particular of him. She was aggressive towards him, then became depressed and began to show signs of mental confusion. She was living in a "fog". During one train journey, she had had to force herself to behave properly; but she suddenly felt a pain in her stomach, lost her self-control, and became incoherent. She had brief spells of depression.

This was the condition Anne-Marie was in when I first met her.

First meeting with the patient

She immediately struck me as an attractive young woman in spite of the look of weariness and exhaustion she had on her face. She had just come out of a state of psychomotor agitation which had lasted several hours, and now she felt puzzled and anxious, with a kind of inflexibility about her. Her eyes were very expressive—they alternately narrowed then opened wide. From time to time she looked as though she was lost in a void. She did not say anything, but since she seemed to be waiting expectantly, I broke the silence: "What's the matter?"

She replied: "The world is coming to an end . . . Clouds, wind . . . Everything is empty." She fell silent, then added: "Put on weight, I want to put on weight. The world is empty . . ."

I commented: "Empty like you feel yourself to be, empty and bereft of everything. And you're so confused that you don't know where the emptiness is, whether it's out in the world or inside you."

Another silence, then Anne-Marie, placing her hand on her stomach as though she were in pain, murmured in a broken voice: "Have a child . . . have a child."

I replied to this: "Your stomach is complaining and demanding a baby."

The development of our dialogue showed from the outset that she was capable of reacting to my remarks in a communicative way. The fact that in a preliminary diagnostic interview I deliberately adopted a therapeutic attitude may call for some explanation. In the case of psychotic patients, I consider it important, from the point of view of the prognosis, to investigate not only their capacity for making links but also the ego's ability to respond to what I call *interpretative stimuli*.

Analysis during the hospitalization

On her first day in the clinic, the nurses reported that Anne-Marie alternated between a puzzled and unbending attitude, outbursts of tears, and manic periods (compulsive dancing). The analytic sessions took place in a hospital bedroom, a single room—not her own bedroom, which she shared with other patients.

As she entered, she hesitated, glanced around the room, then sat down on the bed. "This one is nicer," she said.

"It's better to be alone and by yourself, isn't it?" I commented.

Anne-Marie continued to look all around the room, then stared at a portrait of St Theresa hanging on the wall behind her; or, to be more precise, she looked at the *reflection* of the portrait in the mirror on the wall facing her. At no point did she look directly at me.

She began to wring her hands, then wept bitterly and brought her hands together as if in supplication, muttering something which I could not catch. Then she pointed accusingly to the bed and looked at St Theresa as if to seek forgiveness for her sins. Her imploring attitude became even more blatant when she put her hands between her thighs near her pubis. I interpreted: "You're looking between your legs for your lost saintliness, and you're asking forgiveness for being a sinner."

A few moments later her attitude changed. Still addressing the mirror, she murmured the word "tenderness", then, referring to herself in the third person, she said: "She has no daddy, no mummy and no brothers." To which I added: "And so everything is empty, like the world."[3]

She looked at the white blanket on the bed and stroked it with her hand as though to straighten it out. "You'd like me to straighten things out for you," I said, "because you're feeling very upset."

"Nothing can be straightened," she replied. Putting her hand on her breast, she continued: "I'm searching for my love."[4]

"Your love, your first love," I replied. "You're looking for a mummy, a good mummy like St Theresa." She rocked gently back and forth in a swaying movement. I went on: "Little Anne-Marie is being rocked in a cradle."

Her attitude immediately changed, and she began to undo her hair. I said: "Suddenly there's a lot of anger and everything becomes undone, your head becomes undone." When I said that, she stopped fingering her hair and instead began to unmake the bed. I interpreted: "The bed as white as a breast, which you loved and cherished, now you're dismantling it."

---

[3] The fact that at times I restrict myself to describing "what I think I see" or to reporting what I understand of the patient's internal language calls for some comment. I base this attitude on the feeling I have of representing, in certain situations, the intermediate or "transitional" object, the third-person substitute (like the mirror in the present session), or, as E. Pichon-Rivière (1952) put it, the third party.

I think that in regressive situations where there is such a split between thinking and doing, it is important to be the translator, the person who "puts into words" what is going on inside the patient. This helps the patient to realize the extent of his splitting. As we know, in the pre-verbal period of primary communication, words are felt to be dangerous; in such a situation, a patient may feel the need to communicate by projecting himself into a suitable mouth, through which he can then speak (an appropriate word-object-mouth). The analyst here is like a true auxiliary ego that the patient needs in order to make contact with reality. This resembles to some extent primary mother–baby communication, where the mother picks up and then translates what her infant is feeling. Interpretation is occasionally a verbal explanation of something that has already been anticipated in implied form. Empathy has a lot to do with all of this.

[4] The figurative but "auto-plastic" (Ferenczi) dramatization (i.e. using her own breast) reveals a narcissistic kind of object relation. In other words, everything is expressed in terms of her own body.

These actions were accompanied by pathetic gestures some-where between hysteria and catatonia, pleading for God to forgive her. She showed me her empty hands, then kissed them. I com-mented: "You're losing everything. You're losing what you love. And you're afraid you'll lose me too, and then you'll be left empty-handed. Nothing lasts with you."

After a pause, she said: "Were you supposed to come today?"

I answered: "You didn't think I would come; you were already feeling that you were losing me."[5]

She again unmade the bed and undid her hair. I added: "You're undoing all that with as much spitefulness as if I had never come." She touched her nose and then her hand. She tried to see whether the fingers of her hands would interlock correctly with one an-other. I said: "You're trying to see whether we fit together well, whether we're going to get on well with each other."

"Yes," she replied.

I added: "Probably you're afraid to make direct contact with me, so you're doing it via the mirror, as you did with St Theresa."[6]

At this, Anne-Marie wrapped her head in the blanket. I asked her: "Are you putting yourself inside St Theresa so that she will protect you?"[7]

Her attitude changed once more, and she tidied up the bed. As the session drew to a close, she made as though she had just thought of something but wanted to chase the thought away. I told her this was the impression I had had.

* * *

[5] The external object made her narcissistic style of object relation collapse. Attacks against the frustrating breast occur when its existence as something independent is confirmed. Her disorder is the product of an indiscriminate attack on the object and the parts of the ego bound to it; this is felt as though her impulses were impacting on her own mind.

[6] Using a transitional object is part of indirect or long-distance communica-tion. It is a defence that keeps the relationship at bay and so protects Anne-Marie from her destructive paranoid impulses. It is also a way of controlling separation and unexpected encounters.

[7] Faced with the necessity of recognizing that the object she needs is indeed external to her, her projective identification increases (getting inside the object or hallucinating it in the blanket). This is a typical form of anxiety in schizo-phrenics: it is difficult to live outside one's objects.

In the following session, Anne-Marie was much more calm. She began by lying down on the bed, which gave me the feeling that she was on an analytic couch. I had the impression that she was dramatizing her earlier analysis. I noticed that she was opening and closing her eyes, and speaking alternately in a loud then in a quiet voice; I interpreted: "You feel you are in analysis again. Your position seems to indicate that you want to go on with it, yet you also seem undecided—you don't know whether you should open up or close down (like your eyes), or whether you should have your words travel as far as me."

She scratched her stomach and told me she had a scar on the surface of her skin (appendectomy). Her stomach gurgled, and she said: "That means digesting with a good appetite."

I replied: "You have an appetite for taking me in as something good, like your first love—mummy's breast."

"Yes. Mummy, mummy . . .", she said thoughtfully, as though to herself at first then looking around for me. I said: "You're looking for a mummy to love in me."

She made a question mark with a lock of her hair, and I commented: "You're not sure about me; I'm only a question mark for you." She opened her eyes very wide indeed, as though to observe me. I added: "You're trying to get rid of your doubts about me."

With an apparent intention to make contact with me, she gestured in my direction as though to send something tender. Then her hands made penetrating movements resembling coitus. She said: "I'm thinking of holy water."

"Holy water for you, my holy milk through sexual intercourse," I said.

She answered: "Yes, a strong man like mummy."[8] As soon as she had said that, she looked anxious, as if an unpleasant memory had suddenly surfaced. As though she were in pain, she said: "My spleen is hurting."

---

[8] The inclusion of sexual elements in the transference relationship indicates eroticization of the analytic field. I studied this phenomenon later, finding it a recurrent difficulty in treating psychotics. The relationship to the breast in its nourishing and educational roles (maternal superego) is distorted because of sexualization (it distorts normal sublimation and symbolization). Here, the erotic atmosphere is transferred onto an idealized relationship with the father.

I replied: "Suddenly you're no longer a glass[9] which receives holy water from me, but a spleen which hurts when my words and your memories are not maternal and good [holy water] but irritating and painful.[10] (The erotic transference relationship masks the depressive and paranoid pain).

"It hurts," she insisted.

I responded: "My words are hurting you."

She looked attentively first at the palm, then at the back of her hand; she seemed to be studying the lines on her palm. "Those are the big questions that are puzzling you," I said. "What are you like, inside and outside? What will become of you?"

Anne-Marie paused, then commented: "How strange everything is." One of her hands seemed to be playing with its own shadow, and she moved her legs as though she were marching.

I said: "You're walking towards your childhood, playing with shadows just like when you were a little girl. To be psychoanalysed means travelling all the way back to one's childhood, all the way back to the shadows."

"Yes," she replied, "my shadowy moments."

* * *

---

[9] Anne-Marie is Spanish. The phonetic analogy between *bazo* [spleen] and *vaso* [glass], which are pronounced almost identically in Spanish, is at the root of my association. This is an example of what I call the "phonetic equation".

[10] The fact that I make use of the patient's own words is not designed simply for communicating with her in her own language, but also for dramatizing her words as though they were in fact objects she had brought to her session (word-objects typical of the pre-verbal phase of language development). This is to some extent what happens in child analysis, where the young patient communicates his feelings to us through the roles he attributes to the various playthings in the room. Similarly, when the analyst is inspired by the word-games of the psychotic patient, he re-creates the playful "objects" of his own infantile language. Just as the child puts his play "alphabet" away in his personal box or drawer at the end of the session, the psychotic leaves his picturesque language (word plays) in the analyst-box. In the initial stages of development, the mother is the container into which the infant deposits his objects by projective identification; similarly, the analyst who works with psychotics is converted into a depository for their word plays. A particular way of handling internal objects is expressed through puns and what is usually called "schizophrenic humour". The ability to play indicates the presence of an infantile ego and therefore the potential for communication.

The following day, Anne-Marie had a uneasy look on her face. When I said to her that I had the impression that she felt dubious about me, she responded with tears and trembling. Then she calmed down and held out her hands to me—one open, the other a clenched fist. I commented: "You're in two minds, there are two attitudes in you—on the one hand you'd like to open up, but on the other you want to keep yourself tightly shut." She tried to join her hands together, and became anxious. I added: "You're trying to make all the parts of yourself agree."

She brushed her hands over her eyes as though to see more clearly, and she began to open and close her legs repeatedly.[11] Opening and closing her legs was another way of expressing her ambivalence, this time in genital terms. Later, she behaved like a child trying to get closer to me,[12] and she looked at the interior then the exterior of her hand. I interpreted: "You'd like to come closer to me and set your doubts aside by getting to know me inside out; then you won't be mistaken about me."

She replied with a nod of her head and adopted an attitude of supplication: she seemed to be begging me not to deceive her. She looked at the blanket and traced marks on it. I asked her: "Are you looking for the road to follow?"

"You are life," she said, stroking the blanket.[13] But as she did not look at me as she said this, I replied: "Yes, I am life . . . the life you don't dare face up to." She smoothed the blanket, then rumpled it again. I added: "Tenderness and rage about life and about me."[14]

---

[11] The object relation is becoming erotic. Eroticization of thinking makes it impossible to "see clearly". There is here a topographical displacement from thought (high) to the genitals (low) which downgrades the initial relationship.

[12] She is expressing on the genital level pregenital feelings related to her desire to be fed and joined with the source-object.

[13] The blanket represents the mother who covers and protects her. At the same time, it personifies the source-object that puts her in touch with reality and that is in direct *physical* contact with her infantile ego.

[14] Insofar as the mother is a representation of the reality principle, she is both loved and hated (ambivalence). Reality is both accepted and refused. Bion (1956) argues that the schizophrenic's destructive attacks are aimed not only against reality but also against the perceptual apparatus that puts him in touch with reality ("the apparatus of conscious awareness of internal and external reality"). In other words, the schizophrenic attacks both external *and* internal reality.

She had a puzzled look on her face, and I commented: "You're wondering whether life is worth living or not." One of her hands had been resting on the bed, and now she slowly raised it in the air; the movement gave me the impression of something growing taller. I interpreted this as a dramatization of her own growth. Noticing that her anxiety increased as her hand climbed higher and higher, I said: "Is it worth growing, just to suffer more and more? Maybe it would be better to remain a little girl."

A moment or two later, she said: "I want to have lots of money—with lots of money, I can be beautiful." She continued: "Yes, be good . . . and be able to have a child."[15]

I interpreted: "Having a child means getting better, changing a sterile life into a fertile one; but in order to get better, in order to have your analysis, you need money."

She looked thoughtfully at the blanket and said: "Mummy . . . mummy . . ."

"You'd like me to be a fertile mummy who makes you better," I said. Then she became anxious and said: "Mummy . . . Daddy."

I interpreted this as follows: "Saying daddy after mummy means bringing them together, reuniting them. And you're anxious in case they don't fit together well."

Anne-Marie seemed to disintegrate, and she began pronouncing words with no obvious connection between them: "How, how, odour, odour, sulphur, sulphur, hard, ripe, not ripe." Then she traced a sign of the cross on the bed.[16]

* * *

---

[15] After a playful and sublimated infantile relationship with mother, the fantasy of having a baby again eroticizes the analytic field. Her incestuous fantasies are reactivated in the transference.

[16] It is obvious that she experienced bringing the words "daddy" and "mummy" (word-objects) together as a traumatic reunion of Daddy and Mummy as objects. This reunion takes place in her internal world and is reactivated in the transference; this had the effect of shattering her and making her disintegrate. At that point she experienced the primal scene in hallucination as though she could smell it (odour, odour, sulphur, sulphur); she felt the smell was pursuing her (because of her projected destructive impulses) and abruptly trying to penetrate inside her. The sign of the cross, like the sulphur, was probably a magical means of warding off danger (trying to keep the persecutor—the combined parents—away). I think that for Anne-Marie, sul-

Anne-Marie looked somewhat confused as she arrived for her next session. I found her depressed and in low spirits. She had at first refused to get up in time for her session, but in the end did so—after explaining to the nurse that she could not believe the doctor had come. She went up to the portrait of St Theresa and stood directly facing it (i.e. without the help of the mirror as mediator).[17] Then she kissed her hands and looked at me. I interpreted: "When you thought I wasn't coming, you saw me as bad, bad because I was absent. But now that I am here, you see me differently; you feel my presence to be proof that I'm interested in you. That's why you're kissing me on your hand and daring to look me straight in the face, like St Theresa."

She looked at the picture again and, moved, stretched out her hand towards the saint. She brought one hand up to her breast as though to grasp it.[18] "You're searching for mummy's breast," I said. She clasped her hands, and I added: "You're being united with mummy."

She showed her delight at this by drumming her fingers on the crossbars of the bed, then, suddenly, she made a movement as though she were in pain; she complained that her arm was hurting her. I said: "It hurts when you have to stretch them out so far to call for mummy."[19] She turned around, her back towards me, and coughed several times; then she faced me once again. She traced marks on the blanket with her finger and said: "My stomach is empty."

"Perhaps you're hungry?" I asked.

"Yes," she replied.

I added: "You're trying to map out your own road [the tracks she drew on the blanket] all by yourself, but without me you feel a

---

phur may also mean something like camphor and other similar substances, which, in popular lore, are used as remedies for certain disorders (keeping the demons away).

[17] Now that her persecutory fears had diminished, she was able to dramatize a direct relationship as distinct from the previous indirect and distant one.

[18] The operative mechanism here is introjection of the analyst, who is then re-projected in the shape of an idealized image on to the portrait of St Theresa. In turn, re-introjection of the idealized image is thereupon dramatized in terms of her own body.

[19] The "baby" is upset by the existence of analytic "bars" between her and the therapist.

pit in your stomach. It's as if you were asking me to fill up your emptiness." She stroked the blanket. "When I fill up your emptiness," I said, "I'm like a holy mother who gives good food as white as the blanket."

After a pause, she went behind the bars of the bed and made movements with her hands as though trying to escape. I interpreted: "You get inside me to look for food, but then you're a prisoner and can't escape."[20]

She took hold of the belt of her dressing-gown and held one end out to me; then, hearing a noise, she suddenly became frightened. I interpreted: "Being hospitalized means being inside and being fed by me as though through an umbilical cord. Then suddenly you become afraid I'll prevent you getting out, and the slightest noise frightens you."

* * *

In the following session, Anne-Marie clasped her hands together (joining herself to me) and expressed the desire to take me inside (she felt hungry). She then looked at the lines on her hand and said: "It's fate. Fate is air. Air surrounds us . . . It's space, and it makes everything grow."[21] She made as though to grasp something in the air. I said: "Catching some air?" "Yes, but it's horrible," she replied, clutching at her stomach. After a short pause, she added: "Gentleness."

I interpreted: "Good air is indispensable, like a good fertile mummy that makes everything grow. But air is bad air—an 'ill wind'—when it hurts in your stomach."[22]

* * *

---

[20] Here, there are two juxtaposed meanings which are probably in a very direct relation to the actual moment when they operate. On the one hand, she is an infant trying to break free of the barriers and get inside the mother; but at another moment, she is already captive inside the mother and suffering from corresponding claustrophobic anxieties.

[21] As with the ancient Pythagoreans, there is an equivalence between *air* [ἀηρ], *emptiness or void* [κενον], and *space*. A parallel could be drawn with Plato's idea of the receptacle [χωρα] in which everything is born (and grows).

[22] In babies, abdominal wind and tympanites are related to the persecutory intentionality of the introjected object.

The next day, she welcomed me gracefully, coughed several times (she had a slight cold) and made an effort to blow her nose. "I'm very eloquent," she said.

"Your body's eloquent: the cough for expelling and the blocked nose for not letting anything in."

She replied: "It's something to do with the air. I don't know what's happening to me, I don't have any appetite."

"It's very painful for you to take in air, me or anything else that's outside you. That's why you're closing down your nose and your appetite."

"That's right," she agreed. Pensively, she tried to pull a thread from her dress.

"Are you trying to find the thread?" I asked.

She replied, with obvious anxiety: "I feel I've lost my way and I don't know which road to follow."

Later, she brought up to her mouth a comb which had fallen on the floor. "It's pretty," she said. Her stomach rumbled, and she immediately took the comb from her mouth. She stroked it, then suddenly squeezed it.

"Perhaps you lose things?" I asked. "I am the comb you'd like to take in, but when you hear the noise the 'ill wind' makes in your stomach, you're afraid you will lose me. And so you push my 'comb'[23] away from your mouth."

She again brought the comb up to her mouth, but hesitated over what to do with it. I interpreted: "You don't know what to do with me, whether to take me inside in spite of the risk that you'll lose me because of the 'ill wind', or whether to push me away."

Anne-Marie became very anxious and began to whimper. She put the comb down and, with a thoughtful look on her face, began to stroke the blanket. She kissed her hand and shyly made as though to blow me a kiss. She tried to say something, but instead belched; this startled her. I interpreted: "Words get mixed up with

---

[23] The phonetic equation (in Spanish) between *peine* [comb] and *pene* [penis] is used by the patient to illustrate how confused she is about levels of contact—i.e. between the comb that arranges the hair-thoughts tidily and the erotic genital relationship.

the air. You'd like to say nice things to me, but it's an 'ill wind' which escapes from you."[24]

"My jacket's bothering me," she said, taking it off and inhaling through her nose. "You're getting rid of what's bothering you," I commented, "and you're trying to breathe in 'good air'."[25]

* * *

At the beginning of her next session, Anne-Marie said to me: "You're looking better, doctor."

"Am I your mirror?" I asked.

"Yes, in fact, I do feel better," she replied. With a frown, she added: "But I'd like to be better still . . . and be able to meet people."

She looked at herself in the mirror as if she wanted to see what kind of a state she was in; she looked sceptical. I said: "Are you thinking that nothing will change?"

"In order to change, you have to want to," she replied. "I have no patience. Every time I do things slowly it never works out." With a thoughtful look on her face, she traced question marks on the blanket.

"Are you looking for something unknown?" I asked.

"That's what it looks like," was her reply.

"You're trying to solve your problems all by yourself, without any reference to me?" I questioned.

---

[24] The confusion of relational levels between oral and genital is echoed now between oral and anal. Part of the patient's struggle consists in resolving the dilemma her anus presents to her mouth with respect to object relations. Bad air—the "ill wind"—is an anal depreciation of primary air. Respiratory introjection is the earliest expression of our relationship with the world; "airmother" is the first element of external reality which is taken inside.

[25] When Anne-Marie confuses words with air, good with bad, and becomes anxious when she cannot get rid of whatever she wants to, this is an illustration of how difficult it is for her to distinguish between her different "objects". Such a situation is typical of the inability to work through the *depressive position*—that is, to identify the whole object as distinct from its component parts. It also illustrates the fear of projecting the dangerous air through belching "without really intending to".

She rumpled the blanket, tried to arrange the folds correctly, then flattened them as she smoothed out the blanket again. I noticed that as she did this she was frowning. I interpreted: "They're the lines on your forehead. You don't know what to do with all the things that are worrying you: should you try to arrange them or erase them from your mind."[26]

"That's true," she said, looking towards the mirror. She added: "Putting things in order is terrible."

"Putting things in order means bringing them together," I said. "And it's terrible to bring good and bad together."

"Yes," she replied.

* * *

In the days that followed, Anne-Marie became very depressed and began to refuse her food. She was inflexible and withdrawn and would speak to nobody. She stayed in bed all day long, so I was obliged to go to her room (which, as I have said, she shared with other patients) in order to see her.

When I entered, she hid beneath the blankets. She did not speak or even look at me, and she was obviously very tense. I commented on her frankly negativistic attitude: "You're under

---

[26] The patient's play with the blanket reminds me of Freud's "Mystic Writing-Pad" (Freud, 1925a [1924]). In his discussion of memory, he observed that notes could be written on the surface of the pad, which kept a relatively permanent trace of them until we desire to erase them. In the case of memory, the possibility always exists that engrams can be recalled—though perhaps not in unaltered form—by the act of remembering. Here, the white blanket could also be looked on as a projection screen similar to Lewin's (1946) dream screen, which is based on Isakower's studies of hypnagogy. Isakower (1938) says that the "mist" which envelops us as we are about to fall asleep represents breasts whose convexity has been flattened out; it merges with the advent of sleep as though to capture us and carry us off into its world. For Lewin, this smoothed-out breast is the maternal breast seen from the infant's position as he is sucking at the nipple. In Garma's opinion (1955), representations of the maternal breast seen in close-up (i.e. smoothed-out) are themselves part of the manifest content of the dream. Manifest contents of this type are reflected on circular screens, which also symbolize the maternal breast—but seen from further away, which is why they remain spherical.

cover, protected, because you're afraid. And since you can't trust anybody, you withdraw into yourself."

She hid even more. In the neighbouring bed, another patient, who was worried about the state Anne-Marie was in, told me that she hadn't said a word all day but had complained of pains in her stomach.[27] When she heard what we were saying, Anne-Marie changed position and tried to prop herself up on her pillow. I interpreted: "Now you feel we're taking care of you and you're trying to lean on me in order to protect you from the 'ill wind' that's attacking you in your stomach." She covered herself up again, and I added: "And now you're withdrawing once more under your blanket so that the 'ill wind' doesn't get into me and hurt me."

She nodded in agreement and a few moments later said: "I'm bad . . . bad."

"And since you're bad, everything inside you is lost. That's why you're withdrawing from me, to protect and preserve me."

She made sucking movements with her mouth, and her nostrils fluttered as if she were "sucking in air".[28] I interpreted: "You're trying to take in my good air."

"Ouch!" she exclaimed, clutching her stomach.

"And that's the pain," I said. "Mixing the good air from outside with the 'ill wind' inside."

* * *

---

[27] I generally make use of material that other people in contact with the patient bring me—in the present case, what the other patient told me—because I consider that the patient is part of a group (the hospital) whose different members are called upon to express different aspects or facets of the patient's life. In situations like this one, the operational context necessarily varies, and the correct attitude to adopt is open to discussion. Some analysts—Bion, for example—prefer to ignore everything that is not directly part of the analyst–patient relationship (he argued that when we ignore what is happening outside the strict analytic field, we are better able to detect the specific nature of what occurs in the referential framework of the analysis). Pichon-Rivière and Herbert Rosenfeld, however, took into consideration what other patients, nurses, and relatives said. My present inclination is to insist on the specific nature of the analytic field, while keeping in mind that its "space" may fluctuate. Data on the patient or group situations (as here) may constitute part of the "grammar of behaviour".

[28] As I have already mentioned, the first substance the infant sucks in is air, not milk.

Anne-Marie maintained this negative attitude, and she refused to eat unless the nurse brought food to her in a very kind-hearted way, calling her "my treasure", "my darling", and so on.

Here, fear of taking me in (negativism) illustrated the paranoid elements, but depressive aspects were present too. She inhaled air, then whimpered as though she were afraid of polluting it; she accused herself of trying to steal my affection. She associated this to the fact that she blamed herself for trying to extract money from a married male friend, and to the idea that if she cohabited with him it would be tantamount to robbing his children of their father—and this, in her view, would drive them mad.

At one point, noticing that the nurse had left her a glass of orange juice, I decided to give it to her myself, to see how she would respond. She refused to take any. Recalling that in previous sessions Anne-Marie would become aggressive whenever I was about to leave, I interpreted: "The nurse is kind towards you, she gives you food, calls you her 'treasure' and leaves you good fruit juice. But I'm bad because I abandon you. And so you won't take any orange juice from me."

Again she indicated her refusal, then stroked the blanket to smooth it out. She was avoiding all contact with me. I interpreted this as a refusal of me as a person, as well as of everything connected with me; my words, the nourishment I offered, had become tainted with persecutory intent and perpetuated the hostility that frustrations aroused in her (for example, when I abandoned her at the end of the session). All this increased the paranoid aspect of the transference relationship.

* * *

In a subsequent session, Anne-Marie signalled to me that the blanket was slightly dirty. I pointed out the relationship between the dirtiness of the blanket and the bad and dirty aspects I might have inside me. She insisted, however, on the dirtiness of the blanket, all the while showing me the palm (the interior) of her hand; I had the feeling that there was more to it, but I was unable to grasp just what was at issue. I asked her: "Where is the dirt?"

She gestured to me that the dirtiness was in her hand, and I interpreted this to her: "Right, you said you were bad and dirty. The palm of your hand represents being dirty inside and contaminating my clean parts [the blanket]. And so, in order not to dirty me or the food, you keep yourself at a distance, you refuse to eat and to make contact with me."[29]

She pointed to her stomach and said that everything was mixed up—food, fat, muscles, air.

I said: "Inside your stomach different things are all mixed up, and since you are unable to separate them you hold them all in, afraid the bad parts will get out at the same time as the good ones." (She was very constipated during the whole of this period.)

She traced parallel lines on the blanket, then intersecting ones; I interpreted this as her alternating desires to "intersect" with me or remain parallel to—and separate from—me. She drew a flag, then a line to separate it from another drawing representing, she said, water pipes.

"Water pipes are intestines with faeces," I said, "which you're separating from me—the flag—by a line, so as not to dirty me. That's why you're not eating: you don't want me to be in contact with your faeces."

* * *

The following day at the beginning of the session Anne-Marie sat on the bed and pushed it backwards as though to move away from me. I commented: "You're putting distance between us, just as you did yesterday with the water pipes and the flag."

"I'm better," she snapped impatiently, and exclaimed: "Holy God! Where art thou?"

I said: "Where is your God, your 'flag'?"

She answered: "Each person has to meet Him inside himself. Everything depends on each one of us, from birth until death. Each person has to make his own decisions."

I interpreted: "Now it's a question of choice, between accepting me and not accepting me. That's what was going on these past few

---

[29] In chapter three, I discussed negation with respect to food, and I insisted on the need to interpret the paranoid situation not only as a way of "closing oneself down" in the face of a persecutory world (the external persecutor), but also as a way of preserving the "good" parts that have been externalized from the internal persecutors (e.g. the "ill wind"). Anorexia is a minor form of nutritional negativism.

days when you weren't eating, when you were isolating yourself from me in order not to accept me."[30]

She paused, then went on: "I try to go forward, but if what's ahead of me is worse and it all fails, it would be better to turn back."

I interpreted: "Going forwards means getting close to me, or in this period of your life getting closer to Mr G. You experience that as a failure, and you turn back—just as you moved the bed backwards a moment or so ago." She traced an egg on the blanket, and I added: "You're going all the way back to being an egg again. That's what you've been trying to do with your breakdowns, go back to being an egg, like your younger sister."[31]

"But I've not managed to get back as far as that, unfortunately," she replied, then added: "Babies should be born by spontaneous generation, and not have parents."

As she said this, she began to fiddle with little bits of cotton thread which, according to her, were like soft white bread. She smiled at me when she pronounced her last sentence, and I commented: "Yes, not have parents so they wouldn't have to create links and undo them again. But you can't be completely without links, that's why you're softening me up—so that we can be good friends."[32]

She then traced a Y-shape on the blanket. I interpreted this as: "The y is used for joining words together,[33] and now it is joining us together—not mixing us up, but joining each of us to the other."

* * *

As I arrived for her next session, Anne-Marie was writing a letter. She told me it was for Mr G, and she continued: "I want them to

---

[30] The point here is that when a given symptom—negativism—is seen from a different perspective and under different structural conditions, the interpretation of the psychological situation also changes. I think it necessary to explore as many avenues as possible, because full understanding of the symptom can only come from the experience of multifaceted vision.

[31] I was referring here to the sister who had had a lobotomy. Anne-Marie had told me that this girl was in a state of very profound regression, practically to the point of becoming a foetus again.

[32] There is a pun here in Spanish, based on the phonetic similarity between *buenas migas* [good soft white bread] and *buena amiga* [friend].

[33] In Spanish, "*y*" is the conjunction "and".

bring me the clothes I need. When they hospitalized me here, I wasn't able to pack my suitcase. It's much better when you pack your own suitcase."[34]

She began to trace lines on the blanket, expressing—as we have seen earlier—her need to start moving. Some of the traces were in a forward direction, others backward. I interpreted: "There are two tendencies inside you. One wants to go forward, to get closer to me and to communicate with me; this tendency has the upper hand for the moment and it represents being well again. The other tendency tries to move backwards, to fall ill again, to be an egg again."

She picked up the penholder on the table and spun it round, waiting to see in which direction it would come to a halt. "A compass?" I asked.

"Yes," she replied.

"Are you looking for your own north?"

She smiled and handed the penholder to me. I interpreted: "You're looking for your north in me."

She looked doubtful, as though suddenly afraid to put all her hopes in me. She abruptly spun the penholder again, making the "compass" gyrate crazily. She said: "I was turning, turning . . ."

I commented: ". . . but without knowing where you would stop, spinning crazily because you'd put all your hopes in one person and you feel frustrated."

She drew an aircraft on her writing paper. I asked: "Are you taking off so as not to feel frustrated?"

---

[34] In other words, Anne-Marie was referring to her need to look after herself; she was attempting to find herself through placing her own things in her own body. The suitcase represents her body and its frontiers, inside which she wants to put her "belongings" and thereby differentiate between what is hers and what is not: the differentiation between "me" and "not-me", in relation to her own "internal image". The y session is all about the process by which frontiers are created.

In chapter one, I stressed the importance of the early mother–child relationship (Winnicott's "moments of illusion") as a stimulus for the development of the ego and of its sensory functions. Freud (1923b) argued that the "ego is first and foremost a bodily ego; it is not merely a surface entity, but is itself the projection of a surface." The relationship between the infant and the world takes shape at that frontier.

"Yes," she answered, and she began drawing a dining-room and bathroom. She tried to speak but was unable to do so: she felt a pain coming up from her stomach into her mouth. She had toothache.

"Some things," I said, "are painful to bring out because they might hurt me. Things that go from the bathroom [the intestine] to the dining-room [the mouth]. You don't want to lose me with your faeces-words, so you hold them in with your lips, even though it hurts."

She expressed the same fear of projection in case she hurt someone, when, pointing to her shoe, she said: "I'm annoyed by this strap because it's about to come undone."

"Why does that bother you?"

"I'm afraid in case what I have inside might come out."

"That the faeces might escape downwards?"

"Yes," she replied, looking at her shoes. She went on: "They're different."

"There are two different aspects in you," I said, "like your different shoes. One of them needs repairing, that's your ill part which is also dangerous and hard to keep in check. The other, whole, part is the good one."

While I was saying this to her, she tried to bring both shoes together. She interrupted me with: "The shoe whose strap came undone is offending the other one."

"That is, the ill part containing dangerous things may invade the healthy part if we try to join together and become integrated."

As the session drew to a close, she bit one of her fingers. She was very dependent on my words and gave the impression that she wanted to go on listening to me. I commented that when I have to leave her I was like a nipple she bites out of sheer fury. She agreed, accompanied me to the top of the staircase, and watched me go downstairs until I was out of sight.

* * *

At her next session, Anne-Marie was in bed, in a state of apathy, stone-faced and dissociated. She seemed to ignore me completely. In a disorganized way, she pronounced words I was unable to catch correctly. I interpreted that the more she related to me, the angrier she became when I left; when she bit her finger, she was biting the bad beast and tearing it to pieces because it was going away. Now she felt I was broken and disintegrated like the words inside her.

She looked at me as if noticing me for the first time. She stiffened, her arms and legs crossed. I said: "You're remaining closed so that the strap can't hurt me when I go, so that you won't demolish me with your anger."

She tidied her hair, leaned her head on one arm, then kissed her hand. She looked at me and made sucking movements with her lips. I interpreted: "Now that you can see I'm not demolished, you can come closer again and take me in."

This time when I left, she did not simply accompany me to the top of the staircase; as I crossed through the garden, I saw her running after me, waving to me to come back.

* * *

For some days after this, the room in which I usually saw Anne-Marie was occupied, and the sessions took place in a small kitchen. The following are some extracts from the kitchen sessions.

As she came into the kitchen, Anne-Marie picked up a dirty duster and said: "That's a good duster." She pressed the edges flat, smoothed them out, and spread the duster on the table, resting one hand on it. I interpreted: "Even though it's dirty and bad, like me when I go away and abandon you, you try all the same to see me as good and clean because that's what you need me to be."

She paused, looked at me, and said: "You've got daddy's good gaze." With a movement of displeasure, she rumpled the duster, then smoothed it out again—showing her ambivalence with respect to the father figure.

Another day when she arrived she tried to tidy up the kitchen. Then she sat down and showed me her hands. "They're different," she said. She drummed her fingers on the table as if it were a piano, and she added: "I'm harmonizing."

"You're trying to harmonize all your different parts and keep them in tune: the part that tidies up, like when you tidied the kitchen, and the other part which creates disorder."

On another occasion, she covered part of her face with a lock of her hair and said: "It's dirty."

"Even though you're annoyed because your hair's dirty, it's useful for covering yourself with; the dirtier your hair is, the more cover and protection you have," I said.

"That's right," she agreed, and she touched the tip of her nose with the lock of hair. Then she grasped one of her breasts and said: "It's difficult to keep everything."

"When you see me good like a good daddy, you want me all to yourself."

"Of course," she replied, looking up at me disappointedly.

I said: "But when I'm not like that, you look at me as if I'd turned into something strange; that's when you try to find mummy's breast."

She smiled and made sucking movements with her mouth.

"You're sucking my words like mummy's good milk."

"Yes, that's right," she said, and she began to suck one of her fingers. Suddenly she looked at her hand thoughtfully and said: "There's a mystery here."

"What mystery?" I asked.

"Well . . . the mystery of the yellow room,"[35] she replied. She stared for some time at her fingers as though trying to discover some secret or other. I commented: "Maybe the fourth finger[36] is the yellow one?"

"My brother M has something wrong with his liver." She paused, then went on: "He was always ill, something to do with his liver, he used to turn yellow.[37] I couldn't stand him. Everybody spoiled him; I was jealous of him."

She began to make a grinding noise with her teeth. "You're grinding M up," I said.

---

[35] An allusion to a novel by Gaston Leroux: Le mystère de la chambre jaune.

[36] A play on words: cuarto amarillo [yellow room] and cuarto dedo [fourth finger].

[37] She is referring to the fourth child in the family, her half-brother, the son of her father's second marriage. "Yellow" might also symbolize Anne-Marie's urethral attacks against her brother as yet undifferentiated from a part of the mother's body. In my view, sibling rivalry very often has to do with attacks on part of the mother's body.

"Yes," she replied, touching her nose. Then she added: "I have a grudge against him. If I could, I'd chew him to pieces."[38]

* * *

In her next session, Anne-Marie continued with her transference fantasies concerning the penis. She was in a state of considerable sexual excitement (her movements resembled coitus) and began to masturbate. She stopped suddenly, hid her face in shame and began to pray. I interpreted: "You're trying to struggle against the temptation to take possession of my penis, just as you'd wanted to have M's penis. You feel those desires to be equivalent to stealing, and you're ashamed of that."

She took off her bracelet (a present from her mother), fondled it, then brought it up to her mouth and began sucking it. "With the penis inside," I said, "you can get close to mummy again, and find mummy's breast once more [the bracelet]."

She held the bracelet tightly as though it might fall from her grasp, and, with a distressed look on her face, took it from her mouth. I interpreted: "Just as you can't keep the penis inside after having sex, you can't hold on to my penis even though you're thinking of stealing it. And you feel distress because you don't have a penis with which to get close to mummy."[39]

* * *

---

[38] In this session, we can see how Anne-Marie protects and defends herself against dirtiness (her dirty hair) and how her over-demanding impulses (wanting me all to herself) bring about sudden changes in her choice of object (from father's penis—the nose—she goes quickly to mother's breast). The inevitable frustration, given the intensity of her demands, nourishes her anal aggressiveness: she dirties the hated objects—father, then mother. But since these objects are also needed, in spite of being hated and dirty (through her fault), she preserves them and protects herself thanks to them.

A word here about "penis envy": Anne-Marie appears to be saying that it is necessary to be a boy in order to be loved ("spoiled") by her parents (her father wanted a son). A. A. Pichon-Rivière (1958) argued that hatred for brothers represents also hatred for the mother (siblings experienced as part of mother). Resentment against the original object is expressed in this way.

[39] Fantasies about stealing the penis—*in fine*, the father's penis—and incorporating it orally are expressed alongside genital impulses, in a manner similar to the development of early oedipal tendencies (Klein, 1950). The assumption is that such impulses are subordinate to pre-genital tendencies. As for Anne-

In another session, Anne-Marie was depressed. It was difficult for her to make contact with me. She used one hand to strike little blows on the other, as if she were trying to communicate something to it. I asked her: "Are you transmitting something? One of your hands is saying something to the other?"

She sighed and then began tracing parallel curves on the blanket. I went on: "Now perhaps you're transmitting something through the blanket."

She became anxious, and passed her hand in front of her mouth, saying: "Bread exists when it is eaten."

I interpreted: "Things exist when we bring them up to our lips, taste them and ingest them. I exist for you when you can feel me inside you." (Like a bread-breast or bread-penis or bread-wholeness.)

Marie, penis envy and desire to incorporate the penis increase when frustration becomes very strong. Her first breakdown occurred when she was 18, after she had sexual intercourse for the first time—and with a paternal figure, namely, a man in his forties who was already married. She experienced him as good, but he abandoned her very rapidly. Her other breakdowns occurred in similar situations of overwhelming disappointment, repeating to some extent the traumatic situation of being abandoned by her father. The nymphomaniac episodes that occurred during these breakdowns could be looked upon as a compulsive way of taking in a series of "assorted" penises into which she could project the good (or rather, idealized) penis (her father's whole penis).

From another point of view, incorporation is related to secondary masochism, which, for Melanie Klein, aims at internalizing destructive penises in order to combat the already internalized bad penises, whatever the subsequent threat to the ego.

My interpretation of Anne-Marie's frustrated desire to incorporate the penis after every coitus corresponds to the infant's primary experience (again following Klein) that the mother keeps the father's penis after each coitus. From this springs the fantasy that the mother has several penises inside her.

Another motive for nymphomania, argues Klein, is to anticipate and therefore control the anxiety and pain resulting from sudden intromission of the penis. Yet another aim, with the accent this time on incorporating the penis, is to placate the bad penis and transform it into a good one. In this case, possessing the penis is above all a transitive means of possessing the mother (the penis as a link). The relationship with the paternal penis could also be conceived of as the product of displacement from the nipple to the penis as a substitute for the original relationship with the breast. If this displacement is over-eroticized, it can be used as a defence against weaning. We should note that in this session with Anne-Marie, there is an atmosphere of eroticization which creates confusion among oral, anal, and genital levels.

"I'm thirsty," she said, touching her stomach.

I replied: "Thirsty to welcome me in like good daily bread, like the breasts [the parallel curves] which satisfy your thirst."

* * *

A particular type of relationship between Anne-Marie and me emerged at one point. My habit of treating puns as a way of manipulating word-plays (which, in certain circumstances, is a rudimentary way of re-creating internal objects), is related to what I call playful communication. Occasionally in the therapy another kind of transference play or playful communication appeared. I shall now report an extract in which the dramatization is fairly close to the kind encountered in fairy tales.[40]

Anne-Marie pointed to a picture (the session took place this time in a dining-room), and in a childish voice said: "There's a whale with its mouth open."

"And is it going to eat me?" I asked. "Yes, because you're wicked" was her reply. Looking thoughtfully at the painting, she added: "No doubt the picture contains nice things too."[41]

I interpreted: "It's like you. You sometimes contain ugly things and get angry, like the whale which would like to eat me—but at other times you feel nice and beautiful things towards me."

I had the feeling that both Anne-Marie and I felt the need to express ourselves as if we were dramatizing a fairy tale. When I said to her, "And is it going to eat me?", I was putting in dramatic form her projective identification of the infantile part of herself. In addition, thanks to my countertransference response, the latent playful language in myself awoke—and I played out the role that the situation attributed to me. I believe that with some patients—and in particular with psychotics—in the transference relationship,

---

[40] The infantile ego in counterpoint to the psychotic ego possesses syntonic abilities and is capable of "pretend-play".

[41] The idea that beauty and ugliness can coexist within the same painting—in her own psychic "frame"—is akin to a "discovery", that is, to the revelation that her internal world contains contradictory tendencies. As we know, this is specific to the depressive position, in which the ability to distinguish between qualities of the object appears.

various forms of expression such as dramatization,[42] playing, or story-telling are spontaneously activated.

On another occasion, Anne-Marie showed how ambivalent she felt when she alternated between gently stroking the table at which we sat facing each other, then scratching it with all of her fingers. Terrified by her hatred, she seemed to step back and—perhaps to test the effect—scratch the table only very gradually: first one finger, then two, and so forth. It was as though she were trying to calculate the "amount" of her destructiveness. This led me to ask her, "Are you measuring your hatred?", adding that it was important for her to know not only what her hatred was like, but also just how far she could go without risking losing me.[43]

* * *

Another element that is interesting to explore is the development of the ego's integrative capacity during analytic treatment. In my work with psychotics, and particularly with schizophrenics, I make a point of studying the oscillation between integrative and disintegrative ego processes. The fear of disintegration that exists in each of us is well known, as are the obsessive mechanisms that appear in reaction to this fear. This type of reaction is typical of inflexible personality structures. Schizophrenics combat disintegration by clothing themselves in the armour-plating of character disorders, hence the climate of cold indifference that they tend to generate.

People who are more flexible have greater confidence in their re-integrative capacities and allow their ego more freedom of movement. They can be "scattered" at times (dispersion is neces-

---

[42] Dramatization and play: it is interesting to observe that in many languages the same word can carry both meanings—in German, *spielen*; in English, *a play*; in French, *jouer*. Spanish, however, differentiates between *jugar*, "playing", and *interpretar*, "representing", in the sense of theatrical representation.

[43] We have seen how in the "whale" session, Anne-Marie became aware of her ability to distinguish between the object's good and bad qualities. Here, she was concerned not so much with qualitative as with quantitative differences in her impulses (calculating the "amount" of her aggressive impulses).

sary in order to understand and resolve certain types of problem) but are always able to gather themselves together whenever it becomes necessary to do so. Winnicott (1945) said: "There are long stretches of time in a normal infant's life in which a baby does not mind whether he is in many bits or one whole being, or whether he lives in his mother's face or in his own body, provided that from time to time he comes together and feels something."

In our psychoanalytic work, especially with this type of patient, I think it important to allow for some degree of dispersion in order to be able to pick up the maximum amount of material and construct interpretations whose experiential content is more imaginative. It is almost as though we had to log on to madness in order to detect its manifestations and understand them more fully. I shall now report a session with Anne-Marie in which we can study the degree of ego flexibility and synthetic functioning at different moments.

Anne-Marie was lying down, calm and fairly well integrated. For the first time since she had been hospitalized she was reading a book. I interpreted this as proof of improvement in her condition, since it meant that she could be integrated with something (here, reading).

"Yes, I am better," she agreed. She asked me if I had brought any cigarettes with me, and she explained: "Otherwise I can't talk."

I replied: "If I don't give you something, you won't give me anything either." Her only reply to this was to break one of her fingernails aggressively. I went on: "And now, in a rage because I'm not giving you anything, you break a fingernail."

She suddenly made sucking movements, looked at me, and said: "I have the impression you're tired."

I replied: "You feel I've been 'sucked dry' by you and now I'm tired out—'exhausted'—by your demands. And you feel my milk has turned sour." She coughed, and I continued: "And now that I'm 'bad milk',[44] milk that has turned sour, you're expressing your rage through your bronchial tubes."[45]

---

[44] The Spanish *mala leche* in popular parlance means "in bad faith".

[45] In Spanish, there is a phonetic connection between rage, *bronca*, and bronchial tubes, *bronquios*.

She suddenly lifted the blanket anxiously, jumped up, and said: "I've dirtied the bed." (This was not in fact the case.)

I commented: "If rage can't get out through the top, through the bronchial tubes, it comes out through the bottom, like faeces to dirty me."

She began to be depersonalized and moved her legs rapidly as though she were marching. With one hand she appeared to be turning something inside a recipient, while with the other she saluted, sometimes even standing to attention to do so (she looked like a robot whose circuitry had gone haywire). Puzzled, she said: "I don't know any more . . . I don't know any more." She touched her genitals, and she babbled: "Te-te-te, ti-ti-ti, ke-ke-ke, de-de-de."

"Things are beginning to move too fast," I said. "You don't know what to do any more. Obey me by saluting like a soldier, or make my milk better by churning it, or swallow it somehow or other—through your vagina, de-de-de's milk or through your mouth, mummy's ti-ti-ti."

After this interpretation, she cried; at the end of the session, she tried to stop me leaving.[46]

* * *

[46] The ability to disintegrate and re-integrate quickly during a single session is a sign that the ego is stronger and has increased mobility. When Anne-Marie fragments her words (by babbling or stammering) then reconstitutes them by linking the fragments together, she is in a way reproducing the process of language acquisition. Reconstruction of words, says A. A. Pichon-Rivière (1958), is related to the possibility of creating the original word-object. Babbling is a primitive form of communication (Shirley, 1933, calls it "socialized vocalization"). It is also a playful form of communication. In the session I am reporting, Anne-Marie stimulated in me the need to "be part of the play" and to babble also—that is, to speak her own language. With that language I was able to make contact with her infantile world. When my interpretations are experienced as good, they help to gather parts of the object together (word-fragments and syllables) and contribute to assembling the word-object—that is, they reinforce the patient's reparative capacity. Bion (1956), discussing the conflict between ego and mental apparatus in schizophrenia, says that patients cannot tolerate reality nor the mental apparatus responsible for putting them in touch with reality. Attacks against "internal reality" are experienced as fragmenting or breaking up the mind and, consequently, inner communication. This results in disintegration or fragmentation of inchoate verbal thought, expressed as fragmentation of the words used.

At the beginning of the following session, Anne-Marie was puzzled. She hardly took any notice of me, and she seemed indifferent to her surroundings. She appeared to be seeing something (a visual hallucination). Suddenly anxious, she began to fidget and babbled: "Co-co-co, ke-ke-ke, ti-ti-ti, no-no-no, ye-ye-ye, be-be-be." She grasped her neck, as though to choke something back.

"Tears," I said. She did in fact burst into tears, much as a child would do, and I interpreted: "You think that the doctor went away because of your anger, that you'd hurt him and lost him.[47] And so you don't notice me, you don't believe I'm here."

Anne-Marie looked as though she was in despair. Throwing her head back, she stiffened her body as if she were dead. I interpreted: "If your anger hurts the doctor and kills him, Anne-Marie dies inside me, so she is dead too."[48]

She changed immediately and made sucking movements. I commented: "Perhaps you're sucking me in, recovering me inside yourself again."

She sucked her fingers and said: "De-de-de". Picking up a little piece of biscuit which was lying on the table, she put it into her mouth—but suddenly her other hand seized her wrist and prevented her from eating it.

I interpreted: "Sucking the de-de-de of daddy. I am daddy, but when I am angry I take him away from you." She made a gesture to stop me leaving—"Are you going away?" she asked.

She undid her hair, loosened her clothing, and, grasping the crossbars of the bed, began to babble: "Tan-tan-tan,". To my mind, her gestures were theatrical, and I interpreted: "It's not as much as it looks,[49] you're exaggerating your feelings and showing me that if I leave you, you'll be all undone, deranged and mad. You're doing all this so that I won't go away."[50]

---

[47] The fear of losing me is felt both internally and externally as the consequence of her attacks against me as an internal object and against that part of her mind which is linked to verbal communication with me.

[48] Death is personified in me as persecutory death—I am supposed to wreak vengeance according to the *lex talionis*. I referred to the idea of persecutory death in chapter two in my discussion of Cotard's syndrome.

[49] *Tan* in Spanish can mean "as much" or "more".

[50] In this session, as in the previous one, we can clearly see ego integration and disintegration alternating, this time, however, on a more "sophisticated"

Anne-Marie's hysterical theatricality was also a way of playing out her fantasy of being an actress. When she was a little girl, she said, her father had said she was destined to become an actress. She associated this to her father's desire to see her undertake "virile" activities. In the transference, being an actress (theatre) and being a man—and so, by condensation, "actor"—is an attempt to satisfy her father's desires (actress and male child) in order to win his love. She tried to satisfy symbolically her desire to be a man, to "steal a penis" (as we have seen) by taking cigarettes whenever she could (stealing them from other patients, asking male visitors . . .) and demanding that coffee be served to her so that she could drink it "like a man".

Later, once her condition had improved, the question arose as to the appropriate moment to let her leave the clinic. When I asked until when she intended to stay, she replied: "Until I have everything . . . cigarettes, cream, salts . . . When I'll be more sheltered. I need winter to go away and I don't want to be left all alone."

She looked at me as she said that, and her lips moved as if she were kissing. "I'm kissing the world," she said.

"Am I your world [mother-world]?"

"Yes," she replied.

I interpreted: "I am your world because you've put everything into me. If I'm not there, the world is empty—just as it was when

---

level—that is, theatrical or hysterical (as I said to Anne-Marie). One of the major difficulties we encounter in what are called hysterical psychoses (which are more elaborate than schizophrenia) is the fact that patients can manipulate reality more intelligently and more effectively (hysterical control of objects). Whenever psychoanalysis comes into contact with psychotic elements, the various clinical syndromes (which psychiatry explores one by one in a static way) are seen to follow on from each other throughout the therapy. This is why the issue of how to deal with hysterical phases emerges in every analysis of psychotics.

The need to modify the ambience is greatest in periods of deep regression, given the predominance of paranoid anxieties. When the ego is insufficiently integrated, its efficiency in manipulating objects in the environment is precarious. The presence of hysterical components makes attempts at controlling the environment much more effective; this means that the gains from illness are greater (secondary gain), and the patient succeeds in "controlling" the situation. It is at times like these that the analyst must be aware of what is going on if he hopes to avoid being manipulated by the patient.

I met you for the first time."[51] "Yes," she replied, kissing her hands.

As the session drew to a close, she told me that the night before she had been able to help another patient who was lonely and had neither visitors nor cigarettes.[52]

* * *

In another session, Anne-Marie said: "People shouldn't be judged by the clothes they wear. There are more important things, like lines on the forehead and the look in the eyes. The attention people give us depends on the clothes we wear, and not to have clean clothes is a miserable state of affairs and makes us evil. Wickedness is a means of defence against all the suffering we've had."

I interpreted: "You're telling me not to judge you by the clothes you're wearing. If they're dirty, that's because you've suffered a lot, because people haven't been good to you, so you're asking me to look at your forehead and your eyes."

As I said that, she became sad and began to whimper. She opened her eyes, a look of fear on her face, and said: "I remember Hitler, he was good."

---

[51] If I am her world, she filled up the emptiness of *her* world by put everything inside *me*. Pichon-Rivière (1952) emphasizes the role of the analyst as depository of the patient's good parts and points out that patients tend to protect the analyst from their destructive impulses. Putting the best she had into me was a way of protecting the good part by projective identification, separating it from the bad dangerous part she felt inside herself. What in fact Anne-Marie desires here is to live as something good inside a good depository object. This was what she meant when, at another point in the session, she asked me to give her my hand, saying with great feeling: "I need somebody good like you in order to be able to die"—that is, survive inside me through her best and most valued aspects, the ones she had constantly tried to put inside other people in order to preserve them, while annihilating the bad and dangerous part left inside herself.

The concept of death as Anne-Marie expressed it here leads to a novel way of looking at suicide—a way of destroying a bad persecutory part, and of preserving an idealized part in someone else's memory. Generally speaking, staying alive in other people's memories is a necessary condition for accepting death.

[52] We could conclude from this that she must have "received" something, because she was able to give help. She was able to reconstruct the world—her own world, which in a sense I had helped her to "repair" and restore to her.

I remarked: "He was good, and yet you open your eyes in fear."

"Daddy was egotistical and tyrannical," she said.

I replied: "Yes, but in spite of your resentment you need him, and so you put all the good into him and idealize him."[53]

Now that the acute phase was over, Anne-Marie was able to establish retrospectively the origins of her breakdown. She attempted to arrange in an orderly sequence what she had gone through—finding points of reference in time meant that she was discovering her "own" time and was herself becoming integrated in time. Also, she expressed a desire to widen her horizons (a bigger space for communication) by projecting herself outside the confines of the clinic (beyond the limits of her illness); she expressed the desire to see her father, mother, and younger sister.[54]

Her mother's visit was proof of her affection, though Anne-Marie remarked that her mother was opposed to the psychoanalysis. In addition, Mr G, who up till then had been paying for Anne-Marie's analysis, now began to have difficulty doing so. These two factors increased her feeling of insecurity. During this period, whenever she said in her sessions that she did not feel that people outside were helping her enough, she was expressing the desire to escape into illness.

On another occasion when we were discussing the difficulty that she was indeed having to face concerning the continuation of her analysis, she tossed her cigarette ash out of the ashtray; she was "acting the fool", indicating that, faced with frustrating and inexorable reality, she preferred to seek refuge in "foolishness" and "folly".

To this was added another very real fact—I, her analyst, was planning to leave soon and to remain absent for some length of time. I did not think it appropriate at that point to inform her of

---

[53] In this session, we can see Anne-Marie's reactions to frustration. First resentment, expressed as making demands on her world (parents-world), and then idealization. According to Melanie Klein, idealization is the corollary of persecutory fear. The greater the paranoid anxiety with respect to the bad (frustrating) object, the greater the overestimation of the good object; hence, good and bad objects find themselves further and further apart, resulting in an even greater splitting of the ego.

[54] This was the first occasion on which she expressed a spontaneous desire to meet any of her relatives. Before then, only Mr G, who, as we have noted, had more or less taken on the role of next-of-kin, had come to visit her.

this; when I was just about ready to tell her, something occurred that caught my attention.

In one session, Anne-Marie told me that she was thinking of travelling to a foreign city where she had spent quite a long time previously—she meant Paris, the city I was myself about to travel to. She said also that she wanted insulin treatment again instead of going on with her analysis (her mother had suggested this). Referring to insulin, she said: "It takes effect more quickly and it gives me an appetite." She added: "I don't know why mummy is looking for a quarrel with daddy."

I replied: "You feel mummy is opposed to the therapy—to me—just as you feel she is opposed to daddy. Whereas insulin— that's something your mother agrees to."[55]

Anne-Marie became anxious and started to cry. I asked her why. She replied: "Because you're in such a hurry to go." She began to move her arms mechanically like a robot. She was holding her right arm stretched stiffly out in front of her, when suddenly she felt a pain in her hand. My impression was that she had referred to my haste to go away because she had grasped the fact that I was in a hurry to see her cured and well again. Also, as a result of her excessive projections into me, she felt deprived of life, like a robot, destitute and at my mercy since I was the depository of all she had placed in me. All this combined to distress her and arouse anxiety in her.

When I made an interpretation along those lines, Anne-Marie replied: "I like getting inside people, that way I get to know what they're thinking."

I commented: "Getting inside *me*, you mean, in order to know what *I'm* thinking."

"Yes, I can feel you're in a hurry," she said.

I added: "And being in a hurry means being bad."

---

[55] I thought that the coincidence between her desire to take insulin again and to travel to the very city I was about to leave for (coming towards me) was related to the fact that I was about to abandon her. That would mean anticipating my abandonment by abandoning me first (she could let go of insulin quite easily). Also, insulin was not a person but a thing—so that she could cathect it without compromising herself so much in the future.

"Yes, but it's more than that, there's tenderness, affection, *tendresse*."[56]

"Why in French?" I wondered.

"Daddy went to Paris," she replied. (He had in fact lived several years in Paris.)

I felt surprised and moved by this "perception". I said that she felt I was abandoning her like her father, and that she was making some kind of combination of both of us.

I told her also that what she had somehow picked up was true, I did have plans to go to Paris. I added that before feeling the need to hold me back, she had refined to the maximum her ability to project into me (projective identification).[57]

Abandonment was now the central theme of the analysis. Anne-Marie could not accept the idea that she might *really* lose me—for, to her, that would have meant confirmation in actual fact (proof in reality) of her fantasy that she destroys whatever she loves ("I lose everything"). She therefore took refuge in the certainty of my return.

At another moment, there was an electricity failure in the clinic, and candles had to be lit. Anne-Marie blew them out, because she knew "that the electricity was going to come back again" (I too would come back, and all the lights would go on again for her). She felt abandoned also by Mr G, who could not make up his mind to continue funding the analysis and said that it was the mother's responsibility. One day he was waiting for me at the entrance to the clinic; he transferred the role of "next-of-kin" to me and asked me to hand Anne-Marie a packet of tea and some cigarettes—he could not make up his mind to give them to her personally (he was feeling guilty). He asked me also to tell her that he was no longer in a position to continue paying for her therapy. Anne-Marie for her part perceived Mr G's desire that I take on the role not only of doctor but also his own.

---

[56] Anne-Marie said the word in French.

[57] The ability to be inside someone else, which increases when the situation contains a hint of abandonment, creates a kind of direct but recondite connection—what some people will call "telepathy". This kind of communication is similar to the primary transmission that exists during the "moments of illusion" in the mother–infant relationship.

Given this situation, and realizing that in actual fact Anne-Marie was going to be without any support at all, I suggested to each of them that we meet together to try to clarify matters and define who was to do what (I was the doctor, and "tea and cigarettes" was Mr G). The three of us had a meeting; Mr G took on the role of guilty father which Anne-Marie had attributed to him; I was the depository of the good paternal role, displaced in the first instance from the father to Mr G, then from Mr G to me.

In this triangular situation, Anne-Marie found it impossible to be close to either of us without excluding the other. She repeated in this way her own situation in which somebody was always excluded. As a result, it was impossible to reconstitute a triangle—but another was in fact being constructed: Mr G and Anne-Marie's mother decided to meet me.

During this second interview, it was as though Mr G were absent; he said nothing at all and was completely dependent on the mother's words—as if he had delegated all responsibility to her. The mother admitted that Anne-Marie was being cured of her breakdown thanks to the analysis. She probably did not agree with the procedure itself—but since to her it seemed more or less to be something to do with magic, she preferred not to know any more about it. She could not accept the idea that I had a good relationship with her daughter, just as she did not accept that Anne-Marie and her father got on well together (she blamed him for both daughters' illnesses and, in a barely veiled fashion, accused him of seducing them).[58]

At the end of our discussion, she expressed the wish that Anne-Marie's father take over responsibility for her. She informed me that she had written to him to come and resolve the question.

A few days later, the third triangle was in place. The father came to see me with his second wife, and the three of us had a meeting: father, stepmother, me. He was very anxious and sat down some distance from me, near the radiator. He felt cold and had difficulty talking;[59] he was holding a hot-water bottle, and

---

[58] The mother could not, without feeling guilty over the younger sister's lobotomy, accept the fact that Anne-Marie's condition had improved thanks to "words" (as she put it).

[59] He was suffering from an attack of asthma.

from time to time used his inhaler. He felt very embarrassed by his asthma that day.

His wife sat down next to me, and in fact it was through her that he communicated with me, insisting that he himself was too weak to do so and asking her "to explain . . ." (indirect communication). His paranoid attitude and his fear of breathing reminded me of Anne-Marie and her fears about the "ill wind". He was afraid of me, and as a result he needed an intermediary object (his wife) in the same way that Anne-Marie, at first, entered into a relationship with me through the mirror. In this indirect way, he told me of certain events in his daughter's life.

He addressed me directly only when he related how, during her first breakdown, Anne-Marie had attacked her stepmother and provoked the miscarriage: "She killed my child." This was how he expressed his resentment against his daughter, then directed it against his first wife, Anne-Marie's mother, whom he accused of making their daughters ill (as we saw, the mother made the same accusation against him). He told me he had noticed how much Anne-Marie had improved. He had in fact gone as far as discussing the situation with Mr G and Anne-Marie's mother before contacting me directly.

On the day following this meeting, Mr G phoned me. He was in rather high spirits and informed me that he had discussed matters with Anne-Marie's family and thought that he could come to some kind of agreement with them. The next day, Anne-Marie's father phoned me. He had spoken frankly with Anne-Marie and other members of the family about the situation. They agreed to continue the therapy until my departure.

I then resumed analysis with Anne-Marie, this time under far better conditions: the family group had become more integrated (with respect to Anne-Marie), and they were managing to reach agreement. During her convalescence after her breakdown, Anne-Marie needed a more appropriate family environment so as to be able to project in a more integrated manner. Given the family situation up till that point, it had only been possible for her to adjust by means of her schizoid mechanisms (projecting split-off parts of herself).

The father did not feel able to reorganize the family group all by himself (in the last resort, all the others had delegated to him their own individual responsibility). He contacted me again, but this time with a request for help. His asthma was no better, he did not know what to do, and he felt unable to take on the role of head of the family; he transferred this role to me, taking for himself the part of a son (he, too, needed a father).

* * *

And so we see unhoped-for improvement in Anne-Marie, comprehensible only if we manage to look at things from the perspective of what I might call a "conditional series": a series of mediations, a sequence of situations—with Anne-Marie at the centre—that stimulated the family group and set them in motion (an inductive chain of events). Anne-Marie needed that kind of help in her therapy.[60] She was then the most powerful because the most "regressive",[61] and she urged Mr G to contact her family (through attributing to him the role of guilty father). Mr G, faced with the alternative of taking the situation on board or eluding it, tried first to delegate his role to me (I was—in his name—to give tea and cigarettes to Anne-Marie: I was to "carry the can" for him). When I refused this attempted delegation (in order to preserve my role as analyst: we clarified this point in the first group meeting between Anne-Marie, Mr G, and myself), he had recourse to Anne-Marie's mother and tried to make her take charge of the situation. She in turn (in the second group meeting, between the mother, Mr G, and me) delegated all responsibility to the father. The latter (in the third group meeting consisting of father, stepmother, and me) tried to take charge but did not feel up to handling things on his own; as we saw, he sought my support.

In these meetings, I could observe how Anne-Marie's parents displaced onto their children the deep resentment each felt towards the other (I pointed this out to them). Consequently, to come

---

[60] Previously, in order to be helped by others *and* to keep me, she used her illness (secondary gain from illness). Now, however, she had to demonstrate to her family the value of the therapy and so use the improvement in her condition (secondary gain from good health).

[61] In every pathological group, the most omnipotent member (the one, in fact, who is the most ill) controls the situation when reality is persecutory and distressing; infantile "regressive" mechanisms are mobilized, for they are felt to be the most effective.

together without the possibility of displacing hatred signified danger: the risk of hurting each other. In order to reach agreement and protect themselves from the dangers inherent in reunion, they required an intermediary who could maintain between all of them the distance necessary for avoiding mutual destruction. The intermediary's other role was to be a "good focus" for gathering together the good parts (into which could be projected each person's good integrative parts). They needed me as a good, idealized reparative object. Each member of the group felt responsible for having defensively projected into me his or her own guilt feelings and reparative needs.

They all needed the family group to be reconstituted. The successive triads represented part-intentions on the way to this goal.

By taking the family group as a whole, it might seem I was pushing Anne-Marie into the background. In reality, however, this was not the case, because if we go back to the origin of this "conditional sequence" we can appreciate how everything was focused on Anne-Marie. It is in this sense that I can say that at no time did I consider the family situation separately from my transference relationship with Anne-Marie.

Summary and conclusions

In this chapter I have dealt with the criteria I follow in treating psychotic patients. I began by referring to possible approaches to the patient through various types of communication. The need for communication (felt by both patient and analyst) produces different techniques such as play in children (and fairy-tales), plays on words ("word-playthings") and babbling (primitive vocal expression of a playful type). Occasionally, a form of communication generally thought of as telepathy can be observed;[62] in extreme

---

[62] I use the term to refer to any communication that lies beyond the realms of our present scientific knowledge; I do not mean that I am in any way an adept of parapsychology. Telepathy is probably a referral back to very primitive modes of communication related to our earliest object relations of which we have no direct conscious knowledge.

situations of abandonment, it signifies the increased need to be "inside" the other (projective identification).

Another theme I discuss in this chapter has to do with the analyst's attitude towards his patient. He must be spontaneous and flexible (ego flexibility) and able to tolerate some degree of self-dispersion if necessary to sharpen his powers of detection and understanding. He must be ready to express himself in the language or other means of communication that for reasons of necessity are prevalent at that time in the analysis; he should be able to make his interpretations at the right moment, all the time keeping the "distance" that the patient requires.[63] As there is an opportune moment for interpreting, so there is an optimal distance from which the analyst's ego can reach out to the patient. The use of transitional objects or elements[64] and of indirect communication or communication-"*via*" (in Anne-Marie's case, the mirror or the blanket) has similar meaning: respect for the patient's fears of being violated and abruptly penetrated. Nevertheless, direct interpretation need not imply an abrupt intromission into the patient's internal world. Being direct means aiming for the nodal conflict while searching around for the optimal point (focal distance) in the spatial relationship between doctor and patient.[65]

I emphasize also the handling of the reality principle during therapy. The fact that in the transference difficulties in actual reality are not overlooked is a contributory factor in defining the ana-

---

[63] Here, the countertransference is the clue that guides us and orientates us with respect to the patient's needs.

[64] E. Pichon-Rivière (1952) argues that the transitional element in the transference is a kind of "third-party" element—that is, the oedipal triangle in its various forms is represented.

[65] I have perhaps not emphasized enough the narcissistic aspect of the patient, although I do remark on it incidentally when I refer to the "auto-plastic" introjection of the maternal breast: the mother as part-object or analytic breast taken to be the patient's own (the object loses its original identity and becomes part of the narcissistic territory of the patient's body). There is no ostensible emergence of envy, since the narcissistic object relationship obviates envy. The narcissistic incorporation of the needed and admired object is a defence mechanism that denies the object's otherness. Envy is an acknowledgement that the object is external and independent. The syncretic–symbiotic relationship does not allow for awareness of feelings or judgement with respect to other people.

lyst–patient context as not far removed from everyday reality—the very reality that psychotics try to avoid. Also, the more regressed the patient, the more his fantasies are unlimited and uncontrollable; generating a limit by confronting them with reality is beneficial for ego integration and creating the idea of contours (the frontier between internal and external world), and so strengthening the personalization process. Frustrating situations in reality, such as abandonment by the family or the analyst's departure, necessarily entail confrontation between fantasy and reality—all the more so because such situations may be experienced as reality-testing of fantasies of love (i.e. clarifying the difference between the actual fact of abandonment and fantasies of abandonment).

We were able to observe clearly the repercussions of environmental factors on the development of Anne-Marie's personality. The emotional instability of her parents, the atmosphere of tension in which she lived, and the lack of durable and stable spatial enclosure prevented her to a large extent from becoming integrated.

In this "schizoid" family structure, it was difficult for her to work through the depressive position. She was unable to project herself as a totality and acquire that feeling of personal responsibility which is the hallmark of the depressive position: taking on board one's own impulses. This only went to strengthen her schizoid tendencies, which were a kind of adjustment to the family gestalt.

In analysis with psychotics, just as in child analysis, given the very real dependence on the environment, we cannot escape having to deal with the family. In the case of Anne-Marie, the unexpected results of the therapeutic process led me in the end to take on the role of analyst of the family group. In this way I was able to integrate three aspects of my analytic experience during the course of treatment: child analysis, analyst of adult psychotics, and group analyst.

Postscript

Since 1957, when an initial version of this chapter was drafted, I have continued my research into the analysis of psychotics. In revising this chapter, I realized that I would not have written it today in exactly the same manner. I would, however, still emphasize the transference experience and the phenomenological description of the context. Describing something is always arbitrary and idiosyncratic; just as for an ethnologist, the way we collect data and relate one element to another is already part of our thinking on the question. Interpretation is a formal way of making this process explicit. I do not know whether today I would deal with the family situation in quite the same way as I did then, but I am still convinced that society, with its institutions and structures, is constantly present in every analytic situation; that is why I attach great importance to applying the analytic method to the wider social and environmental framework.

Today, in 2001, now that I have overcome my strict ideological dependence on Kleinian concepts—I look upon them now from a somewhat more distant perspective—I no longer believe that we can treat severely psychotic patients without the help both of their family and of a psychiatric institution. I feel rather pleased, in fact, at my approach to Anne-Marie's family, since I consider them to be vehicles or mediating agents for split-off parts of the patient herself. I now realize that I was one of the pioneers in my intuitive use of psychoanalysis to gain a fuller understanding of the dynamics of a family situation in which one member is psychotic.

CHAPTER SIX

Countertransference

While it is now widely accepted that we cannot speak of transference without also considering countertransference, it is nonetheless still important to distinguish between the two.

The structure of the analytic setting involves a very particular—indeed quasi-unique—type of experience. The encounter takes place in a given space and at a given time, both of which components participate in the construction of the operational field. Willy and Madeleine Baranger (1969) made an interesting contribution to the question, while, from a dynamic point of view, Kurt Lewin (1963) studied the idea of a field containing forces that operate constantly on its structure. Lewin makes use of the principle of contemporaneity or historicity to criticize the strictly genetic point of view then prevalent in social issues.

The phenomenologists, in particular Merleau-Ponty (1945), went even further. The field can be looked upon as a kaleidoscopic landscape, the appearance of which changes according to the time of day and the perspective adopted by the observer. The latter's position in this environment is never completely neutral—his very presence participates in and modifies the field.

The issue is to what extent we can maintain objectivity without being alienated by the phenomenon itself. Some situations engender new events. The act of revealing or unveiling "organizes" the observed material and makes it meaningful. In psychoanalysis, patient and analyst participate in a shared experience; they inhabit the space of the session in a particular manner, each with his own rhythm and experience of time. The dialectic mobility of the exchange intrigued Freud almost as soon as he began to shape his technique. At the Nuremberg Congress of 1910, Freud discussed the analyst's responsibility and the risk he ran of losing his objectivity when he let himself be influenced by his patient (Freud, 1910d). In 1912, he was able to identify several aspects of the phenomena he was to call transference (1912b).

For Freud, transference is an experience based on the transposition of infantile *imagos*[1] onto the analyst. He drew a distinction between "positive" transference, based on affective and sexual factors, and "negative" transference engendered by hostile feelings. In Freud's view, while the phenomenon was particularly intense in the analytic context, it was not specific to that situation.[2]

In his paper on transference love, Freud (1915a) emphasizes the importance of the positive dimension, but he shows also that falling in love with one's analyst may be a sign of resistance on the part of the patient. We must not let ourselves be taken in by countertransference narcissism, he writes; we have to keep our self-control and try to understand what is going on inside us—hence the importance of the training analysis. Analysis, says Freud, should be undertaken in a state of frustration. Nevertheless, the analyst should not dismiss the patient's feelings of love; he should

---

[1] A concept introduced by Jung in 1911: an unconscious prototype based on infantile relationships which depends on the manner in which these experiences have been perceived and fantasized. The *imagos* are the model for future object relations.

[2] In psychiatric institutions, even in patients who are not treated by psychoanalysis, transference phenomena—sometimes very intense—can be observed in various forms: for example, an exaggerated erotic ambience. Erotic transference plays an important role in the analysis of psychotics and is one of the major problems in the daily life of psychiatric institutions. Herbert Rosenfeld (1950) made a thorough study of the question, as I myself did in a seminar on the psychoses at the Milan Institute of Psycho-Analysis in 1971 (unpublished).

look upon them as something that is "real"—but *real in fantasy*, not tangible reality. Transference love is always a new edition of former unconscious models (imagos).

Transference is a useful tool for the analyst, but, as Freud points out, it may also serve the patient's resistance,[3] resulting in a dynamic ambiguity between opposing forces or principles. What are the respective positions of analyst and patient in this situation, and what is modified in the "field" where the phenomenon occurs? It is not simply a matter of "two-way traffic" between impulses or projective and introjective mechanisms; several significant elements are present in the space and time of the analysis, in particular two living bodies, two individuals, who perceive and influence each other in the drama of the transference.

Heinrich Racker (1959) studied the question in his exploration of the analyst–patient relationship. He calls concordant identification the identification of the analyst's ego and id with those of his patient. Understanding this process maintains the empathy of the encounter. However, it may happen that the analyst loses sight of his patient and can see only his own image as though reflected in a mirror. This situation is what Racker calls complementary identification: in the countertransference, the patient represents for the analyst the receptacle into which he projects the objects of his own personal world. Grinberg (1963) draws a distinction between the complementary countertransference and what he calls projective counter-identification. In the former, the analyst is faced with conflict: in identifying with certain aspects of the patient (his internal objects), he confuses them with his own objects. In projective counter-identification, the analyst's reaction is to a considerable degree "independent" of his own conflicts, because the emphasis is on the patient. Nevertheless, the process is much more complex: the patient's projections always have an impact on the analyst, who can never be wholly "independent" of the transference phenomena. The analyst has to acknowledge his "functional dependence": patient and analyst are each modified and influenced by the presence of the other. The point is to estimate to what extent the patient's

---

[3] From the perspective of the countertransference, there may also be resistance on the analyst's side.

projections manage to modify or even alienate the analyst's identity as analyst by disrupting him as a person. The identity that the patient attributes to his analyst by projective identification is a function of his fantasy world, but it cannot be revealed independently of the physical presence of both protagonists. In other words, every fantasy is materialized by means of physical acts: the voice itself is physical presence and, as such, induces something in the other just as other aspects of the patient's attitude do.

When I use the term induction, I am referring to a "real" or "physical" phenomenon, an influence that stimulates the other protagonist's capacity for picking up the message being sent to him and unconsciously taking on the role he is being asked to play. There is a kind of simultaneous concentration of space and time; what is expressed and "suggested" by one partner is taken in and dramatized by the other. In his discussion of projective counter-identification, Grinberg (1963) writes of non-verbalized messages being "acted". This kind of communication may have the effect of compelling the analyst to act—to *do* something instead of speaking (thought turns into act, and comprehension actuation). We could say that the analyst is acting out, he has become an "actor" of his patient's unconscious fantasies, incarnating the *dramatis personae* of the latter's internal world. The more psychotic the patient, the more his powers of induction increase. Omnipotent control of reality and all it contains is particularly sharp in psychotics and young infants because their paranoid anxieties are so pronounced.

There is a form of induction that stimulates the other person's normal accessibility. This is not the same as pathological induction, which is an obstacle to true communication precisely because one party is manipulating the other. In such a confrontation no message can be truly received, all *logos* having been replaced by a power struggle.

Following Freud, most research into countertransference has emphasized the infantile *imagos* projected into the analyst and arousing the appropriate response in him. The analyst's personal world is the *locus* in which many "events" exist, depending on the way in which he introjects the patient's message. I would like to explore this introjective aspect and the destiny of the internalized object. My starting-point will be the distinction that Money-Kyrle (1956) makes between normal and abnormal countertransference.

In normal countertransference, the patient expresses something in the presence of the analyst, who picks up the message and assimilates it into his ego; the analyst can then work over what he has assimilated and attempt to formulate an interpretative hypothesis.

If this interpretation, projected by the analyst into the patient, clarifies the issue, we could say that the former has succeeded in communicating with the latter. In normal countertransference, the analyst is truly able to take in, introject, and assimilate what the patient projects into him, and to re-project into the patients what his thoughts on the issue are. In such a case, the empathy cycle is successfully completed.

In abnormal countertransference, there are several possibilities. In the first place, the analyst may find it hard to listen to what his patient is saying; he may not be able to perceive the message or to hear him properly. In other cases, the analyst is able to take the message in but cannot assimilate it or understand what the patient has projected. The patient's material thus becomes, in the analyst's internal world, a kind of isolated object, a foreign body—either it remains in his thinking like an autistic enclave or it is projected into his body (hypochondriac defence). In the latter case, the analyst may suffer from some somatic ailment. Finally, the analyst may get rid of this foreign body by re-projecting it onto the patient as a kind of discharge. The patient is "used" by the analyst not as an object for communication (normal projective identification), but, rather, as a reservoir or dumping-ground for something that he has not managed to assimilate. His own anxieties have been aroused by the patient's projections (abnormal projective identification, not conducive to communication).

I would like to illustrate with some clinical examples the vicissitudes of the countertransference and different aspects of the interrelationship.

It is often said that in child analysis the countertransference is a difficult problem to overcome. There are real difficulties in the fact that, for the child, the analyst supplants the parents; what often occurs, particularly with inexperienced analysts, is that an unconscious tendency to "steal" the mother's place is set in motion, thereby increasing the split between the "good analyst mother" and the "bad mother" in the external world. Also, inexperienced analysts are often afraid to activate fantasies in the child which might awaken unresolved infantile anxieties *in the analyst*. My first example is that of a 2-year-old boy.[4]

In one session he told me that his "naughty little doggy" had got into the garden and stolen everything it could find. After telling this story, the boy began to take the toys out of his box with impetuous movements, as if he had claws-teeth that greedily took and devoured everything the analyst-mother contained in his-her body. Then he began to play with water, turning on the tap and soaking little bits of wood which he identified as babies. I interpreted this, saying he was taking possession of the contents of the analyst-mummy, swallowing it all with his hands-mouth and absorbing it into his own body as though he was swallowing up and drowning the babies he put there.

This little boy could not tolerate his destructive orality, which he had projected into the naughty little doggy. As a result of certain countertransference problems, I omitted from my interpretation any reference to the biting and grinding he expressed in his play; I said nothing about his teeth-fingers-claws. The boy himself drew my attention to this omission. Later in the session he left the therapy-room in a state of fear, then returned with his child-minder. He snuggled up close to her like a little baby at mother's breast, fell asleep after this hallucinated satisfaction, then woke up again a few minutes later. He began to make biting movements with his mouth, then brought one finger up close to the child-minder's mouth, all this with a look of alarm on his face. She then said that just recently the boy had begun to bite people. This behaviour coincided with feelings that his legs had been bitten (paresthesia).

He had shown me the part of his body (mouth and teeth) related to his cannibalistic tendencies and had also signalled that

---

[4]This analysis was done in English. The child was 22 months old; I saw him five times a week for one year. He had very few words at his disposal, but he could play—this to me meant that he was able to communicate and that therefore the circumstances were perfectly adequate for beginning analysis. There are times, of course, when children cannot play. This is important with autistic children, for it is precisely the inability to symbolize and dramatize symbols through play which constitutes the central problem.

the persecutory mouth had been projected into the mother-child-minder (and before that, into the dog). He had tried to escape from that persecution by running out of the therapy-room, the analytic locus cathected with oral cannibalistic meaning. Helped in this way by the child, I was able to get in touch with my own oral cannibalistic tendencies—the kind of impulse that for personal reasons I had omitted to mention in my earlier interpretation. In other words, when I succeeded in facing up to my own orality—initially denied—I was able to complete my understanding of the message and make good what I had left out.

The next example has to do with role dramatization (changing roles) and the phenomenon of induction. The patient was an adolescent girl with autistic tendencies. During one particular session she appeared to be almost asleep. It was as though she was "absent". I felt compelled to wake her up by talking to her.

I had the impression, nevertheless, that the actual interpretation was not in itself important; what mattered was the need to stimulate the patient and wake her up from her lost world. I was, as it were, to act like an alarm clock. I said to her that it was as though she were absent, lifeless almost, and I reminded her of one of our recent sessions. In that earlier session, she had identified with the fireplace in the consulting-room, a fireplace in which no fire was burning; she had said that she needed someone, a good mother, to give warmth to her inanimate body and breathe life into it. I added that she had now become that part of herself which had fallen asleep, and her sleepy words could not make contact with me. As a result, I represented the live part of her as well as the live mother.

The patient's face began to change colour (her cheeks became "fiery"), and she became more lively and began to smile. I pointed out this change to her, adding that I had been the firewood she had needed to kindle her fire.

She came closer to me, bending her body forward and holding on with one hand to the chair on which she was seated. She said she was afraid to get close to anybody, because when she did so she felt she became so amalgamated with the other person that she lost her own personality. I replied that when her sleeping part had been awakened, an impulsive part had been aroused at the same time; that part wanted to take possession of the object by amalgamating with it (here, the analyst in the transference) and getting inside it with her fingernails, just as she did when she clung to the chair.

In another session, this patient was quite the opposite—very lively, and very much awake. This time I was the one who was feeling tired and drowsy; I found it difficult to keep my eyes open. The patient responded to my attitude by playing the part I had played with her in the previous session. She became more and more energetic as she spoke and was angry with me because I was sleepy. In this transference situation, with its exchange of roles, the analyst dramatized the patient's sleeping autistic aspect, while she played out her lively—and life-giving—part.

Analyst and patient had, as it were, dramatized the latter's split-off parts. It was only when I was able in my countertransference to communicate with my own sleeping part—my own autistic aspect—that it became possible to integrate both parts. The interpersonal relationship between analyst and patient had become true communication because it was at last possible for the two split-off parts in the transference to integrate and communicate with each other.

* * *

I would now like to say a word about countertransference in relation to the analyst's ability to hear, listen, and understand, and to stress the fact that there are perhaps different stages to the process of "taking something in".

The analyst is able to handle these essential functions insofar as the unconscious fantasy awakened in him by the material projected by the patient can be heard, listened to, and understood. I will take as an example an adult patient suffering from psychosis. During one session, I had some difficulty in listening to and concentrating on what the patient was saying. It was as though I were impeded in my attempt to understand the sequence of events.

A few moments later, the patient reported that as he was driving to his session he had been "impeded" by the traffic and had thought he would not arrive in time. After a slight pause, I was able to connect this with my countertransference feelings, and I said to the patient that on several occasions recently he had experienced considerable difficulty in communicating with me—it was as though he had been "impeded" by his "internal traffic". Here, in the session the patient had felt this "impeded" part of himself loosening its grip as he deposited it in the analyst. Then, however, he realized that if I was to be the depository for that part, I would be "impeded" in my communication with him.

After this interpretation, the patient's contact with me improved, and I myself responded by being more able to concentrate—I was feeling more integrated in my role as analyst.

After a short time, however, the patient again felt impeded; it was as if he had re-introjected the "impeded" part of himself that he had previously deposited in me. His speech became monotonous, with almost no emotional content whatsoever. There was a split between the words he used and the content of what he was saying, a split similar to the one between him and me as analyst—and similar to the split inside himself between his syntonic part and the impeded uncommunicative part (disrupted endopsychic dialogue). The transference response was the dramatization of the patient's unconscious fantasy: as soon as he became able to make contact with someone (or with himself—integration), one part of him cut off all communication. This was his jealous infantile part (the triangular situation[5]), jealous of the good contact between his ego-syntonic aspect and me.

Once I could become aware of these different roles (the patient's impeded part, his autistic and infantile parts), I was able to acknowledge and understand what was going on in the session and express it in an appropriate form.

Another patient, more psychotic than autistic, used to speak in a manner that had a very peculiar impact on me. Her voice was monotonous and bland, and her aim was not to communicate with me but, as she said herself, to *bore* me—and to *bore into* me. She was indeed so "boring" that I could not concentrate on what she was saying. I could feel in my body that insidious persistent voice boring into me; it was as though her words were drops of water

---

[5] In envy, says Melanie Klein (1957), the situation is dyadic. Often, however, the parental couple conceived of as a unit is a source of envy; this envy provokes the infant into attacking the combined parents in an attempt to break the link between them.

falling inexorably and rhythmically, drilling holes in my body. This countertransference feeling was confirmed by the patient, who said: "My words bore holes, they are boring a tunnel. And out of this tunnel, a child will be born."

I interpreted that what she was saying was indeed boring, but at the same time the baby inside her was trying to bore its way inside me, the analyst-mother, in a "bor*n*ing" way.[6] Once she had induced in me the availability to be bored and had bored into me, the baby could again emerge from the tunnel and bore towards the outside world, while still retaining the possibility of boring back into me whenever it might want to. The patient was unable at that moment to communicate with me in any ordinary fashion, because she needed (as she put it) to create underground passages in order to penetrate my body, especially when I was asleep. She wanted to put me to sleep through sheer boredom, settle down inside me, and then observe and control my thinking.

In my final example, I discuss in more detail another issue concerning transference and countertransference, which I encountered with Alice, a young female patient aged 25 years suffering from an acute psychotic condition,[7] whom I treated while she was in hospital.

She was the youngest child of a very religious family; her father was a Protestant clergyman and her sister a missionary. She had been admitted to hospital after a suicide attempt. In the month preceding this, she had suffered from periods of confusion during which she could not identify time and place correctly—she did not recognize certain places, and she was unable to state at what time a given event occurred. She told me that one day she had wanted to go to a specific place but had been unable to do so. She would, for example, start off in the wrong direction, or mistake the time of an appointment. This was also the case with her sessions—she would lose her way in the building and fail to turn up on time. Not

---

[6] This is another example of what I call a phonetic equation: using two words of similar sound [boring/borning] to express two meanings that are different but related in fantasy. The two words become a single aural *signifier*.

[7] See also my chapter on "Delusional Space" (Resnik, 1997a) in which I discuss other aspects of this patient's analysis.

only was she confused, she was fragmented and disseminated throughout space.

A musician, she played the organ in church; she was also professor of gymnastics in a high school and taught some quite unrelated subject in a primary school too. Her dispersion was characterized by difficulties in concentration and consequently in thinking. She complained that her thinking had stopped (as in a mental block). She was living in a dream (dream-world) from which she could not wake up. She said: "Instead of thinking, I dream." In her nightmares, she would hear noises and threatening voices shouting to her that she was mad.

Her fear was expressed in several ways, in particular by ideas of reference and of influence: she felt that people could see what was going on inside her and could control her. From time to time, she would feel that everything was strange and unreal (derealization), and on occasions even her own personality seemed foreign to her (depersonalization).

In our first interview, the patient was distant, rather frightened, tense, and anxious. I asked her some questions, to which she made no reply. Suddenly she began to tremble, making compulsive shaking movements with her head as if to remove something from her ear. I pointed out that this movement was repeated every time I spoke to her; she replied that she was not listening to a voice but to a noise she was trying to get rid of by shaking her head in this way. "Sometimes," she added, "the noise turns into a voice which says I'm mad." She began a dialogue with the voice, saying: "Be quiet! Be quiet!" A few moments later the voice disappeared; she told me that it was even more frightening when the voice broke up into a multitude of little voices calling out to her from all sides. This situation made her feel all the more insecure and all the more insane; she had the impression that the whole world had become foreign and hostile.

In another session, she began to tremble when she heard a radio broadcast in a neighbouring room, the ticking of a clock, and church bells chiming. When I made a little noise to clear my throat before talking to her, she again became anxious and shook her head compulsively from side to side. I reminded her of the earlier session, in which she was afraid of all the tiny voices calling her mad; when I made a little noise just before saying something, she immediately interpreted it to mean that I too was saying she was insane. She was feeling invaded by the noises from the radio and the clock; my throaty noise meant that I was about to speak, to force my way inside her with my noises and word-sounds and thereby invade her too. She felt the need to isolate herself and to withdraw into herself; consequently she became more tense (stiffening herself defensively). As soon as my words got inside her, she tried to shake them out of her ear. It was difficult to communicate with her because as soon as I spoke she got rid of the message (defence by driving the message away).

I realized that during this phase of the therapy the formal aspects of the analytic setting (the furniture in the room, my way of talking, etc.) often had more impact on her than the actual content of what I was saying: she was more sensitive to the world of things than to that of representations. Word-things made her react, not symbols. This is an example of the downgrading of symbol-objects to that of thing-objects—a concrete world in which the object is reified. Hanna Segal's *symbolic equation* is a reference to this downgrading of symbols and the equivalence between the symbol (secondary object) and the thing-in-itself (primary object).[8] When this world of things began to move—for example, whenever I spoke—she took this to be a concrete action *against* her rather than as a message addressed *to* her.

Throughout the first months of her treatment, the patient was plunged into a state of confusion, with hallucinations and illusions.[9] Occasionally, she would be so agitated that the staff could hardly cope with her—she was rebellious with them, just as she was with me in the sessions. Her reactions were unpredictable, and she was difficult to handle. For instance, she was abrupt and demanding with those around her (nurses and patients) and would not accept the ordinary rules of group life. Her behaviour in the group was, however, slightly different from that in the ses-

---

[8] For Kant, the thing-in-itself is unrelated to any human act of representation; that is, it is without the *ob* of object.

[9] Hallucinations are perceptions *sine materia*, whereas illusions result from projecting a hallucinated object onto something and in so doing creating distorted perceptions.

sions; thanks to the fact that I could observe both aspects in her, I could see her more as a whole person. The boundary between inside and outside was unclear, and the analytic field sometimes stretched beyond its normal frontiers. On some occasions, her external behaviour illustrated and confirmed the fantasies analysed in the sessions; her responses were sometimes a defensive dramatization of unconscious fantasies that she did not bring to her sessions.[10]

To return to the issue of the countertransference. The difficulty with this patient was the unpredictability of her reactions. Her verbal language and gestures were not at that point a true symbolic communication; she expressed herself through acts by means of which she tried to force her way inside me. She used induction in order to project into me parts of her body—for example, her throat and the persecutory voice that said she was insane (projective identification). My problem was related to the way I ought best to speak to her as analyst, given that my throat and voice were already cathected with paranoid intentionality which distorted the meaning of anything I might say.

Another habit she had was to speak to me about different topics at the same time; by drawing my attention in opposite directions, she was able to split and disperse me.

As I have frequently observed with other psychotics, this patient did not only hate reality; she hated also her own mind for putting her in touch with reality.[11] She tried to drive me insane by attacking my mind and my thinking because I was putting her in touch with the reality she tried to ignore. By creating dispersion in me, she could project her own dispersion in order to be rid of it. Patients associate in ways that lead us along unknown paths, and sometimes into dead ends or along diverging roads—and this tends to make us feel split-off from our own ego. This impact on the normal countertransference prevents the analyst concentrating and—ultimately—thinking.

---

[10] It is important to draw a distinction between "acting-out" or "acting-in" and "message expressed through behaviour". A child will "act-talk"—that is, he expresses what he has to *say* by *doing* something.

[11] See also Bion (1959).

After periods of elation, depression, and ambivalence towards the therapy, the patient was able to acknowledge that the analysis was indeed helping her. She became more cooperative in the sessions and also within the wider hospital community. I attempted in my countertransference to work through her attacks on my mind and not let myself be alienated by her manipulative behaviour. I had to accept that her world and her defences were capable of interfering with my own integrity.

Paula Heimann (1950) argues that the countertransference is an instrument that guides us towards a better understanding of our patients. The analyst's unconscious is a useful aid to understanding the patient's unconscious. This intimate connection is expressed as an implicit dialogue in which the analyst's emotional response and attitude are as important as those of the patient. Winnicott (1947) explored the hatred that the analyst may feel in his countertransference, especially in the case of psychotic patients. What can the analyst do in order to tolerate and work through this feeling? It is probably the feeling that the analyst is being manipulated (omnipotent induction) which kindles this hatred. It may also be the expression of a narcissistic wound—the analyst fails to understand something and finds it difficult to tolerate this failure/failing. There has to be some kind of curiosity for the unknown, the mysterious, and the incomprehensible if he is to be a true explorer—and a readiness to discover the unexpected. It is obvious that the countertransference is a subtle and difficult experience to work through; it is not simply a question of saying out loud to the patient what our feelings are. One of the dangers of the countertransference in treating psychotics—particularly when the analyst is inexperienced—is that of idealizing the psychotic world, for the patient may well perceive this and use it to reinforce his own narcissism. Psychotics occasionally use the fascination that their world has for the analyst in order to captivate him and beguile him into admiring its opulence and complexity. If the analyst falls into this trap, he will only reinforce the omnipotence of the patient's psychotic part.

Racker (1959) defines the countertransference as an essential instrument for understanding the transference situation, and he also points out the "danger" inherent in all analytic work (loss of one's identity as analyst). This brings me back to the question of the analyst's formal role as opposed to his informal one (i.e. that assigned to him by the patient). How are we to maintain a playful disposition without being alienated by the scenario itself? Bion (1959) describes the good-mother-analyst who is able to take in the anxieties of his patient's infantile part and to assimilate them into his ego through the interplay of the transference. How are we to re-project the message once we have worked it through in such a way that it brings comfort to the patient and diminishes his anxiety? In the countertransference, the analyst has to deal with the patient's infantile aspects and imagos (unconscious prototypes of object relations), and this situation awakens in the analyst his own infantile experiences. The transference itself, as I have shown, can guide us towards a better understanding of ourselves (countertransference), and in turn the countertransference influences the transference. Each protagonist—patient and analyst—participates in and modifies the analytic field; it is therefore necessary to adopt an attitude of operational ambiguity between transference and countertransference, between ob-jectivity and sub-jectivity.

A thorough exploration of what is at issue in the countertransference is, to my way of thinking, a crucial element of the psychoanalytic approach. For essentially didactic reasons, I have devoted a separate chapter to it, but the reader will appreciate that the question underlies everything that I say in this volume.

CHAPTER SEVEN

The experience of space
in the analytic situation

Hesiod's chaos[1] is probably the first expression of the experience of the universe. In Orphic cosmogony, the original chaos becomes organized "rhythmically"—that is, under the influence of time. For Heraclitus, organization requires movement for its structuring function to operate. All movement in time implies covering distance in space.

Whatever the perspective, spatial or temporal, what is common to all cosmogonic theories in ancient times is the desire to know one's position in the universe. The idea of place [τοπος] is in itself a way (in fantasy) of putting limits and boundaries in space, within which something may be contained. Plato's *Timaeus* discusses Heraclitus's conception of movement and becoming, the principle of which [χωρα] is also the locus or receptacle in which the elements of the universe are contained.

---

[1] Etymologically, Χαος is related to Χαχω [yawning, gaping]. In chapter four, I showed how the cavity of the mouth, the primary hole, plays an essential role in the genesis of spatial experience.

179

Plato's idea of the receptacle is particularly interesting in that it opens on to a connection between models of thinking: in the one, the container–contained relationship (space); in the other, transformation and change (time).

In psychopathology, too, these two models can be connected. In this chapter I endeavour to explore the dynamic experience of space and time and how it develops in the transference and the analytic setting. One of the crucial ideas I emphasize is that of spatialization of time.

Pierre Janet gave a series of lectures in the Collège de France in 1927 and 1928, in which he argued that the idea of duration[2] derived from the continuity of human behaviour. Primitive behaviour, on the other hand, is organized in space only. From the time when the individual becomes a "mobile body" able to move about in space, he learns how to conquer distance (on condition that he recognize his separateness). A spatial act becomes structured in time through the experience of separation. If the transition from space to time is not worked out "in time", it may become explosive. We see this phenomenon very clearly in acute psychotic crises, where time is fragmented and dispersed throughout space.

For Bergson (1972), the basic issue in the spatialization of time is the fact that successive moments are always impregnated by simultaneity. He pointed out that both normal and pathological spatializations of time exist.

In his exploration of schizophrenia, Minkowski (1927), working from a Bergsonian perspective, studied how the flow of time can be transformed into immobile and mechanical space, which the psychotic can then control by means of a symmetrical delusion. The schizophrenic is deprived of the ability to assimilate anything that has to do with movement and duration; he tends to construct his behaviour according to purely logical and mathematical principles, with a tendency towards excessive rationalization and spatialization. Duration is paralysed or negated; time does not count. Everything is spatialized either in thought (morbid rationalization) or in the body and external space (morbid geometry). In both

---

[2] For Bergson (1972, p. 114), duration is characterized by invisible continuation of movement.

cases, symmetry and stereotypes occupy in a mechanical and obsessive way the space where living experience should be. All recurrent space is sealed within its own repetitive cycle; it is not open for communication and becomes disorganized. Immobilization of the experience of time is certainly present in pathological spatialization as described by Minkowski—but the converse exists too: excessive mobility of thinking and fantasy is also typical of the mental processes of schizoid and schizophrenic individuals.

Minkowski (1927) quotes Anglade, who compares the schizophrenic to a book in which page numbering has gone haywire—all the pages are there, but they are dreadfully mixed up. If I may be permitted to continue the metaphor, I would add that the binding is often defective, and some of the pages tend to drop out. Part of my task as analyst is to discover where they have gone, to locate them in space and decipher the messages inscribed on them (spatial semiology).

The principal aim of this book is to explore the analytic phenomenon and the setting in which it takes place, not only from the therapist's point of view, but also from that of the patient. The analytic field is not experienced as a static space; change and movement are its hallmarks—it does not stand still.

This implies that we distinguish between categories of experience and the analytic possibilities that are contained in that space. It is part of my task in the transference to explore the experience of intra-body space as well as that of inter-body space. The body is the container for a space in which an internal world can be experienced as one's own, a space where mental processes operate. The body-container is also in a dynamic relationship (interplay) with the space outside it. The body-container occupies a locus in space; this is what I take Descartes to mean when he writes of *res extensa*. My work with schizophrenics has given me the opportunity of studying spatial phenomena and the flexibility and dramatization with which they become manifest in this type of patient.

As always, a clinical example and the detailed examination of a session will help me to make these points clearer.

Mr F, who suffered from a thought disorder, had, at the time in question, been in analysis for three years. He was 36 years of age and had had a previous analysis for a character disorder. What drew my attention in the analytic work with this patient was the contrast between his external presentation as a clean, shy, and meticulous person working apparently quite normally as an assistant cashier, and the very severe thought disorder that remained undetected in his everyday behaviour. I call this kind of condition *mental schizophrenia*: any infirmity appears to be concentrated in the sphere of thinking, which remains split off from praxis. It is of course the case that if someone were to investigate the meaning of his behaviour, his disordered thinking processes would become obvious because of his incoherence and inconsistency.

Mr F's emotional life was stunted—in fact, almost non-existent. His mental expression usually lacked emotion, and his body let nothing of that kind pass. He experienced his body as a sort of a robot that he could manoeuvre so as to accomplish whatever was required of him at work and in social relationships. He lived in a mechanical, withered world.

During the analysis, he discovered his inability to have an authentic relationship with internal and external reality. His body was a machine called upon to perform certain acts that reality demanded or induced it to do. His whole world operated according to this machine-like conception of reality. Everything that occurred obeyed the laws of mechanics and had no existence in terms of human intervention. His robot-body was "thrown" into space [*res extensa*] without any real relationship with other people or other things. The patient did have some awareness of the external space in which his body moved, but this space was emotionally impoverished.

In the session I am about to report, he disengaged from external reality and concentrated on his body and intra-body space.

Mr F began by saying: "Where are my private thoughts? What am I thinking?" Then he went on: "Russell Square is in my mind." (He worked near Russell Square, in London, and it was as though Russell Square had just made its way into his mental space for him to visualize.) "I'm seeing it," he said, "I'm there." ("Seeing it" means that Russell Square occupies a *locus* in his internal world, as a visual and factual event: he is looking at something concrete and real.) "But, if I think about it, I discover that I'm not in Russell Square, I'm here, in your consulting-room." When he realized that he was in my consulting-room, it meant he felt that he was not in Russell Square; he appeared to be stirring from some intermediate state between sleep and wakefulness and discovering that his body was contained in the room.

Mr F then began to turn his attention to his internal world or internal space, which he discovered to be private and belonging to himself. This is the space where phenomena occurred. He was trying to make contact with what he called his private thoughts. He knew the word "thought", but what interested me was the idiosyncratic meaning he attached to it. Sometimes he called "thoughts" what in fact turned out to be images or impressions. There are also, as when he spoke of Russell Square, elements of the outside world that simply occupy space in his internal world (these are neither images nor thoughts nor anything else that could come to the conscious part of the mind). It is as though some fragment of reality could move about inside his internal space without being transformed in any way.

He said of this phenomenon: "Russell Square is in my mind." After this, Mr F moved "with" Russell Square "to" Russell Square, near his work (he was spatializing as far as there). This happened when he said he could see Russell Square, but the tone of his voice and his body language[3] made it plain that his thinking had been transported to the site occupied by Russell Square in external reality.

When he said, "When I think about it, I realize I'm in your consulting-room", he was indicating another position for his spa-

---

[3] In this instance, he was making actual walking movements. Occasionally he would express his mobility by "jumping" or "flying". When he is in space, his notion of time tends to accelerate, and changes of location take place so rapidly that it becomes difficult to follow him. He "spatializes" from one place to another, using more or less rapid methods to do so, depending on the needs of the moment. Schizophrenic thinking obeys its own spatial logic. Sometimes movement takes place on foot, or with jumps—at others, the laws of gravity are abolished and the individual begins to fly; again, sometimes only certain elements fly off, hence the dispersion. His is a wandering mind, he is forever rootless; it is impossible to know where he is at any given time; he does not rest easily. His aim is to spatialize time. He has no time to stay, nor—as the analytic situation demands—to reactivate past experiences so that they can be analysed.

On other occasions, the situation is quite the contrary. He seeks to negate time, paralyse it, petrify it. When all movement is "congealed", thinking itself becomes catatonic. There is no life; the only experience that can exist is that of death. Flight into mobility and petrification are both ways of escaping from the analytic situation.

tial mobility; he was again in the formal space of the analytic session.

He went on, "Russell Square is like going to the countryside", and he made a gesture as though he were indeed leaving for another place. Then he said, "I'm in the countryside", making another gesture as though to indicate that he was coming back. I interpreted: "Your mind went for a walk in the country and now it has come back. You say you're interested in your private thoughts, but this is a way of neglecting anything private and going towards something 'public'—the outside world."

The problem was how to make public here with me in the session (and not in Russell Square) these private thoughts. (In other words, in his mind, Russell Square was a convenient way of carrying his private thoughts away from the actual session.)

"Yes," replied Mr F, "but Russell Square is near my work. And I go there to get away from the noise in the office where I work." As he said "noise", he gestured towards his head. I answered: "At present, you feel inside your head something you call 'noise' and you're running away from it by leaving your body—which is the work-place for thinking."

"And I go to Russell Square," Mr F added, "in order to be alone." (i.e. isolated from his internal noises). In other words, Mr F was going towards open space not in order to communicate with external reality but so as to escape from noisy internal reality. "Now I have a picture[4] of Russell Square," he said (as though the camera had stopped and with it the experience of time). He is alone, but time is paralysed—nothing can happen, nothing unexpected.

He went on: "Now I feel I *am* Russell Square", to which I made the comment: "You are well and truly inside, but alone, there's no contact with your noises." (He had transposed Russell Square to his own body so that every experience—in Russell Square and in his body—was converted into a single one.) Then he fell silent, and this silence appeared to put him in touch with his body, with his intra-body reality, as if trying to understand something of his inner solitude. With this reflex innerness, he was trying to comprehend

---

[4]Mr F uses one of two terms: *picture* when he means a static image, and *scene* when the image is mobile.

what was happening inside his own world—the world that inhabited the space inside his body. This became all the more the case when he said: "I'm ill. I'm not a human being, I'm a thing." This was how he became aware of his thing-body and tried to make it more human; he was trying to be a person, he was striving to come alive.

He said: "I don't understand why I was suddenly Russell Square, then why, when I don't feel human, I feel cut off from life. It's very upsetting to feel separate, but it's painful too to be with someone and have feelings."

It is important to note that here Mr F was referring to the fact that he had *feelings* inside himself—not just *noises*, as before. This distinction shows that different categories of experience were possible inside his "inner space"; each has its own semantics, expressed in different ways in the analytic time. "Noises" were something he ran away from, "feelings" help him to find himself again and to become aware of his body in his endeavours to become a person.

"Being a person is painful," said Mr F. Then he paused, and his attitude became that of someone about to leave (i.e. he was leaving the pain of being himself). "I'm not with myself, part of me has gone to the beach in Dorset where my parents live. It's like going away on holiday, but I feel lonely, I'm not with myself any more" (split between thought and body, or between container and contained).

At the end of the session, I pointed out to him that splitting (running away from himself) was one way of avoiding a painful—but integrating—encounter. Mr F agreed with this: "When I imagine myself on the beach in Dorset, I feel divided in two: I am there, and here too. But if I think about it, I realize I'm here because I'm talking to you." I commented: "Thinking means linking the Mr F here and the Mr F over there; when both are reunited, a single Mr F is 'present'."

Again mobility is used in order to avoid the encounter with himself in the setting of the session, where conflict could be confronted. Yet Mr F insists on holding on to mobility as a defence against confrontation *in situ*. He said, "I'm back from Dorset," adding: "I see Dorset in my thoughts." If we look at this in terms of container and contained, the sequence is as follows. Firstly, Mr F hides away in Dorset, using it as a reservoir for that aspect of himself which escapes from the *hic et nunc* of the session. The second step consists in incorporating Dorset as an identifiable component of his internal space. Dorset is a fragment of reality which moves: there is "transportation" from one place to another (transportation is the word used by another schizophrenic patient to describe this phenomenon), but no transformation of perception, no true process of symbolization.

At that point, Dorset was no longer an image: it had become something concrete occupying space in his mind. Later, Mr F said: "Now I see a picture of Dorset, and I can also see a picture of the sea."[5]

He went on: "I don't know whether what I see is a picture of the sea or whether I really am at the seaside."

For Mr F, there was ambiguity between existing as a picture and existing as a thing, or, to put it another way, a lack of clarity between perception and the concrete world of action. In the latter, either the body moves "in reality" or reality moves into the body-space, but there is in any case no transformation (no symbolic process). When it comes to perception, the mind is able to take in an experience and transform it into something different (the object and its image.)[6]

---

[5] Mr F could also speak French, hence the phonetic equation *mer/mère*. In any case, the symbolism sea/mother is common to almost all languages.

The body as reservoir of different types of experience is in a dynamic relationship (interplay) with space outside the body. The body-as-reservoir (or receptacle) raises the question of the *locus* it can be said to occupy in space. This, as I have mentioned, is my understanding of Descartes's *res extensa*.

[6] Descartes, Leibniz, and Hume all discussed the relationship between the image of an object and thinking about the object. Sartre (1965) drew a distinction between the image-thing and the image-thought (a copy of the object in the imaginary). Leibniz tried to establish a continuity between the two modes image and thought: the image is coloured by intellect. There is a type of experience in the internal world, he argued, by which a mundane object attains the category "image" by means of sensory (perceptual) transformation; the development of ideal experience gives an image categorical value through which it becomes functionally appropriate for thinking. Thought is the result of integration between the spatial relationship with the object world and the construction of personal time—in other words, the organization of experienced rhythm within the personal body space.

If Mr F were to accept that the sea is an image, this would imply acceptance of the fact that the sea was not with him, that it has a separate existence independent of his own. The image of the sea is not the sea; Mr F would have to be able to accept the absence of the original object and admit of a reproduction: the *image* of the sea— Sartre would have said that the sea now exists as an image within himself. (Displacement in space of a transforming experience is part of the process of symbolization; time transforms spatial experience, or, to put it another way, time expresses the inherent mobility of the object of experience.)

Mr F continued: "If I am there, by the seaside, I'm not imagining it, I am there."

In the reality of the analytic situation, there is a split between Mr F's mind and his body[7] which dramatizes his intention to be concretely united with the sea-mother-analyst. (He would like to take me in as mother and project himself into the sea—this would enable him to go to the seaside on holiday or at weekends, when there are no sessions.)

When Mr F was in a frame of mind that allowed him to be aware of his problems, his principal preoccupation was how to think. Bion (1962) argues that thoughts develop before the apparatus required to cope with them—thinking is a development forced on the psyche by the pressure of thoughts—they are not the *product* of thinking processes. They are, however, the result of a complex perceptual and cognitive process that implies intellectual activity of some kind. For Leibniz, a thought image results from intellectualization of a sensory image; there is a dialectic structuring movement between the primary perception that stimulates mental processes and the configuration of these processes that attributes to them an imaging and thinking character.

Mr F's analysis was the starting point that enabled me to formulate certain concepts that I have since explored with other patients, concepts that are related to the development of mental processes and their expression through language. For example, excessive mobility of thinking split off from the body is an escape

---

[7]This split illustrates in fantasy the dualism typical of certain religious beliefs and philosophical thinking.

mechanism, a defence against true thinking ability, and is typical of schizophrenics and schizoid personalities. In classic psychiatry, Bleuler (1950, p. 29) referred to this as "psychotic distractibility". Here, Mr F became aware of his mental mobility and said abruptly, "I go away and then come back, but in reality I ought to be here", "I'm here and there", or even "I'm everywhere" whenever his projective identification was excessive. Because of his mental dispersion, Mr F could be in several places at the same time (his avidity was enormous, and he did not want to lose anything). He was connected to everything and separated from nothing. Whenever his paranoid aspects became dominant, his intention was to be everywhere in order to control all spaces simultaneously. Projecting himself suddenly out of his body, in particular through language, was experienced by Mr F as though sounds and words were jumping out of his body.

Language is inseparable from action. Vocal language, said Merleau-Ponty (1955), before being linguistic, is another form of movement. When Mr F became anxious, any hint of separation was intolerable. Projection by means of words was experienced as an extension of body space as though he possessed pseudopodia that could reach far out into space; there was a complete absence of separation (even in projective identification there is some measure of separation). When an infant learns how to play with sounds through babbling, he makes contact with objects in external reality with the help of these pseudopodia-sounds; he takes into his internal reality what he grasps hold of, and he establishes provisional identity between the sound and the experience—which thereafter begins to take on meaning (the intermediate stage between vocal extension and projection of sounds). There is a gap between sound and experience that makes possible an encounter out of which may emerge an appropriate symbol. But before we can cross that gap, we have to acknowledge its existence, and therefore the existence of separation—it is this, argues Melanie Klein (1960), that is decisive in working through the depressive position. Accepting that a word as transmitted is different from the original object is a transition to a new situation (from expansion/extension to projection). One of the problems schizophrenics have is that they cannot make up their minds to "come out"; they live inside their objects instead

of forming a relationship with them.[8] Inter-space is not acknowl-
edged—they leap over it and settle down inside other containers.
This is similar to pathological projective identification that neutral-
izes normal processes of communication. There are two dangers
inherent in leaping over space: falling down, and annihilation
through total dispersion. The tendency to go out into space in
order to lodge inside objects (projective identification) is part of the
spatialization process; by spatialization, I mean any ego mechanism that tends towards the mere *occupation* of space as contrasted
with *living* in space.

When I speak of dispersion—the simultaneous occupation of
different *loci* in space—I am alluding to one of the fundamental
pitfalls of every attempt at helping schizophrenic patients: their
referential conception of the world. In ideas of reference, every
aspect of reality is read as concerning the egocentric patient. This is
due to what I have called massive dispersion: since the patient is
"everywhere", everything is somehow related to him.

I want now to illustrate some of the vicissitudes of spatialization—for example, massive projection and the subsequent delusional transformation of the world (delusions of reference are one
instance of this).

In the case of Mr F, displacement and dispersion alternate with
topologically precise projections. When he says, "I am in such-and-
such a place", he means that at that moment he is not dispersed—
he is split, because of course his body is in fact present in the
session. At one point he said: "I am in Euston station, and I'm
reading the word 'Euston'." "I know what Euston is," he added
(the word "Euston" tells him in what kind of place he is). He went
on: "Now I'm back here, and I realize that once again I went away
somewhere else. There is a space outside here, and another one
inside me." Then: "Sometimes it's as though I had a hole in my
head, with a space that comes and goes. A space that can go
through the hole and come back the same way." "Everything
which is beyond my eyes is space . . . Sometimes I want it back

---

[8] Living inside one's objects is one component of the schizophrenic conception of the world: other people are not individual persons, but receptacle-
things.

inside me" (mobile space which, depending on its position, can be internal or external). "Now I can't distinguish between the space outside and the one which is behind my eyes."

On another occasion, he said: "Space is everywhere." Then: "Now I am half-awake" (in other words, he is also half-asleep— that is, in an ambiguous state between sleep and wakefulness). "It's easy to be outside myself. Now I'm in Hornsey, in the library near where I live; I'm standing by the door outside the library." I interpreted that he was transporting the analytic library (analytic learning) to Hornsey. He was seeking to achieve integrative organization in his thinking (the library), but he stayed outside.

"Now I've no space inside me," said Mr F. I commented: "Space escaped through the hole, and so you've no more space inside you, where your own library and learning could develop." Learning is evacuated out of his body; in other words, he is "outside" all learning (at the door of the library).

The hole to which he was referring could at that point have an anal signification: evacuation. This is a hallucinated aperture he "invented", something that has little to do with ordinary loci, an aperture for evacuating space. The intentionality of the aperture could also be oral, when he uses it for taking in mobile space.

"That point about space is interesting," said Mr F. "It's enigmatic," he added, as though interested in understanding it. "I can see this space, but what about all the others?" he went on, as though trying to solve the enigma. "I have some connection with something which I didn't have before. If I go for a walk on my own in the evening, I try to think."

And so at the end of this session he became aware of his body and of himself as inhabiting it in space. When Mr F takes a walk in the evening and tries to think, he is trying to communicate with his intra-body space and with the contents of his internal world. The discovery that he possesses a world of his own and that it is part of the experience he has of his body is an important step on the road to personalization (an integrative process resulting in the acquisition of the concept of being a person). Incarnate space secure within the body is a domain on which can be mapped the development of mental processes. On the other hand, mobile space in its comings and goings does not have the capacity for integrating a mind. (I draw a distinction between the mobility of internal space, the container, and the mobility of its contents—elements to be evacuated defensively.)

Discussion

After I had delivered the above lecture, a discussion took place with the audience, and this is reported below. For me, every lecture should be an invitation to dialogue.

* * *

Could you be more explicit about the different categories of thought, when you distinguish, for example, the image of Dorset from the word "Dorset"?

People who work with autistic children or psychotics have often observed that when patients write their name on a sheet of paper, this can imply—from the patients' point of view—that the written word (their name) is the manner in which they are themselves spatialized on the piece of paper. It is an example of concrete thinking in which only displacement exists and not symbolic transformation—or, if the latter does exist, there is always a symbolic equation between the word and the person it is supposed to represent. The word "Dorset" in this context takes on the quality of concrete reality; it exists in fact and is neither image nor thought.

In another session, Mr F reported that when he comes into his office he behaves like a camera: he has an aperture through which he can look at the employee sitting next to him. When he looks at his co-worker, Mr F feels he is taking this other person inside him, and so he no longer feels empty. From a perceptual point of view, what I am trying to show is that a component part of reality is taken *as such* into his personal space without any transformation. This precedes imagination and thought. It is the world of displacement, and it obeys the physical laws of the external world.

At one point in that session, Mr F showed that he had some awareness of his illness when he said that his camera was not working properly and he would have to take it to be repaired by a specialist firm called Kingsley (he was, therefore, "leaving" the session and on his way to Kingsley's). Then he said that he again felt himself to be "in" the session, and that the word "Kingsley" was in some way connected to the word "Resnik". I pointed out that each had a "k", and that perhaps this was a link between him and me. He was taking me into his mind as someone who specializes in repairs. The significance of the "k" as a nexus could be the starting point for a semantic investigation that might enable us to discover other significant components in the word "Kingsley".

Other than "Resnik" and the connection through the "k", might the word "king" not be significant?

Exactly. Taking the "k" as a starting point for a linguistic investigation, it is obvious that the word "king" (inter alia) plays an important part. It links my first name, Salomon, with King Solomon. His idealization of me in his internal world, together with the fact that he believes me able to "repair" him, does indeed confer "kingly" status on me. But in reality I am neither a king nor the letter "k"; I am a psychoanalyst who has undergone a series of transformations inside Mr F's world. This process is evidence of a "transforming" capacity, which is quite different from simple "transportation"— the simple moving of things from one place to another without any modification. The word "king" inside Kingsley would be part of a more developed process similar to symbolization, taking on the quality of a morpheme—a meaningful unit.

I have the impression that your practice of psychoanalysis emphasizes the formal aspects of thinking rather than content or emotionality.

When you live in a world as concrete as that of the schizophrenic part of the ego, understanding of that world is initially accessible only through its formal aspects, because it is much more difficult to understand in terms of content. For example, in such a world, the letters of the words "Kingsley" and "Euston" are as concrete as a three-dimensional picture of a human being. Also, classifying things into container and contained is quite arbitrary. Every formal container has (semantically) meaningful content, and everything that is "contained" should also be looked at from a formal perspective.

The categories "container" and "contained" are part of a conception of the world connected with the idea of recipient or receptacle. But there are other conceptions: a mystical view of the world would see things in terms of infinite time and space, and not in terms of container and contained. My intention is to study the formal aspects of language insofar as they enable me and the patient to establish a common linguistic instrument. In the symbolic process, differentiation between container and contained is evidence that it is possible to distinguish between an object and its representation. The ability to move from primary to secondary object is related to the capacity to be depressed and to accept separation. When Mr F was able to accept the *image* of the sea, it meant he accepted separation from the sea *per se*—in other words, he accepted its absence.

What relationship is there between thought, image, and language?

It is necessary to distinguish between two types of mental process here: mental thoughts and verbal thoughts (i.e. ready to be put into words). As I pointed out earlier, images express the primary ability to accept the absence of the object (the absent object is represented by the image). Thought is a particular type of image that contains a "thinking" quality.

Verbal thought is a more specialized expression of the mind. It is related to the ability to accept the linguistic environment of everyday reality, and to the capacity to take in conventional meanings of language devices. It requires acceptance of space and physical separation, as well as the ability to go forward in order to communicate and transmit messages.

What part was played by transference interpretations with Mr F? I did not have the impression that you made this kind of interpretation, at least in the ordinary sense of the term.

To my way of thinking, transference interpretations are extremely important, because it is only within the transference relationship that the psychoanalyst can bear witness to what is going on. But looked at from the patient's standpoint, it sometimes transpires— as we saw with Mr F—that he is not "in" the session at all (except when it becomes transposed to the seaside via introjection followed by projection as far away as possible). His transference relationship was taking place elsewhere, in a location where I was not able to bear witness. Following the spatial "adventures" of the session in the transference means recovering space and bringing it back inside the analytic setting where the roles of patient and analyst can be formally identified. Once that condition is satisfied, even very slight changes can be made visible. Endeavouring to interpret as occurring in the session, "in the transference", something that in fact is spatialized outside the frame of reference would be inoperative and inconsequential with respect to the phenomenological reality of the given experience. If a patient alludes to his past and claims for example that as a child he was beaten, he is referring to something that I did not witness. But if I feel that the patient is beating me with his words, with his way of addressing me, I would interpret that the child in the past is now present in me and being beaten by him (by his words).

I had the impression that the transference interpretations you mention led to a kind of reification of you as a person.

The important issue is surely what meaning I have as a person from the point of view of the patient. If he treats me like a thing and sees me as Dorset or the seaside, I must follow this scenario and my interpretations must be coherent with the role I am allocated. Yet this same patient will suddenly change his attitude and realize that I am not the seaside, not Dorset, and not even "in" Dorset. Just as a psychotic part of the patient's ego tends to reify reality, so there is another non-psychotic part able to reflect on and modify its perception or the intentionality of its experience.

How do you make patients understand what reification means?

If I am part of a reified world, the important thing is for me to manage to put this into words from the point of view of my role as a thing-person. A psychoanalyst takes on a whole series of ambiguous roles which gradually become clearer as the analytic exploration progresses.

What is fundamental is that each participant sees the other in a dynamic perspective; the analytic discourse is there to guarantee these dynamics. In this way, communication within the patient's own world—between different aspects of his ego—is established, with the aim of achieving internal harmony.

What was Mr F's attitude towards time? He spreads himself out mentally and flits from one place to another; this would appear to indicate that time passes very rapidly.

One of the features of schizophrenics and schizoid personalities is their tendency to spatialize their own personal experience of time (this was Minkowski's point too). Thanks to dispersion, the patient stops thinking and feeling, he runs away from the pain of encountering himself. There is disintegration and expulsion of internal time. Nonetheless, it is true to say that temporal elements are encountered even in spatialization, particularly concerning matters of rhythm and speed. For example, shifting rapidly from place to place implies some notion of time, accelerated time. When such patients begin to improve, a major step is the establishment of a personal reference to space via appropriate re-internalization of the various projected part-spaces. With psychotics, re-internalization of the dispersed parts of their fragmented body does not necessarily take place according to the laws of anatomy and physiology (false restoration[9]). Reorganization brings in its wake the reintegration of dispersed "lost time'. When time has been recov-

---

[9] I find it necessary to make a distinction between reparation and restoration, while at the same time stressing the link between these two terms. To procure again [Lat. *re-parare*] has also the meaning of restoring or mending, whereas *restaurare* means to give back what has been lost, removed, or destroyed and hence has to do with faithfulness towards the form and matter of the original object. This highlights a problem that Freud tried to solve in one of his less well-known papers, "Constructions in Analysis" (Freud, 1937d). One of the aims of psychoanalysis, for Freud, is to recover, through the transference, the original truth or inaccuracy (or misunderstanding) of the repressed situation. He states (p. 127): "In madness, as the poet has already perceived, there is a fragment of historical truth." Perhaps we should differentiate between delusional and non-delusional logic. In any case, the restorer (the analyst, with the help of his patient) must, while respecting the "historical truth", call it into question if the need arises in order for the self to be correctly constructed. The link with Klein's concept of reparation is that any mental construction is in fact a re-construction; this has to do with early catastrophic experiences and primitive feelings of guilt. In my recent research on delusional thinking, I take very much into account a further statement by Freud in the same paper: analytic work consists in "liberating the fragment of historical truth from its distortions and its attachments to the actual present day and in leading it back to the point in the past to which it belongs".

ered, the analytic atmosphere becomes alive. Re-temporalization of projected space is the therapeutic converse of spatialization of time.

I wonder whether, in this type of case, there is a common primal experience in which both time and space are mixed.

I answered this point to some extent in my remarks on the implicit temporal aspects of spatialization. There is a sense in which we could say that time is expressed in terms of space, or space in terms of time. For example, a patient may speak of his childhood, his past-in-time, with an intentionality that is spatial—that is, he is in fact removing the child from the session and placing him in a point somewhere out in space called "childhood", far from present time.

CHAPTER EIGHT

A profile of
the schizophrenic mind

When we approach the world of the schizophrenic patient, one of the problems we encounter is a difficulty in perceiving sense and structure in his message. His thinking is so distorted that the rules that ordinarily apply to the way we think are of no help to us in our attempts at understanding. Bleuler (1950) had underlined the importance of thinking disorders in schizophrenics and had observed also their difficulty in associating; the associative process, he argued, is blocked. This corresponds to a global split in the personality.

Minkowski (1927) investigated the schizophrenic's lack of contact, not only with respect to thinking but also in his relationship to the world (loss of vital contact). This schizoid tendency—loss of contact with other people—is related on the intra-psychic level to loss of contact with oneself. There are communication disorders first with oneself (inner dialogue) and then with the outside world (external dialogue).

The schizophrenic is usually described as malfunctioning because of his "tendency" to cut himself off from reality. The paradox is that, being cut off in this way, he manages to set up a kind of

"psychotic equilibrium" which allows him some degree of adjustment to reality.

One of my patients who suffered from a hypochondriac delusion claimed that his stomach made terrible noises; when on business, he slept in hotels, and his neighbours were inconvenienced
by these noises and hammered on the bedroom walls while he was
asleep. This patient was an expert in electronics, and his splitting
enabled him to maintain his delusion "separate" from his everyday work. During treatment, splitting decreased then disappeared;
having to face up to his ill part placed him in a state of crisis. Such
an encounter is always distressing because it calls into question the
patient's entire system of adjustment. At that point, he had a significant dream: *he saw a very ugly and deformed girl approach him.
There was something about her that made him think of his fiancée, whom
in reality he found beautiful and attractive. The girl in the dream seemed
impatient to speak to him, but her voice was covered by noises from
outside, noises like someone hammering on the wall. He himself felt very
ambivalent: he wanted to speak to her, yet at the same time did not want
to. He was struck by the transformation in the young woman, and his
feelings were confused and contradictory.*

I interpreted these associations as follows. He identified the
woman approaching (i.e. getting close to him) with his own distorted feminine part; his delusion was expressed spatially by
means of physical deformity. In the dream, the noises from his
hypochondriac stomach are projected outside, as in the hotel, and
their uncontrollably violent re-introjection prevents him talking
(thinking)—that is, prevents intra-psychic dialogue between the
two parts. His masculine part, the one that can go on working and
adjusting to life, has difficulty in facing up to his delusion, personified partly by the girl in the dream and partly by the noise disseminated throughout space and obstructing inner dialogue.

The psychoanalyst is the mediator of this encounter, which
takes the form of a psychotic crisis. Normally, the split personality
goes through periods of confusion that are necessary steps on the
way to the self's reintegration. The patient's dream is a semiological illustration of these different aspects of dissociation—bivalence,
ambivalence, and confusion. During the analysis, the patient was
unable to tolerate any differentiation between his beautiful fiancée
and his ugly (mad) feminine part. He was envious of her physical

harmony and could not bear his own dissonance. He forced his own discordant self into harmony (his fiancée); he deformed her by his madness, and his delusion took possession of the admired object by projective identification. Splitting protected him from painful reuniting—the awareness of his inner chaos was masked by a split that enabled him to give the appearance of being orderly and competent in whatever he did.

During the treatment, reintegration entailed the disappearance of the frontier between both parts of the self (breakdown in defensive splitting), which in turn led to a state of confusion. (This latter idea is borrowed from Herbert Rosenfeld, 1950.) He employs it operationally: confusion is an intermediate stage between splitting and reintegration. It can therefore be evidence either of improvement or of regression.)

My patient was in a state of confusion when his adaptive splitting began to fade. Analysis of the situation and clarification of the confused relationship enabled him to reach a new level of unification—but the transition to this new state was painful because it meant abandoning the delusion cathected by his own narcissism.

Adjustment was no longer based on his split personality, but on a "whole" personality. As I pointed out, every psychotic has a non-psychotic as well as a psychotic part. Bion (1957a) emphasizes that differentiation between them is important both for theory and in practice. When we speak of the non-psychotic (i.e. neurotic) part, we think of what Freud called repression; reaching that level requires an advanced degree of differentiation of the psychic apparatus. The ability to discriminate between the repressed and the repressing parts of the ego is crucial. The psychotic part of the ego knows nothing about repression, because it employs other mechanisms—fragmentation and massive projection. It cannot be integrated in thought because everything is projected out of the mind, and as a result the internal world is—at least in that part—empty, deserted, and impoverished. What ought to be an apparatus for thinking is no more than a device for ejecting inner experience. The ego's movement is centrifugal: it does not bring "thinking images" together. The main reason patients that have for adopting such manoeuvres is their inability to bear the anxiety of meeting themselves.

Hanna Segal (1956) discusses the schizophrenic's incapacity to tolerate depression, and Melanie Klein (1935) argues that it is the impossibility of working through the depressive position which obstructs whole-object relations and ego integrative processes. Depression has to do with loss and separation, the possibility or otherwise of tolerating mourning, and the differentiation between internal and external reality; as such, it is related to symbol formation and word-representations. For symbolization to be effective in thought and speech, differentiation between the primary object and the secondary object representing it is required. If there is failure here, thinking becomes reified; components of thought acquire a concrete persecutory intentionality with occasionally a hint of depression (paranoid depression). Instead of having elements suitable for thinking at his disposal, the schizophrenic feels haunted by persecutory objects which he attempts to evacuate. Thinking then becomes an operation by means of which undesirable thought-things are eliminated.

Thinking itself is reified; the mind and its texture become substance (in the material sense). One female patient had the impression that when she cried, her ideas liquefied; occasionally they solidified, or else vaporized (her thoughts "evaporated"). "When I speak," she said, "I feel my words to be hard and bruising." From time to time her word-thoughts were experienced as air, which she could then blow into a balloon; but it was not simply air that she expelled, sounds too came out. Hence, speaking was a way of expelling air and noise. Sometimes also her worries were metaphysical and related to her body ("Is it made of wood, or glass, or iron . . .?") or to her existence (was she "a living being or a corpse wandering throughout the land"?)

In surrealist literature, Leonora Carrington (1944) gives an example that clearly illustrates the experience of a body's "schizophrenic" texture. She describes her feelings as she walks through Madrid during her illness: "I was still convinced that it was Van Ghent[1] who hypnotized[2] Madrid, its men and its traffic, he who

---

[1] "A Dutch Jew, a Nazi agent" (Carrington, 1944, p. 72).

[2] The transformations that the world undergoes during the schizophrenic crisis are rooted in the omnipotent projections of a delusional ego that cathects external reality (psychic and physical) with widespread paranoid intentionality. The schizophrenic's environment constantly functions with reference to

turned the people into zombies." One evening she read in a newspaper that a new technique of hypnotism had reached Madrid: "I was at the door of the hotel, horrified at seeing in the Alamada people go by who seemed to be made of wood" (p. 73). Her body image was fragmented and spatialized into the multitude of bodies walking along the street. Her physical texture—woodenness—was fragmented and multiplied, and inhabited other people's bodies.

She tried to reorganize her fragmented body: "I began gathering a week ago the threads which might have led me across the initial border of Knowledge." She wanted to become as she had been before, but the word "threads" indicates that her integration was to be that of a puppet—with herself pulling the strings (her woodenness was at the mercy of an unknown force, and she wanted to control it herself).

The feeling of transformation in the body was reflected in the transformation of internal and external worlds. Her personal world was turned upside-down; time, the inhabitants of her world (internal objects), and parts of her ego were all glued together, at the mercy of forces that prevented them moving and immobilized her internal world, her vital rhythm.

She relates how, at the beginning of her crisis, she was fleeing the Germans and had managed to reach Spain. Suddenly, her car came to a halt; the brakes had jammed. "I heard Catherine say: 'The brakes have jammed.' Jammed! I, too, was jammed inside myself by forces that were foreign to my conscious will, which I was sure was paralysed by the pressure of my anxiety acting upon the mechanism of the car. This was the first stage of my identification with the external world. I was the car. The car had jammed on account of me, because I, too, was jammed between Saint Martin and Spain. I was horrified by my own power."

One of my patients had the following experience. She used to say that she felt like a piece of cheese walking in the street and upsetting people because of the smell. One day, as she was on the way to her session, she decided to visit the ducks in Regent's Park,

---

him and speaks about him through the metamorphosis of objects that become capable of speech and action. Bleuler called this intentionality of the surrounding environment *ideas of reference*. It is indicative of the passage from allocentrism to egocentrism so characteristic of the schizophrenic world. See also Resnik (1957).

just opposite my consulting-rooms. She had brought bread along, and she threw some to the ducks. Later, while she was on the couch during the session, I had the impression that though her body was there, her mind was elsewhere. After a minute or so, she said: "I'm in the park and I'm throwing crumbs to the ducks, but as soon as they stop eating they become very bizarre. One of them is facing up to me angrily, the second is running away, and the third looks absolutely out of its wits." Then she physically drama-tized the situation by moving like a duck: the piece of bread which represented part of herself "ducked" back inside her body. The patient had projected one part of her "bread-like" bodily nature into the duck, then re-introjected the contents of her projection mixed with the object into which she spatialized herself (this mix-ture is what Bion, 1956, calls the bizarre object: from what she said of the ducks, we can see that she had evacuated her feelings of anger and persecution, as well as her madness, into them).

As I have already said, the schizophrenic is afraid of reality and dislikes the mental apparatus that puts him in touch with it. Bion (1957a, p. 48) gives an example in which the fragmented part of the personality is concerned with sight; if this part is projected onto a gramophone, the patient may feel that the machine is watching him. If the fragmented part has a connection with hearing, how-ever, he will have the impression that it is listening to him. Hallu-cinations, says Bion (1958), are the result of expulsion by means of the sense organs (which, therefore, can be felt to expel as well as to receive).

The attack may also be directed against the self, taking the form of an explosive and catastrophic fragmentation experienced as the end of the world. If the detonation takes place within the frontiers of the body, implosion is the result.

The patient's psychotic part attacks his own mental apparatus, but at the same time the non-psychotic part needs to learn and acquire knowledge—but what kind of knowledge can there be when thinking is impossible? Knowledge may imply using om-nipotent means to get inside what he wants to know (magic and telepathy). Curiosity is divorced from real knowledge—it is more a voyeurism than an authentic quest for learning. The patient may take possession of the source object which he narcissistically in-vests—thereby destroying all possibility of a relationship with it.

The admired object is located within someone else's body, and the patient endeavours to force his way inside. Penetration does not signify exploration, it may imply occupation and possession: the schizophrenic does not enter into relationships with objects in the world—he occupies and inhabits them.

He dislikes open space: if he opens up to space it is merely in order to get inside other objects. He jumps over space; the risk of being in space is falling. "Being-with" means taking risks, and Heidegger's *Mitsein* is out of his reach. Verbal thought is in the body; when it becomes a voice and gives out aural signals—that is, when it becomes external to the body—the phobic anxiety about open space increases. In such cases, speech is not necessarily a communicable message: the signified is hidden in the signifier when it leaves the envelope-body, and thus avoids going naked in open space. The signified moves through space inside a capsule-object: the signifier. Astronauts inside their spacecraft do not communicate with space, they look out at it. When they leave the containing object, however, and walk around in space, they are in free-floating communication with a new aspect of the universe. Going forth into the unknown is an ontological experience just as fraught with anxiety as is birth itself.

Normally the signifier is the mediator between the signified and the part of reality towards which the message is directed. In "abnormal" cases, as we see in schizophrenics for example, the signifier is used as a defence against fragmentation and annihilation. That is why schizophrenics need to project themselves "inside" objects rather than "onto" them.

Melanie Klein defined projective identification as a mechanism that allows the patient to force himself into his objects. Herbert Rosenfeld draws a distinction between normal and pathological projective identification: the former is used for communication, the second for controlling, attacking, or taking possession of the object—I would say for spatializing inside the other person. Projective identification is one of the forms of spatialization that consists in transcending the frontiers of the body, projecting oneself from one "territory" to another—or, in the case of hypochondriasis and conversion hysteria, from thought to a part of the body.

Another form of spatialization, which I call expansion, consists in the tendency to occupy surrounding space without losing contact with the starting-point (hence the difference with projective identification); in other words, the frontiers of the body expand. One example would be the patient who believes he is a hippopotamus, becoming constantly bigger and fatter until he occupies all the space around him (global expansion). This is megalomania of the body, a kind of omnipotent hugeness which envelopes the whole world.[3]

It is important to evaluate the qualitative and quantitative aspects of projective identification—sometimes quantitatively massive and dispersed, at others qualitatively omnipotent and invincible; occasionally, both aspects are simultaneously present (e.g. in the schizophrenic's unconscious fantasy of the end of the world).

Introjection may be experienced as the converse of projective identification. Where speech is used not as a symbolic element of communication but as a device for occupying space, the message becomes reified and thinking impoverished. In mental deterioration, the thinking apparatus becomes an instrument for "evacuating" conflict instead of an instrument of communication (one of the fundamental ideological elements of this attitude is using other people as things—receptacles for everything that begins to spill over). When the psychotic externalizes the contents of his mental life, all that remains is empty space. When this void becomes charged with anxiety and engenders in the patient a fear of being engulfed, it too is projected into the external world. The inner void is thus externalized like a glove turned inside-out, and so reality itself is turned into an empty outer-ness: the whole world has become a void. This entails a negativistic and nihilistic attitude with respect to the environment.

Questions of space remind me of Mr F, whom I mentioned in the previous chapter. The reader may recall that he used to say: "I have a hole in my head, and I have the impression that my 'space' comes and goes through that hole." The ability to think implies awareness of an internal space in which mental processes can develop. Awareness of our body-space is a fundamental part of mental processes. In his poem *Proprioception*, Charles Olson (1965)

---

[3] In chapter two, where I discuss Cotard's syndrome, I refer to Séglas and the delusion of enormity. The patient who becomes constantly bigger and fatter is immortal (time) and huge and limitless (space).

speaks of the cavity of the body, the space into which organs are thrown as if the body were a dumping-ground for whatever is tossed into it rather than a lively and coherent space. The ontological experience of being thrown into the world is here expressed conversely: a world of organs is thrown inside the body.

The following example illustrates another form of spatialization. A young schizophrenic artist said that he had submitted a painting for his teacher's appraisal; the theme was a piece of wood. The teacher looked at it and commented: "That's not a painting. It's as though you had really put a piece of wood onto the canvas." The patient called this phenomenon "transportation".[4] This was no symbolic process, but the actual conveyance of something from one place to the other.[5] From a technical point of view, this is an important concept—as it is for psychoanalytic theory. I remember a female patient who, during her psychotic crisis, kept running a thread through the holes in a button. The meaning of this seemed abundantly clear as to its sexual implications, yet when I made an interpretation along these lines, the patient made no apparent reaction. When I looked at her face, I noticed she was tense and blushing as though she were having an orgasm. In other words, what appeared to be a representation was experienced by her in a very concrete manner: she was not symbolizing coitus, she was experiencing it as an actual fact. Her imagination was reified, eroticized, and transformed into action. Imagining and thinking constitute a network of internal object relations, an intra-psychic grammar that is more or less coherent, depending on the unconscious models of external reality (primal scene, etc.). Internal reality, intra-communication, and intercommunication are manifestations of a dialectic process, with each element being the corollary of the other.

Melanie Klein argues that all contact is based on the ability to differentiate between internal and external reality. However, when we think about it, relationships with others and with oneself are a potentially painful experience, since every differentiation implies separation. The infant's ability to face up to separation

---

[4] The term meant both translation—movement in space without transformation—and transposition: the object ended up being part of the painting.

[5] This is related to concrete thinking, and Hanna Segal's *symbolic equation* (Segal, 1957).

from mother is the starting-point for what Klein calls the depressive position. Before this phase, the object relation with the mother is split; satisfying experiences are equivalent to the "good breast", and frustrating persecutory ones are the "bad breast", the two forming the schizo-paranoid position. A similar splitting takes place with space and time.

In the depressive position, both relationships come together, so that the "good" and "bad" breasts are recognized as two aspects of a single whole object. The infant has to acquire the ability to work through contradictory feelings, with an intermediate phase of ambivalence, before reaching whole-object relations. Separating means leaving, losing, going from one stage to another, abandoning one reality for another, accepting contiguity (space) and succession (time); it means also tolerating gaps and interruptions in order to achieve a constructive spatio-temporal conceptualization of reality. Psychotics cannot tolerate discontinuity, experienced as separation; they resist the passing of time and differentiation in space. They therefore try to suppress separation and their unbearable fear of open spaces (basic agoraphobia) by spatializing themselves inside the other person's body—but when they do so, they lose their own identity and their personal experience of time.

In one of my group psychotherapy sessions (the group was composed entirely of chronic psychotics), a patient reported that recently he had gone out with a young lady; this was something new for him, because up to that point he had found it difficult to talk to women. This is what he said: "I took her hand and kissed it. Then I felt myself becoming very anxious. I was afraid my kiss had made her pregnant." In analysing this patient, I realized that, for him, the kiss was a way of occupying the other person's space and getting inside the young woman like a baby. Sitting opposite him in the group was another patient, also schizophrenic; this man said arrogantly: "Why go out with girls and have problems? I don't have to go out with real girls, and so I don't have all the worries that go with it. I can feel everything sitting in my armchair; I've no need even to move." He continued: "One day, I dreamt I was meeting a 'marvellous spirit': it was a spirit-woman, a woman without a body. I had an extraordinary affair with her. I'm sure I could always find her again in my dreams, forever and ever."

These two patients were expressing different conceptions of the world. The former was trying to make contact with a reality object, the young woman, but he failed in his attempt because of his psychotic model of object relations. He negated the object as such, negated distance and discontinuity, and forced his way inside. He was a stowaway inside her, becoming like a foetus thanks to the magic cathexis and omnipotent penetrating capacity of his kiss. For the second patient, the only valid reality was what he called his "dream"; it is a reality that eradicates all problems of distance between him and the desired object. The spirit-woman free of all physical constraints represented the infinite liberty, omnipotence, and magic of his own thinking—from his own armchair, he had the power to impregnate the whole universe.

However, the same patient reported another dream in which he admitted his need to "descend" to other people's reality: "There was a very tall building, a skyscraper, and I was on the roof, hanging by a rope which went all the way down to the street below. I was looking down with a mixture of fear and curiosity. I wanted both to enter the building and to go down in order to make contact with the world below. In the end, I decided to go down. When I reached the bottom, I found myself in a supermarket and I wanted to buy a few items; it was a self-service." The building was the containing mother, the body-dwelling in which he lived. Contrary to his previous attitude, in which his dream-body contained the whole universe, he became aware—with a certain degree of apprehension—of another reality. There was an "up on top", an idealized infantile situation, "heaven", the roof of the building, the breast from which he was hanging; and there was also a "down below", an adult situation, the both-feet-on-the-ground reality to which he had to descend. But once on the ground, he no longer had the breast; he still had to eat, yet there was no one to provide him with food. In the supermarket, there was no mother to serve him, he had to do it all by himself (self-service)—that is, he had to grow up and go about his business like an adult.

When I had my first interview with this patient, prior to beginning therapy, he told me that he wanted to be cured of a "building" problem. "I live in a very tall building," he said, pointing to his body, "and when I have problems, I store them away in a bedroom and lock the door. But when the room is full, I have to use another one. Now there's so little space left, just a maid's room I can hardly move around in, I can hardly breathe when I'm in it. I don't have enough room, I can't go on like this, it's suffocating me." His body was a building in which he compartmentalized his problems. The things he put inside began gradually to invade his living space, as in Ionesco's *Amédée*—the corpse (persecutory death) invades space and annihilates time. Indeed, my patient used to say: "I'm a living corpse."

Body language is very important for understanding speech. Thoughts that are split off and projected into the body become part of the semantics of the *soma*. Painful experiences (paranoid and depressive) in thought are "thrown into" the body, and are revealed in movements (gestures, attitudes) or somatic conversions.

As I mentioned earlier, vocalization in the pre-linguistic period is connected to the body just like any other gesture: vocal sounds are felt to belong inside the frontiers of the body. In order to become symbolic messages, they have to accept separation from the original object and cross over the intervening space. Speaking is a way of letting oneself move *towards* other people; it requires recognition of space as the medium through which relationships with others become possible. Going out into the world means running the risk of failure and falling down in space—a replica of the existential anxiety of falling into the world [*Fallen in der Welt*]. When an infant is learning to walk, he "falls down" several times before he is able to move around correctly; he has to overcome the anxiety of falling and being cut off in order to walk on his own two feet. He has also to face up to the anxiety of "going forth" in sound—leaving his mouth-cavity for the unknown, and so separating from his body-mother. Speaking is an adventure in space, equivalent to learning to walk with symbols. It involves classifying space into internal and external.

In internal space, mental thought has to travel in order to become explicit and be transformed into verbal thought. The trajectory implies distance and therefore separation. As the *logos* moves around in the mind, it passes through many levels: *legere*, gather together and reunite; *ratio*, rationalize, conceptualize; *legein*, say, talk, discursive act. There is, in other words, an inner language whose origin lies in the way the object is perceived; the mind transforms presentation into re-presentation, object into image, image into thought. *Legere* enables thoughts to evolve and become concepts. "Thinking," wrote Valéry, "is an immediate activity mingled with all sorts of internal discourse, precarious glimmers and beginnings which will know no future. But there are also such abundant and fascinating potentialities that they embrace man even more than they bring him closer to his end."

One patient said to me: "Sometimes in my head I have things which look like thoughts, but I can't translate them into words. Occasionally, it's an impression or an idea put into my thinking, or behind my thinking, or even further away than that. Sometimes I can't get them to speak up. They're fleeting images which come and go in a flash. I don't feel I'm the author of these impressions, it's as though I had no personal imagination. I'd like to invent things then set them free in order to express myself. But in order to speak, you need to be able to speak to yourself."

"The capacity to communicate with oneself by using symbols is, I think, the basis of verbal thinking," writes Hanna Segal (1957). She continues: "Not all internal communication is verbal thinking" (in the case of the patient I have just mentioned, there were what he called "flashes"), "but all verbal thinking is an internal communication by means of symbols—words." We could say also that someone who communicates with himself is in contact with representations of his unconscious fantasies. People who have good communication with themselves are constantly forming symbols. The difficulty with schizophrenic and schizoid patients derives from the fact that they cannot communicate with themselves. Freud, Jones, and Klein all agreed that symbolization is one way of resolving conflict by communicating with the environment as personified by the superego. To call objects in the outside world by their conventional names implies coming to a compromise with society. In the depressive position, argues Segal, symbols are formed not only from whole-objects destroyed and re-created, but also from part-objects split off from the self. In Greek, *symbol* means to put together; its function is to integrate inside with outside, connecting together elements of different mental processes and enabling us to enter into relationships with other people in time and space. Kostas Axelos (1962) writes: "The *logos* forces man to leave his own world, the world of dreams, and throws him out into a world of light." He goes on: "The *logos* is a link which enables intercourse with the world. A link which, as it matures, is directed towards knowledge."

Speech may be meaningful even though it is not a vehicle for communication: the key lies in the intentionality. For instance, it is often observed that neurotic patients show a change in attitude shortly before a holiday break: they become more anxious, and they try to transmit their anxiety, to the analyst so as to create guilt feelings in him and thereby prevent his "abandoning" them. With psychotics the situation is much more concrete. They try to "impregnate" the analyst with their anxiety, and hence "take up residence" inside the analyst's body, with the aim of forcing the analyst to carry them with him on holiday. The intention behind this projective identification is not communication but manipulation of the other person. The objective is to transform the analyst into a cradle for carrying the patient-infant with him. Thanks to this psychotic mechanism, the omnipotent infantile part becomes master of the situation.

The patient may use other means to take possession of the analyst—for example, through erotic transference. Herbert Rosenfeld (1967) describes the psychotic patient's tendency to eroticize the transference in order to obstruct communication. Eroticization covers all manner of relationships with other people (language, emotional relationships, learning, etc.); no distinction is drawn between sexual and non-sexual, and there is no sublimation. The infant who over-eroticizes his relationship with the breast will have difficulty feeding, because food becomes erotically cathected, and this interferes with the normal development of incorporation–introjection—hence the fact that some children have trouble digesting. Rosenfeld adds that some of the analyst's interpretations may stimulate erotic transference and make the situation very hard to manage. If the erotic transference is interpreted at the outset on the oedipal level, the patient goes into a state of confusion and hallucination, and often he shows signs of negativism; it then becomes difficult to continue the treatment. Since the patient is unable to differentiate between fantasy and reality, the analyst's interpretation may be experienced as an invitation to or even concretely as sexual intercourse. In her discussion of the symbolic equation, Hanna Segal (1957) points out that if the analyst interprets the material of a schizophrenic patient by saying that he has a fear of castration, he may experience that as a real castration. Similarly, if you say to a schizophrenic woman patient that she finds you attractive, she may take that as an invitation to act. She may also, on the paranoid level, take the interpretation (the analyst's words) as a penetration or other sexually violent act. If the analyst is unable to respond adequately, the eroticization of the transference may trigger an acute crisis and create a situation extremely difficult to resolve.

In order to control the erotic transference, interpretations should apply to formal aspects—that is, in terms of ego mechanisms such as splitting and projective identification—rather than to content, precisely because of the obstacles to symbolization. That is to say, the patient ignores the symbol as such and transforms speech into action. Contrary to the widely held idea that the psychotic is utterly detached from reality, everything is in fact *too* real. I discussed this question privately with Enrique Pichon-Rivière, and we came to the conclusion that the analyst should use figurative, formal, and dramatic language in order to get operationally closer to the patient's world. At a seminar in the British Institute of Psycho-Analysis in 1959, Melanie Klein and Herbert Rosenfeld argued that when ego splitting and projection are intense (massive projective identification), the self tends to *fuse* with its objects. This fusion–confusion implies also a lack of differentiation between the original object and its symbolic representation: what ought to be a symbol becomes a concrete object, inappropriate for communication. Speech becomes a technique for invading, occupying, and manipulating reality. Erotic transference is not merely the manifestation of unconscious fantasies, it is an erotic *act*. The patient lives in a world of factuality.

In the erotic transference there is no true interpersonal relationship, no whole-object relation, only a part-object one: the analyst is one element of a supposedly whole part-experience. Rosenfeld explains that a situation that looks oedipal in the transference is experienced as though the "whole" analyst were simply breast or penis. The relationship to the analyst-breast tends to be highly sexualized, and this hinders the normal "nutritive" relationship. There is, too, no differentiation between nipple and penis. Instead of being a source of nourishment, the breast becomes a sexual organ. Eroticization of the nipple-penis is dramatized in the psychotic's compulsive masturbation. In his delusion, the patient believes that the nipple belongs to him, that he can seduce it, excite it, and extract from it all the milk he needs. In homosexual patients, masturbation may be accompanied by delusional ideas or hallucinations tending to prove that they have beautiful breasts—and consequently that they are the object of everyone's admiration.

In her analytic sessions, one of my female schizophrenic patients became aroused as soon as she lay down on the couch; she dramatized her excitement visually, calling it "sexual looking". She could see vaginas everywhere—in the fireplace for instance, or in an abstract painting hanging on the wall. She identified me with a vagina. What she called sexual looking was her way of getting into my vagina-body through looking; she could spatialize into any containing object whatsoever. She did, however, from time to time feel imprisoned and claustrophobic once she was inside. The situation was a complex one. At the beginning of the session, even before lying down, she engulfed me with her eyes and introjected me through her mouth-eyes. The analyst-vagina captured by her looking was then projected in a hallucinatory way onto everything that surrounded her. I became the principal receptacle for her projections, a desired and exciting aperture, the vagina as part-object. As soon as she became able to see me as a whole object, a person, she began to feel guilty about her "delusional sexuality". She realized she had degraded the source-object, the breast, by eroticizing and transforming it; like all narcissistic patients, she used contempt to avoid acknowledging how important her desired object was and how vital was her relationship with the source of nourishment. Failure to acknowledge the source-object and denigrating it are ways of masking admiration for the breast; the patient's envy denies any such appreciation.

In the analytic situation, contempt in the service of envy can be expressed in a variety of ways. One of these, as we have seen, consists in eroticizing communication. Another patient, David, a young painter, used a similar technique. Whenever I said something during the session, he would become exhilarated and say: "That's exciting!" Later he added: "My penis is excited," and, a few moments afterwards, "I have indigestion." I pointed out to him that the sexualization of my words-nourishment was giving him a pain in the stomach; sexualized food, said Melanie Klein, is the starting-point for psychosomatic disorders.

David also defended himself against envy by means of arrogance and role reversal. He would ignore my interpretations and talk to me arrogantly, as if I were his pupil or his patient. Occasionally he would be King David, and I would be his son Solomon; he claimed that I should show deference towards him, because sons should respect their fathers.

Envy negates all distance between the admired object and the admiring subject. The latter takes possession of the source-object by means of projective identification and may even drape himself in its clothes to such a degree that he becomes almost convinced that he *is* the object (delusion), the source of all food in the universe, and that the whole world is dependent on him. He may even have the impression that other people envy *him* (his own envy is fragmented and projected), or, conversely, that they idolize him and turn him into a mystical charismatic figure, the source of all truth. All this is typical of delusional self-centred thinking. Egocentrism is related to narcissism and represents one of the most powerful forces of resistance that the psychotic opposes to psychoanalysis.

In one session, David said to me: "I feel like a mutilated baby, and my thinking also feels mutilated, like after a lobotomy. I remember a girl in the hospital who used to dance like a sexy baby and attracted everybody's attention. I am a good boy, a patient who consents to his treatment . . ." I answered that this eroticizing baby was Davia[6] (Davia represents his seductive feminine part), who was present in the session with us; she was trying to arouse desire in me through her dancing. David was using a scene of sexual seduction in order to assert his power and cause me to lose my attitude as analyst. However, he did want to become "a good boy and a good patient".

He replied: "I'd like to impress my parents by showing them I'm a beatnik who has a lot of success with women, a famous avant-garde artist."

---

[6] Davia was a character of his own creation, about whom he often talked in his sessions.

I replied that in fact it was the daddy-mummy-analyst he was so keen to impress; I was the one he wanted to captivate.

"I would like to be a famous author," he went on, "so that my father[7] would fall magically in love with me." He fell silent. Then: "I'm hungry."

I commented: "When you become omnipotent and everyone falls magically in love with you, the child inside you feels abandoned and can no longer be fed by mummy-analyst." He had begun to make sucking movements, and I went on: "While Davia is dancing, your mouth is hungry." While the seductive part (Davia, the beatnik, the writer) was trying to conquer the source-object and possess it in order to become the source itself (so that it could feed itself), the infantile part needs the analyst and acknowledges the distance separating it from the source-object.

"Yes," said David when I gave him this interpretation, but I had the feeling that he really meant "No"; he was moving away from me and beginning to disperse mentally. Then he seemed to concentrate again, as though he were coming back towards me, and said: "I'm wasting my time, I'm elsewhere, I'm mixing everything up. It's difficult for me to know who I am. Just now I feel I'm Alexandra." (He was referring to a woman who dresses in old-fashioned clothes, combs her hair with a parting in the middle—"a split-hair girl" is his term—and refuses obstinately to change. Alexandra represented that part of himself that refused change.) "Now you've become hostile and old-fashioned like Alexandra," he said to me.

I interpreted that, in order to say "Yes", he had had to get rid of the Alexandra part that always says "No"; and if I had become hostile and old-fashioned, it meant that he had put Alexandra into me (projective identification of the patient's feminine and old-fashioned part which he forced inside my body). The David who said "Yes" was the hungry infant who accepted food. Alexandra represented the arrogant narcissistic ego who could not bear to be nourished by someone else. Yes and no may be manifested at the

---

[7] David often experienced the transference situation in relation to his father. Here, he was enticing his father by being alternately a famous writer and Davia. Occasionally he would use his father as a mother-substitute—the penis as a substitute for the nipple.

superego level[8] (the *law-of-the-father*, as Lacan, 1966, puts it) dramatized in the nipple of the mother-breast—which says "Yes" to the infant's mouth when it opens up and lets the milk flow, and says "No" when it cuts off the supply. Projection of Alexandra into me and distortion of my role are typical of the delusional transference. The delusion is characterized by the certitude that I was indeed that person;[9] during the same session, this certainty disappeared but the role remained—this time as a playful dramatization. David had already given me an example of delusional transference in one of our first sessions together when he spoke of his original crisis thus: "I was alone in my bedroom when I was surprised by my father coming in; a bit frightened, I suddenly saw him paralysed and changed into a photo."

Later, he told me how he had experienced this event: "I had the impression that my eyes were cameras."

In another session, David was blinking his eyelids—as though to take a photograph. This was his technique for introjecting me via his eyes, just as he had done with his father, by transforming my three-dimensional body into a two-dimensional image; his aim was to paralyse me and make me a prisoner of his eye. Back in his bedroom, he could then "project" my by now compliant image onto a wall (two-dimensionality) or beside him in his bed (three-dimensionality) in order to obtain an invented—or delusional—analytic session.

The entire visual-perceptual system of this patient was used, not for introjecting reality experiences, but for projecting delusional content.

Paralysis of the persecutor can be expressed also in terms of time: persecutory time. For Peter Pan, for example, time was paralysed. Time did not move on: Peter Pan knew no change, his body never altered, he never grew. To accept the passing of time, we

---

[8] For Kleinians, the superego is an internal object with, of course, a specific function.

[9] Delusional certainty begins when a distorted perception is experienced as irrefutable and indubitable—and, therefore, to some extent de-humanized. The pathological nucleus, argues Money-Kyrle (1967), is not the oedipal situation as such, but its misconception. He draws a distinction between normal unconscious distortion and pathological distortion; the latter engenders delusions.

have to accept death, we have to realize that life is limited and finite: this the infantile ego cannot accept.

Occasionally, the schizophrenic experiences time quite differently. His rhythm, like his mental processes, may accelerate. Thinking is fragmented, it penetrates different places simultaneously and is spatialized. Diachrony becomes synchrony. Anything that might represent linking is intolerable; the narcissistic ego invades and attacks it from within. "Your interpretation," said David, "seems to me to be full of holes. There are gaps in it, and it lacks continuity."

I replied that the part of himself he calls Alexandra was back inside his body, and it was angry with the link that existed between David and me; it resisted any link that might bring my words together. With its teeth, it broke up the continuity of what I was saying; and it was attacking not only the words, but also the mind in which they were created. The patient's psychotic part rejected any kind of nexus.[10] He was unable to accept linking either to external reality or to internal reality; he refused all organization of internal and external language.

Omnipotence, negation of distance, attacks on linking, negation of time, spatialization of time, disruption of rhythm (acceleration or paralysis), occupation of other people's space (territorial avidity), contempt for the source-object (envy), resistance to any kind of dependence, eroticization of thinking and communication—all these are part of the self-centred narcissistic conception of the world, typical of the psychotic part of the personality.

But there is another part of the self—opposed to the psychotic part—that is characterized by recognition of the limitations imposed by reality, toleration of distance and respect for linking, desire for recovery and growth (accepting the passing of time), acknowledgement of other people and their rights, acceptance of dependence and forbearance of envy, and capacity for admiration.

---

[10] Bion (1959) argued that attacks on linking were related to the primary Oedipus complex. The prototype link for the unconscious is the nipple–penis. I should add that there is some ambiguity in this concept of "attacks on linking" because of separation anxiety and also of the fact that it is unbearable for the psychotic to be reminded of and to think about a traumatic experience.

With omnipotence relegated to the background, this healthy part can acknowledge its own ignorance and need for learning; its playfulness and creative abilities are still intact in relationships both with other people and with the self (capacity to tolerate self-criticism with humour).

These two contradictory conceptions of the world make up the self as a whole. In psychotics, the former pattern is dominant and opposes the syntonic tendencies of the latter.

In analysis, communication between the infantile ego and the schizophrenic ego plays a major role. The syntonic part makes use of infantile models[11] and is capable of communication; it is through this part that we can more easily approach the schizophrenic aspects. The infantile ego retains the capacity to communicate through play. Schizophrenic humour calls upon this aptitude of the infantile ego in puns, for example. In schizophrenics, words become playthings—word-plays—which provide speech with structure and dramatization. It is in language combination (syntax) that the playful inventive part acquires a symbolic character, not in its habitual content.

The self's oscillation between two poles, alternating between the psychotic and the non-psychotic parts, brings instantly to mind Samuel Beckett's *Endgame*.[12] The "game" is played between Hamm and Clov, who, to my way of thinking, personify these two conceptions of the world.

As the saga unfolds within a bare interior, we find gathered together Hamm, his father and his mother, and Clov, his servant. I wonder, indeed, if I am entitled to use the word "unfolds", when in fact nothing "happens", for the dramatic content of the play does not lie in action as such.

The self-centred ego is—naturally enough—centre stage.

---

[11] A distinction should be drawn between normal and abnormal infantile egos. The former is capable of empathy, whereas the latter is still tied to omnipotence and admiration for the psychotic ego.

[12] Since the original (French) version of this book was published, I have come more and more to feel that the world of Beckett is very close to that of the schizoid personality and the delusional person. In 1997, I gave a related lecture (in Italian) on "The Memory of Silence" to a symposium organized by the Teatro Verdi in Pisa under the direction of Roberto Scarpa (Resnik, in press).

Hamm: Back to my place! [. . .] Am I right in the centre?

Clov: I'll measure it.

Hamm: [. . .] Put me right in the centre!

Covered with an old sheet, Hamm is sitting in an armchair on castors. He is blind. High up on the right and left walls there are two small windows, their curtains drawn—two eyes for looking at the outside world. Clov is Hamm's servant. Hamm had adopted him as a child, and Clov has remained dependent on him ever since. Hamm cannot see or move, but he can speak and give orders and he has remained omnipotent in his mind.

"What's the weather like?" asks Hamm, "Look at the earth."

"I've looked," replies Clov.

Hamm: And the horizon? Nothing on the horizon?

Clov: What in God's name could there be on the horizon?

Hamm: And the sun?

Clov: Zero.

In the foreground, two dustbins are standing side by side. Hamm's mother and father have been thrown into them. They are treated like children and are prisoners of their container. They are very dependent on Hamm and ask him for affection and food; their requests are only parsimoniously satisfied. Hamm is as hard as the plain biscuits he gives them. Clov, the infantile ego, wants to separate from Hamm and escape from this unbearable situation.

"Finished," says Clov. "It's finished, nearly finished, it must be nearly finished." But Hamm represents omnipotence for Clov, the omnipotence which up till then has always subjugated him. Little by little, drop by drop, Clov has accumulated hatred and resentment to the point where he can say: "If I could kill him, I'd die happy." Hamm realizes this: "Don't stay there [i.e. behind the chair], you give me the shivers."

Clov's main task is to stand by the window and tell Hamm what is going on outside. But one day he decides to leave and escape from this symmetrical space—"ten feet by ten feet by ten feet"—where time stands still: "What time is it?"—"The same as usual."—"Well?"—"Zero."

Then something does happen. It is due naturally enough to the fact that Clov looks out of the window—the only aperture in their closed world. He witnesses an accident, and brings his account into this nothingness, this life-in-death. "Oh dear oh dear," says Clov.

Hamm: Is it a leaf? A flower? A tomato?

Clov: A person, it's a person.

Hamm: Coming or going?

Clov: Immobile.

Hamm: Sex?

Clov: What does it matter—looks like a kid.

Hamm: What's he doing? What's he looking at?

Clov: I don't know what he's looking at . . . his navel.

Hamm: Maybe he's dead.

Clov: I'll go and see.

Hamm: It's finished, Clov, we're finished. I don't need you any more.

Clov: That's good. I'm leaving you.[13]

Clov leaves. Hamm sees him go, in spite of his blindness. He brings a large blood-stained handkerchief up to his face.

The four characters are the inhabitants (internal objects) of a skull, a body, or a mask. The drama is played out inside a closed space cut off from the living world. Even the outside world is nothingness. "Outside of here," says Hamm, "it's death." Hamm, the omnipotent ego, cannot see—he has no need to see, he knows.

Yet, at the point in the play when we first meet him, Hamm is beginning to doubt his power. He realizes he needs Clov in order to see. He is more and more aware that his power is crumbling. He is in a quandary. His omnipotence denies the curiosity he feels for the outside world. He has no need to move, but someone else

---

[13] This entire passage exists in the (original) French version of the play, *Fin de partie* (1957, pp. 103-104), but not in the English version, which was published in 1958.

has to take on the task of mediating with reality. Clov, the infantile ego, is the intermediary between Hamm and external reality.

Like Hamm, Clov is at an ambivalent stage. On the one hand there is his dependence on and admiration for Hamm, and on the other his attempt to dis-illusion himself, his need for contact with another kind of reality, and his desire to go forward into open space. Realizing that he is a prisoner, he begins to hate his master, the admired object that for so long had been the centre of his world.

Clov has no parents; Hamm is everything to him. The infantile ego is unable to make contact with the parents. Hamm, the narcissistic ego, has dealings with them; he is the intermediary between them and the infantile ego. Hamm cannot tolerate normal dependence on the parents, and he does not put great store by these primary objects—indeed he is contemptuous of them and introjects them without love or warmth. He takes little care of them, abandoning them, prisoners in their dustbins, to a slow death. His whole attitude is aimed at reinforcing his power and avoiding all acknowledgement of dependence: to acknowledge dependence would be a terrible narcissistic wound. His arrogance negates and masks his capacity for appreciation. For Hamm, admiration is tinged with envy; he refuses the very thought that he might not be envied by everybody else. His throne is tottering, his empire crumbling and falling to pieces; his blood-stained handkerchief is the sign of a crime of which he is also the victim.

When Clov says, "If I could kill him, I'd die happy", he ties the death of the Other (Hamm, in this instance) to his own. His hatred is stronger than his desire to live. This is the hatred of the servant for the omnipotent master, the one who comes between him and his parents, between external reality and himself; but it is also resentment against the fallen idol, against dis-illusion.

Hamm knows that another reality exists, but that it is out of his reach. So he tries to invent his own reality, to eliminate the frontier between him and Clov, to negate the latter's identity and any kind of other-ness.

He is convinced that Clov's fate will be his own. He sees himself in Clov as in a mirror. "One day you'll be blind, like me. You'll be sitting there, a speck in the void, in the dark, for ever, like me.

One day you'll say to yourself, I'm tired, I'll sit down, and you'll go and sit down. Then you'll say, I'm hungry, I'll get up and get something to eat. But you won't get up and you won't get anything to eat. [. . .] You'll look at the wall a while, then you'll say, I'll close my eyes, perhaps have a little sleep, after that I'll feel better, and you'll close them. And when you open them again there'll be no wall any more. Infinite emptiness will be all around you. [. . .] Yes, one day you'll know what it is, you'll be like me . . ."

His prophecy is full of sadness, and he pronounces it without conviction. His weariness is both the sadness of his body and the physical manifestation of his mental omnipotence: immobility expresses his incapacity to seek out food or any other object he needs. In denying separation in space, it negates the bridge, the paradoxical proof of discontinuity.

Everyday reality, with its wakefulness and open eyes, negates his power. He has to close his eyes and dream of a reality in order to find the frontiers of his kingdom again. When he wakes up, he loses them, the walls no longer exist. There is no identity any more, death is the only king. His body dissolves into infinity or becomes infinitesimal—"a little bit of grit in the middle of the steppe".

Hamm's inner emptiness is projected into the outside world and ends up invading all space. Clov tries to perceive an accident in this desert. The accident ends the play, with the arrival of a child sitting looking at his navel: the child is the sign of separation, the seal of deliverance. The infant is looking at the spot where the umbilical cord is cut, the wound, the mark of emancipation from Hamm and Hamm's existence inside Clov. Liberation is painful, recovery is agony. In schizophrenics, this divorce is difficult to withstand; it is experienced as mutilation—the psychotic and nonpsychotic parts have lived together for so long. They were united within the space of a single body and in the same time; being apart implies a new outlook on the world, transformation of the inner world, and a new system of values.

Growth means giving up a world invested with all that is prolific: all the good qualities of the ego (intelligence, imagination, etc.) were attributed to the ill part. As one of my patients put it: "Getting better isn't worth it, it's not worth losing my creativity and becoming ordinary like everybody else; if I open my eyes, I'll see I'm lost in the crowd."

Growth and good health imply death and rebirth. In *Endgame*, Clov breaks free of a closed symmetrical world in order to be reborn. He abandons Hamm who, to the very end, refuses to acknowledge his decline: clinging desperately to his arrogance, he embraces death in one last defiant gesture, the emphatic supremacy of his universe.

Postscriptum

A ll that I have learned during these last years[1] has led me to think again about those ideas and concepts that seem to "go without saying" in analytic circles, those that perhaps have not been critically investigated until now.

As I mentioned in the introduction, I was particularly eager to entitle this book *The Delusional Person*. The reason is implicit in the first chapter, "Personalization", based on Winnicott's ontological message according to which the patient should always be seen as a person and not as a conglomerate of "objects" and ego mechanisms. The other reason is the one I mentioned in my introductory "self-reflections" concerning Luisa Alvarez de Toledo's dictum about analysis taking place "from person to person". I should perhaps have indicated that my papers on personalization and Cotard's syndrome were read in 1958 in Ronald Laing's house while he was himself correcting the proofs of *The Divided Self*; we used to meet almost every week as friends in my first years in

---

[1] I refer in particular to the eleven years I spent in London with the Kleinian school.

London. He was very encouraging towards me and my work, and I have a very good and stimulating memory of him. I met Laing through Dr J. Sutherland of the Tavistock Clinic, after he heard that I was interested not only in groups but also in phenomenology. In fact, Laing was eager to learn about Merleau-Ponty's lectures that I attended at the Collège de France. In our meetings, I presented several papers, including one in which I discussed my concept of "implosion". Like Laing, I was always concerned with the psychotic as a person.

Donald Winnicott also was very encouraging towards me and my first papers. As to my "person-to-person" relationship in the transference with Herbert Rosenfeld, I remember in particular that he used to call me a "non-conformist analyst". At first, I took this as criticism, then I realized that he appreciated the fact that I could not accept being or doing what I didn't feel was "right" for me. I came to understand that my "mask"—or perhaps my own "self"— was stronger than "I" was, and that I just could not betray my true feelings and way of being. Later still, through my experience as a teacher, I was more able to appreciate how my students at university and future analysts in analysis with me could benefit from respecting their own "mask" and style of being and working.

I did not create a Kleinian school in France or in Italy, for that was not my aim, but people said to me that I did help them to discover their own true being, style of working, and "school" of thought. I believe that we should attend "good" schools, but also that we should at some point be able to be *ourselves*—without, however, forgetting what we have been taught. Some of my great teachers, such as Pichon-Rivière and Bion, helped me develop my own ideas rather than simply be their pupils.

Language, thinking, and personal identity are inseparable. The psychoanalyst cannot approach the patient's world unless and until he can grasp something of the language used in that world. He must take account of the semantic data expressed in each encounter. Not only words, but sounds, noises, gestures, silences, a particular atmosphere—all these become (for patient and analyst) instruments for forging the specific discourse within the analytic field. The sign-word can be remarkably transparent in "as-signing" meaning, or as part of a significant system. Words do not exist in isolation, and it is impossible to understand sign-words or sign-gestures without taking into account the extent of their potential connotations. Each item of information is part of a structural complex that obeys clearly defined rules.

In psychotics—or, as I prefer to say, in the psychotic part of each patient as a person—structural guidelines (verbal and non-verbal) are more idiosyncratic. The psychotic does not share the ordinary conventions of language or an everyday conception of the world. Any neologism he may invent can be a condensation of several meanings (polysemic neologism), or refer to a particular aspect of his situation or his internal world (specific neologism). The patient's invented world may be revealed through his strange or bizarre behaviour (neologism in action); this is often the case at the onset of a schizophrenic crisis, when the first changes in perception of reality (delusional distortions) take place. The objects in the world exist only insofar as they are related to the patient (the self-centred conception of the world). The patient's intentions are projected onto people, objects, and landscapes and transform their nature and meaning: pathological projective identification is at the root of delusions of reference. This referential world is part of the patient's personal cosmology.

I believe, as Freud did, that there is an intrinsic connection between dreaming and psychosis. Those who have lived in a psychotic world will often say that it was almost as though they were asleep. In such cases, as in dreams, hallucinating is something "familiar". Not long ago, a patient suffering from schizophrenia explained—or rather communicated—to me how he felt as if he was going mad: "It was as though my dreams were coming out of the front of my head, out of my eyes; my dreams were out there in front of me." As his condition improved, I asked him what he felt about his dream-world. "Is there any logic to it?" I enquired. "There's a sort of intimate, private logic, in which emotions are like dreams without being exactly the same thing." He told me that residual aspects of his dreams were mixed into his daily life; this reminded me, of course, of Freud's concept of the "day's residues" [*Tagesreste*] as building-blocks of every dream.

In working with psychotics, the analyst sometimes loses his formal role and personal identity; he becomes one of the *dramatis personae* of the patient's internal world, playing the part that the patient attributes to him. Projective identification, whether quantitatively massive when it fragments or qualitatively omnipotent when it concentrates on one object—or, occasionally, both—never respects the character of the object as such. This continues until the patient is able to wake up from his delusion or dream-world and discover other people as individuals. Thereupon, the analyst too can recover his identity and his role as analyst. Generally speaking—and this is very much the case with schizophrenics—discourse is not simply an expressive sequence rhythmed by the passing of time, it is also a spatial structure of being, specific to the patient's *Weltanschauung*.

"Recovery" from the delusional world is often experienced by the psychotic's narcissistic ego as a *"deflation"* of his egocentric conception. I have developed the concept of "narcissistic depression", a state in which the patient experiences coming back to "normal life" as a sacrifice, a painful process of mourning for the lost psychotic illusions. Those illusions have to do with the ego ideal. Although in the patient's past history there is an ideal ego, an object, loss is experienced as a "hole" in the ego itself. The patient feels that he is losing "capital", made up of normal and delusional illusions, expectations, and hopes. The subsequent disillusion can be catastrophic, and confrontation with internal and external reality (reality principle) may plunge the narcissistic ego into chaos: the world of ordinary reality, which until then the patient had denigrated or negated, is restored—but there is a price to pay. In every analysis, neurotic or psychotic, to become oneself means to become aware of who one is and who one is not—one's true or false self (Winnicott). In the case of psychosis, fragments of "archaeological" value, normal aspects of the self, coexist with pathological remnants, distortions of reality that refuse to die off. Narcissistic depression has therefore to do with a painful mourning process and the new "balance sheet" that has to be drawn up: what is true, what is false, what is valuable, what is worthless, and so forth. The process of reparation has to do with suffering and pain. Suffering implies a capacity for supporting [*sub-ferre*] pain; it is not the same thing as pain itself. In pain [*poenire*], there is the idea of torment, as well as that of guilt. Psychotic patients are very fragile—they do not have any "support" for pain, hence their need to deny it through anaesthetic manoeuvres such as freezing (see

Resnik, 1999) or transforming themselves into inanimate or petrified beings.

The patient has to be helped to discover the meaning of this fragmented and frozen world. He also needs to know the significance of the different parts projected into that mixed-up world. Ego-restructuring is a difficult and complex task, for the patient has to abandon the rules and regulations that were part of a personal "culture" and logic.

One of the analyst's difficult tasks is to encourage patients in their endeavours to confront internal and external reality and to harmonize their own idiosyncratic language with that of conventional usage—as Bion (1962) said, "the problem is the resolution of conflict between narcissism and socialism". The inner dialogue that replaces splitting is experienced at first as painful and distressing. Successful negotiation of the depressive position—global perception of the split-off parts—is strengthened by intra-psychic and interpersonal dialogue (in the transference) between illusion and disillusion, both normal and pathological.

The individual again becomes a person in his own right and acknowledges other people as person-objects. The relationship between "I" and the world implies abandoning the narcissistic object relation; this encourages opening-up to the outside world and to various areas of the internal world which had been detached from the ego.[2]

The analytic situation implies that the roles of patient and analyst be clearly defined. It demands also an agreed or functional dependence. The narcissistic ego resists this: patients refuse to acknowledge that they are dependent on the source-object of which they have so much need—and as a result they refuse to recognize the identity of the desired object. They feel our help to be wounding, as though we were belittling the idealized image they have of

---

[2]Chronic psychosis is marked by dis-union and disjunctive mutilation of the ego, which is fragmented and dispersed throughout surrounding space (hospital, family, etc.). This entails atrophy and impoverishment of the self. The psychiatric institution has to take in all these ego fragments; but if it merely reacts like a "passive" recipient, the patient will adjust to this and become "institutionalized".

themselves. The narcissistic ego clashes with the infantile ego, which needs nourishment and help and wants to grow; the narcissistic ego rejects true dependence. Yet if the analysis is to work, patients will at some juncture have to accept functional dependence in the relationship and acknowledge that they are not self-sufficient. The narcissistic personality will not admit its admiration for the source-object; it is capable only of resentment and envy. Analysis is to some extent a narcissistic wound for every patient, because it reveals that he needs help—nobody can be mouth and breast simultaneously.

In the narcissistic relationship, as Herbert Rosenfeld pointed out, the frontier between ego and internalized object is lost; the ego believes that the object was always part of itself (false primary narcissism). "Envy has no memory"; the patient forgets the identity of the source-object as being distinct from his own. In the transference we can witness a dramatization of this type of experience when patients tell the analyst that they already know what the latter has just said. This is equivalent to saying that the analyst has nothing of value to offer. Patients steal what is offered "like a thief in the night", and they go on to deny all knowledge of the theft. They believe that it had always been their property: whatever the narcissistic ego captures loses its original identity. Constant repetition of this results in a negative therapeutic reaction. If the idea is imparted to the patient that he is the one who is self-analysing, this may confirm the feeling that there is no need to be dependent on the analyst. If the analyst falls into the trap of not making any comment or interpretation, all he will do is reinforce the patient's narcissism.

The analytic setting enables us to study the encounter between a genetic or diachronic perspective and an actual or synchronic one. For Merleau-Ponty, both perspectives are contiguous in language. The present envelops the past, and the past is always a "past present". Meaning brings life to speech just as the experience of time breathes life into the space of the body. Each individual has his own way of dramatizing his or her personal history in the *hic et nunc* of the transference. A patient's frame of mind is reflected in the patterns of object relations that is reactivated in the transference.

For the patient, the relationship with the analyst is a situation that opens onto both past and present. It is the field in which two forces are deployed, transference and countertransference, playing constantly on two levels: between patient and analyst, and from person to person. Even though these two levels come close together at times, for operational reasons a distinction between the formal and informal roles of each participant is necessary. Transference and countertransference are the expression of a "normal" conflict within the analytic setting. The relationship between patient and analyst is, as it were, an encounter between two different worlds (another form of the "two cultures"). There is therefore an ethical issue: how are we to approach the other person's world without invading it, without "contaminating" it with our own system of values? Analysing someone demands respect for difference and acceptance of other-ness; it is an attempt to help the other person, or at least to awaken within that other person the capacity to be helped. Dependence is inevitable between patient and analyst. Each needs the other in order to construct the analytic laboratory and to share out the work. The relationship begins with a "contract of employment" in which certain rules are stipulated— they may be modified later, in a more restrictive or a more flexible way (every exchange has its own rules; in analysis, to a considerable extent they evolve as the therapy progresses).

The analytic work is a linguistic and ontological investigation, and each of these factors is intimately bound up with the other: it is through the medium of language that we try to make contact with the most fundamental aspects of other human beings. Patients are *not* a collection of signs or symptoms; they are *persons*, in conflict with *their* world and with *the* world at large. Each of us has his or her *Weltanschauung*. It must not be forgotten that delusions and hallucinations are *also* attempts at making the universe meaningful.

How we conceive of the world is related to imagination, perception, and representation. Traditionally, "imaginary" phenomena were considered to be in opposition to "real" phenomena; imagination was a function of consciousness. But images are not a mere reflection of reality; they are a way of "seeing" it. The mental representation of a perceived object is the product of a complex

process of transposition in unconscious fantasy and transformation in time.[3] The image is a step towards symbolization. (Objects
in the external world can be vividly represented in the unconscious.)

Beyond the language of psychoanalysis, there is that of the
patient, in the way that he is able to experience it and formulate it.
The work of analysis enables the analyst to undertake a linguistic
investigation into the patient's internal world. A semiology of the
imaginary in its widest sense is required in order to reach some
understanding of a personal world. For some psychotics, what
goes on in thought is just as concrete as what happens in their
stomach or some other part of the body. The body itself may be
experienced as something abstract, unreal, almost non-existent—
and may even be denied altogether.

In psychotics, endopsychic language may become immobilized
and robotic ("catatonic thinking"). Time is paralysed, then spatialized. Nothing can happen, all experience is petrified.

I have continued to develop over the years some of the views
that were still in gestation in this book. I hope that I will shortly be
able to present at least some of them to my readers.

---

[3] It "takes time" to move through space. During this time, the object perceived is transformed into an image.

REFERENCES

Abraham, K. (1908). The psycho-sexual differences between hysteria and dementia praecox. In: *Selected Papers on Psycho-Analysis.* London: Hogarth Press, 1954.

Abraham, K. (1911). Notes on the psycho-analytical investigation and treatment of manic-depressive insanity and allied conditions. In: *Selected Papers on Psycho-Analysis.* London: Hogarth Press, 1954.

Abraham, K. (1913). The ear and auditory passage as erotogenic zones. In: *Selected Papers on Psycho-Analysis.* London: Hogarth Press, 1954.

Abraham, K. (1924). A short study of the development of the libido viewed in the light of mental disorders. In: *Selected Papers on Psycho-Analysis.* London: Hogarth Press, 1954.

Alvarez de Toledo, L. G. de (1954). The analysis of "associating", "interpreting" and "words". *International Journal of Psycho-Analysis, 77* (1996): 291. [Originally published as: El analisis del "asociar", del "interpretar" y de las "palabras". *Revista Psicoanalitica Argentina, 11* (3).]

Axelos, K. (1962). *Héraclite et la Philosophie.* Paris: Editions de Minuit.

Baillarger, A. (1890). *Recherches sur les maladies mentales.* Paris: Masson.

Baranger, W., & Baranger, M. (1969). *Problemas del campo psicoanalitico.* Buenos Aires: Ediciones Kargieman.

Barbé, A. (1939). *Psychiatrie.* Paris: Masson.

231

Beckett, S. (1957). *Fin de partie*. Paris: Editions de Minuit.

Beckett, S. (1958). *Endgame*. London: Faber & Faber.

Bergson, H. (1920). *Essais sur les données immédiates de la conscience*. Paris: Alcan.

Bergson, H. (1972). *Mélanges*. Paris: Presses Universitaires de France.

Bick, E. (1968). The experience of the skin in early object-relations. *International Journal of Psycho-analysis, 49*: 484.

Bion, W. R. (1955). Language and the schizophrenic. In: M. Klein, P. Heimann, & R. Money-Kyrle (Eds.), *New Directions in Psycho-Analysis*. London: Tavistock Publications, 1955.

Bion, W. R. (1956). Development of schizophrenic thought. In: *Second Thoughts*. London: Heinemann, 1967.

Bion, W. R. (1957a). Differentiation of the psychotic from the non-psychotic personalities. In: *Second Thoughts*. London: Heinemann, 1967.

Bion, W. R. (1957b). On arrogance. In: *Second Thoughts*. London: Heinemann, 1967.

Bion, W. R. (1958). On hallucination. In: *Second Thoughts*. London: Heinemann, 1967.

Bion, W. R. (1959). Attacks on linking. In: *Second Thoughts*. London: Heinemann, 1967.

Bion, W. R. (1962). A theory of thinking. In: *Second Thoughts*. London: Heinemann, 1967.

Bleuler, E. (1950). *Dementia Praecox or the Group of Schizophrenias*, trans. J. Zinkin. New York: International Universities Press.

Burdach, K. F. (1838). *Die Physiologie als Ehrfahrungswissenschaft, Vol. 3* (2nd ed., 1832–40).

Carrington, L. (1944). Down below. In: *VVV, 4* (February).

Chaslin, Ph. (1912). *Élements de sémiologie et clinique mentales*. Paris: Asselin & Houzeau.

Cotard, J. (1882–1884). Du délire des négations: perte de la vision mentale dans la mélancolie anxieuse. In: *Études sur les maladies cérébrales et mentales*. Paris: Ballière.

Cotard, J. (1888). Délire d'énormité. In: *Études sur les maladies cérébrales et mentales*. Paris: Ballière.

Cotard, J. (1891). *Études sur les maladies cérébrales et mentales*. Paris: Ballière.

Czermak, M. (1986). Signification psychanalytique du Syndrome de Cotard. In: *Les passions de l'objet. Études psychanalytiques des psychoses*. Paris: Clims.

De Saussure, F. (1967). *Course in General Linguistics*, trans. W. Baskin. New York: The Philosophical Library.

Federn, P. (1959). Ego-psychological aspects of schizophrenia. In: *Ego Psychology and the Psychoses*. London: Imago.

Frazer, J. (1959). *The Golden Bough*. London: Macmillan.

Freud, A. (1936). *The Ego and the Mechanisms of Defence*. London: Hogarth Press, 1937. [Reprinted London: Karnac Books, 1989.]

Freud, S. (1894a). The neuro-psychoses of defence. *S.E., 3*.

Freud, S. (1900a). *The Interpretation of Dreams. S.E., 14*.

Freud, S. (1910d). The future prospects of psycho-analytic therapy. *S.E., 11*.

Freud, S. (1911c [1910]). Psycho-analytic notes on an autobiographical account of a case of paranoia (Dementia paranoides). *S.E., 12*.

Freud, S. (1912b). The dynamics of transference. *S.E., 12*.

Freud, S. (1914c). On narcissism: an introduction. *S.E.,14*.

Freud, S. (1915a). Observations on transference-love. *S.E., 12*.

Freud, S. (1915b). Thoughts for the times on war and death. *S.E., 14*.

Freud, S. (1923b). *The Ego and the Id. S.E., 19*.

Freud, S. (1923e). The infantile genital organization. *S.E., 19*.

Freud, S. (1925a [1924]). A note upon the "mystic writing-pad". *S.E., 19*.

Freud, S. (1925h). Negation. *S.E., 19*.

Freud, S. (1926d [1925]). *Inhibitions, Symptoms and Anxiety. S.E., 19*.

Freud, S. (1936a). A disturbance of memory on the Acropolis. *S.E., 19*.

Freud, S. (1937d). Constructions in analysis. *S.E., 23*.

Freud, S. (1950 [1895]). A project for a scientific psychology. *S.E., 1*.

Garma, A. (1955). Vicisitudes de la pantella del sueño y del fenómeno de Isakover. *Revista de Psicoanálisis* (Buenos Aires), *12* (4).

Garma, A. (1956). *Genesis psicosomática y tratamiento de las úlceras gàstricas y duodenales* (3rd edition). Buenos Aires: Editorial Nova.

Greenacre, P. (1953). *Affective Disorders*. New York: International Universities Press.

Grinberg, L. (1963). Psicopatologìa de la identificatión y contra-identificatión proyectivas y de la contra-transferencia. *Revista de Psicoanàlisis* (Buenos Aires), *23* (2).

Head, H. (1920). *Studies in Neurology*. London: OUP/Hodder & Stoughton.

Heidegger, M. (1927). *Sein und Zeit. Jahrbuch für Phänomenologie und phänomenologische Forschung*. [*Being and Time*, trans. J. Stambaugh. New York: State University of New York, 1997.]

Heimann, P. (1950). On countertransference. *International Journal of Psycho-Analysis, 31*.

Heimann, P. (1952). Certain functions of introjection and projection in early infancy. In: M. Klein, P. Heimann, S. Isaacs, & J. Riviere (Eds.), *Developments in Psychoanalysis*. London: Hogarth Press and the Institute of Psycho-Analysis.

Isakower, O. (1938). A contribution to the patho-psychology of phenomena associated with falling asleep. *International Journal of Psycho-Analysis, 19*: 331–345.

Jakobson, R. (1969). *Langage enfantin et aphasie*. Paris: Editions de Minuit.

James, W. (1950). The consciousness of self. In: *The Principles of Psychology, Vol. 1*. New York: Dover.

Jones, E. (1919). The theory of symbolism. *British Journal of Psychology, 9*.

Jones, E. (1925). *Traité théorique et pratique de psychanalyse*. Paris: Payot.

Jung, C. G. (1911). *Wandlungen und Symbole der Libido* [*Psychology of the Unconscious*]. Princeton, NJ: Princeton University Press, 1916.

Kahlbaum, K. L. (1874). *Die Katatonie oder das Spannungsirrensein*. Berlin: Hercker.

Kanner, L. (1935). *Child Psychiatry*. Springfield, IL: Charles C Thomas.

Kanner, L. (1943). Autistic disturbances of affective contact. *The Nervous Child, 2* (June, No. 3).

Klein, M. (1927). Criminal tendencies in normal children. In: *Love, Guilt and Reparation and Other Works 1921–1945: Writings, Vol. I*. London: Hogarth Press, 1975. [Reprinted London: Karnac Books, 1992.]

Klein, M. (1928). Early stages of the Oedipus complex. In: *Love, Guilt and Reparation and Other Works 1921–1945: Writings, Vol. I*. London: Hogarth Press, 1975. [Reprinted London: Karnac Books, 1992.]

Klein, M. (1930). The importance of symbol formation in the development of the ego. In: *Love, Guilt and Reparation and Other Works 1921–1945: Writings, Vol. I*. London: Hogarth Press, 1975. [Reprinted London: Karnac Books, 1992.]

Klein, M. (1935). A contribution to the psychogenesis of manic-depressive states. In: *Love, Guilt and Reparation and Other Works 1921–1945: Writings, Vol. I*. London: Hogarth Press, 1975. [Reprinted London: Karnac Books, 1992.]

Klein, M. (1936). Weaning. In: *Love, Guilt and Reparation and Other*

Works 1921–1945: Writings, Vol. I. London: Hogarth Press, 1975. [Reprinted London: Karnac Books, 1992.]

Klein, M. (1940). Mourning and its relation to manic-depressive states. In: *Love, Guilt and Reparation and Other Works 1921–1945: Writings, Vol. I.* London: Hogarth Press, 1975. [Reprinted London: Karnac Books, 1992.]

Klein, M. (1946). Notes on some schizoid mechanisms. In: *Envy and Gratitude and Other Works 1946–1963: Writings, Vol. III.* London: Hogarth Press, 1975. [Reprinted London: Karnac Books, 1993.]

Klein, M. (1950). Our adult world and its roots in infancy. In: *Envy and Gratitude and Other Works 1946–1963: Writings, Vol. III.* London: Hogarth Press, 1975. [Reprinted London: Karnac Books, 1993.]

Klein, M. (1955). On identification. In: *Envy and Gratitude and Other Works 1946–1963: Writings, Vol. III.* London: Hogarth Press, 1975. [Reprinted London: Karnac Books, 1993.]

Klein, M. (1957). Envy and gratitude. In: *Envy and Gratitude and Other Works 1946–1963: Writings, Vol. III.* London: Hogarth Press, 1975. [Reprinted London: Karnac Books, 1993.]

Klein, M. (1960). A note on depression in the schizophrenic. In: *Envy and Gratitude and Other Works 1946–1963: Writings, Vol. III.* London: Hogarth Press, 1975. [Reprinted London: Karnac Books, 1993.]

Klein, M. (1963). On the sense of loneliness. In: *Envy and Gratitude and Other Works 1946–1963: Writings, Vol. III.* London: Hogarth Press, 1975. [Reprinted London: Karnac Books, 1993.]

Kraepelin, E. (1907). *Introduction à la psychiatrie clinique.* Paris: Vigot.

Lacan, J. (1966). Le stade du miroir comme formateur de la fonction du Je. In: *Ecrits.* Paris: Le Seuil.

Lévy-Bruhl, L. (1928). *Les fonctions mentales dans les sociétés inférieures.* Paris: Alcan.

Lévy-Bruhl, L. (1949). *Les carnets de Lucien Lévy-Bruhl.* Paris: Presses Universitaires de France.

Lévy-Strauss, C. (1958). *Anthropologie structurale.* Paris: Plon.

Lewin, B. (1946). Sleep, the mouth and the dream screen. *Psychoanalytic Quarterly, 15*: 419–434.

Lewin, B. (1951). *The Psychoanalysis of Elation.* London: Hogarth Press.

Lewin, K. (1963). *Field Theory in Social Sciences.* London: Tavistock Publications.

Marcel, G. (1927). *Journal métaphysique.* Paris: N.R.F.

Merleau-Ponty, M. (1945). *Phénoménologie de la Perception.* Paris: Gallimard [reprinted 1952].

Merleau-Ponty, M. (1955). *La relation avec autrui chez l'enfant*. Paris: Centre de Documentation Universitaire (Sorbonne); Geneva: Delachaux & Niestlé, 1968.

Meyerson, I. (1948). *Les fonctions psychologiques et les oeuvres*. Paris: Vrin.

Minkowski, E. (1927). *La schizophrénie*. Paris: Payot.

Minkowski, E. (1968). *Le temps vécu*. Neuchâtel: Delachaux & Niestlé.

Money-Kyrle, R. E. (1956). Normal counter-transference and some of its deviations. *International Journal of Psycho-Analysis, 37*.

Money-Kyrle, R. E. (1967). On cognitive development. *Scientific Bulletin of the British Psycho-Analytical Society and the Institute of Psycho-Analysis, 18*.

Morris, D. (1966). *The Naked Ape*. London: Jonathan Cape.

Nunberg, H. (1961). On the catatonic attack. In: *Practice and Theory of Psycho-Analysis, Vol. 1*. New York: International Universities Press.

Olson, C. (1965). *Proprioception*. San Francisco, CA: Four Seasons Foundation.

Palazzoli-Selvini, M. (1963). *L'Anoressia Mentale*. Milan: Feltrinelli.

Pichon-Rivière, A. A. (1958). Dentition, walking, and speech in relation to the depressive position. *International Journal of Psycho-Analysis, 39*: 167–171.

Pichon-Rivière, E. (1952). Quelques observations sur le transfert chez des patients psychotiques. *Revue Française de Psychanalyse, 15* (January–June, Nos. 1 & 2).

Racker, H. (1959). *Estudios sobre Tècnica Psicoanalìtica*. Buenos Aires: Editorial Paidos.

Resnik, S. (1957). "Le délire de référence." Paper read at a conference held at the Sainte-Anne Psychiatric Hospital, Paris.

Resnik, S. (1963). "Early Analysis and Character Formation." Communication to the Congress of Child Psychiatry, Rome.

Resnik, S. (1986). *L'esperienza psicotica*. Turin: Editore Boringhieri.

Resnik, S. (1987). *The Theatre of the Dream*. London: Routledge.

Resnik, S. (1997a). Delusional space. In: J. L. Ahumada, J. Olagaray, & A. K. Richards (Eds.), *The Perverse Transference & Other Matters. In Honor of R. Horacio Etchegoyen*. New York: Jason Aronson.

Resnik, S. (1997b). Borderline states. In: *Psychoanalysis in Argentina: Selected Articles (1942–1997)*. Buenos Aires: Argentine Psycho-Analytical Association.

Resnik, S. (1998). Being in a persecutory world: the construction of a xorld model and its distortions. In: J. H. Berke, S. Pierides, A.

Sabbadini, & S. Schneider (Eds.), *Even Paranoids Have Enemies.* London: Routledge.

Resnik, S. (1999). *Temps des glaciations: Voyage dans le monde de la folie.* Toulouse: Érès.

Resnik, S. (in press). The memory of silence. In: R. Scarpa (Ed.), *Le parole del teatro: Samuel Beckett.* Turin: Bollati.

Rosenfeld, H. (1950). Notes on the psychopathology of confusional states in chronic schizophrenias. *International Journal of Psycho-Analysis, 31:* 132–137. Also in: *Psychotic States.* London: Hogarth Press, 1965.

Rosenfeld, H. (1952). Transference phenomena and transference analysis in an acute schizophrenic patient. *International Journal of Psycho-Analysis, 33* (4). Also in: *Psychotic States.* London: Hogarth Press, 1965.

Rosenfeld, H. (1958). Some observations on the psychopathology of hypochondriacal states. *International Journal of Psycho-Analysis, 39* (Parts 2–4).

Rosenfeld, H. (1967). "Problems Occurring in the Psycho-analytical Treatment of Schizophrenic Patients." Paper read at a conference held at the MacLean Hospital, Boston.

Sartre, J.-P. (1965). *L'imagination.* Paris: Presses Universitaires de France.

Scheler, M. (1913). *Nature et formes de la sympathie.* Paris: Payot.

Schilder, P. (1950a). *Brain and Personality.* New York: International Universities Press.

Schilder, P. (1950b). *The Image and Appearance of the Human Body.* New York: International Universities Press.

Schilder, P. (1951). *Introduction to Psychoanalytic Psychiatry.* New York: International Universities Press.

Schreber, D. P. (1955). *Memoirs of My Nervous Illness,* trans. & ed. by I. Macalpine and R. A. Hunter. London: Dawson.

Scott, C. (1948). A problem of ego structure. *Psycho-Analytic Quarterly, 17* (1).

Segal, H. (1956). Depression in schizophrenia. *International Journal of Psycho-Analysis, 37.*

Segal, H. (1957). Notes on symbol formation. *International Journal of Psycho-Analysis, 38.*

Séglas, J. (1895a). *Leçons cliniques sur les maladies mentales et nerveuses.* Paris: Asselin & Houzeau.

Séglas, J. (1895b). Le délire des négations dans la folie systématique hypocondriaque. In: *Leçons cliniques sur les maladies mentales et nerveuses*. Paris: Asselin & Houzeau.

Séglas, J. (1895c). Le délire des négations dans la mélancolie. In: *Leçons cliniques sur les maladies mentales et nerveuses*. Paris: Asselin & Houzeau.

Shirley, M. M. (1933). *The First Two Years*. Minneapolis, MN: University of Minnesota Press.

Sollier, P. (1903). *Les Phénomènes d'autoscopie*. Paris: Alcan.

Stern, W. (1962). Psicologìa general desde el punto de vista personalistico. In: *Biblioteca de Psicologìa General, Vol. 1*. Buenos Aires: Editorial Paidos.

Wallon, H. (1975). Les origines de la pensée chez l'enfant. In: *Les moyens intellectuels, Vol. 4*. Paris: Presses Universitaires de France.

Wernicke, C. (1900). *Grundiss der Psychiatrie*. Leipzig: Thieme.

Winnicott, D. W. (1945). Primitive emotional development. In: *Collected Papers: Through Paediatrics to Psycho-Analysis*. London: Tavistock Publications, 1958. [Reprinted as *Through Paediatrics to Psycho-Analysis*. London: Hogarth Press, 1975; reprinted London: Karnac Books, 1992.]

Winnicott, D. W. (1947). Hate in the countertransference. In: *Collected Papers: Through Paediatrics to Psycho-Analysis*. London: Tavistock Publications, 1958. [Reprinted as *Through Paediatrics to Psycho-Analysis*. London: Hogarth Press, 1975; reprinted London: Karnac Books, 1992.]

Winnicott, D. W. (1952). Anxiety associated with insecurity. In: *Collected Papers: Through Paediatrics to Psycho-Analysis*. London: Tavistock Publications, 1958. [Reprinted as *Through Paediatrics to Psycho-Analysis*. London: Hogarth Press, 1975; reprinted London: Karnac Books, 1992.]

Winnicott, D. W. (1953). Transitional objects and transitional phenomena. *International Journal of Psycho-Analysis, 34*: 87–99.

Winnicott, D. W. (1956). Primary maternal preoccupation. In: *Collected Papers: Through Paediatrics to Psycho-Analysis*. London: Tavistock Publications, 1958. [Reprinted as *Through Paediatrics to Psycho-Analysis*. London: Hogarth Press, 1975; reprinted London: Karnac Books, 1992.]

INDEX

and erotic transference, 211
evaluation of aspects of, 204
excessive, 78
and expansion, 62
identity attributed to analyst, 166
of infantile part of self, 146
manipulation, 210
normal, 167, 203
pathological, 36, 67, 93, 189, 203, 225
protecting good part of self, 152
and separation, 188
pseudopodia, 94, 188
psychopath, 15
psychopathological disorders, 20
psychopathology, 180
psychosis(es) (*passim*):
    child and adult, 3, 4
    chronic, 227
    communication in, 117
    delusion in, 19
    and disavowal, 46
    and dreaming, 225
    hysterical, 151
    mono-symptomatic, 84
    post-partum, 30
    transference, 14
psychotic aspects of personality, 19
psychotic crisis, 26, 28, 71, 198, 205
    acute, 3, 97
        and body language and verbalization, 119–162
psychotic depression, 70
psychotic distractibility, 188
psychotic part of ego, 112, 176, 199, 216, 225
    and non-psychotic part, 20, 194, 199, 202, 217, 221
psychotic patient(s) (*passim*):
    analysis of, 12, 14, 46, 151, 161, 164
    and communication, 89–118
    confusion in, 85
    and distortion of reality, 18
    and erotic transference, 210
    and hatred in countertransference, 176
    language of, 225
    semiological study of, 31–42
    and transference psychosis, 14
    treatment of, 119–162
        and family, 161
    work with, 2
    worldview of, 225

Pythagoreans, 132

Racker, H., vii, 165, 176
Rascovsky, L., vii
rationalization, 180
reality:
    omnipotent control of, 166
    principle, 57, 120, 129, 160, 226
    -testing, 85, 161
realization, 29
reciprocal induction, 92
regression, ix, 5, 49, 75, 85, 112, 139, 151, 199
reification, 194, 200
reintegration, 198, 199
re-introjection, 16, 36, 80, 102, 131, 198
reparation, 50, 57, 60, 83, 226
    concept of, 195
    false, 91
    vs. restoration, 195
repetition compulsion, 78
repression, 19, 28, 46, 199
resistance, 20, 164, 165, 213, 216
Resnik, vii–xii, 3, 10, 13, 19, 22, 41, 63, 104, 172, 192, 201, 217, 227
rhythm:
    in analytic relationship, 10, 98, 164
    biological, 15
    and body image, 28
    and experience of time, 216
    and historicity, 113
    internal, 15, 16
    -mask, 99
    masturbating, 98
    and spatialization, 99, 195
    and structural mobility, 114
    and thought, 186
    of transference, 19
    see also movement
Rodrigué, E., 2
role reversal, 213
Rosen, J. F., 75
Rosenfeld, H., xi, 2, 8, 75
    analysis with, viii, 3, 224
    and analytic field, 136
    and confusion, state of, 85, 108, 199
    and destructive narcissism, 14
    and eroticization of transference, 164, 210
    and narcissism, 8, 228
    and projective identification, 93, 203
        excessive, 85, 211